AF538369

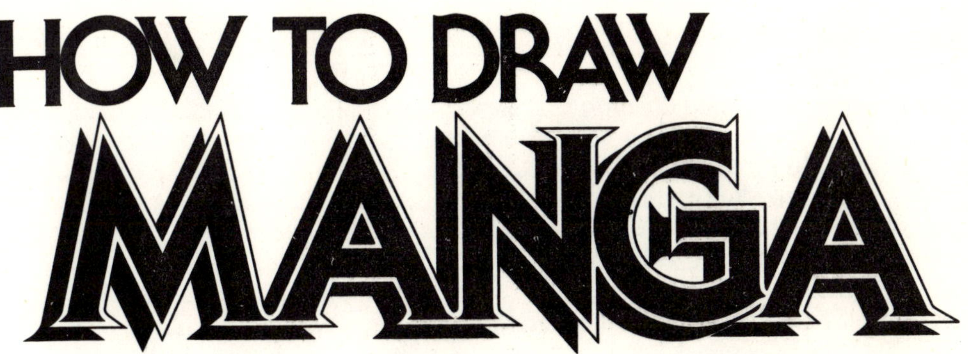

Male Characters

Representation and Techniques

Table of Contents

HOW TO DRAW MANGA: Male Characters
by Hikaru Hayashi

First published in 1998 by Graphic-sha Publishing Co., Ltd.
This English edition was published in 2002 by Graphic-sha Publishing Co., Ltd.
1-9-12 Kudan-kita, Chiyoda-ku, Tokyo 102-0073 Japan

Planning & Production: Yasuo Matsumoto, Jun Matsubara, Kento Shimazaki, Miki Murakawa, Tomo Otake
Cover Drawing: Kento Shimazaki
Reference Work: Jun Matsubara, Kiyoe Yokoyama, Yasuo Matsumoto, Miki Murakawa, Kento Shimazaki, Yukai Asada, ACHA
Composition & Scenario: Hikaru Hayashi (Go Office)

English Cover Design: Shinichi Ishioka
English Edition Layout: Shinichi Ishioka
English Translation: Língua fránca, Inc. (an3y-skmt@asahi-net.or.jp)
Japanese Edition Editor: Motofumi Nakanishi (Graphic-sha Publishing Co., Ltd.)
Foreign Language Edition Project Coordinator: Kumiko Sakamoto (Graphic-sha Publishing Co., Ltd.)

Distributed by
NIPPAN IPS
11-6, 3 chome, Iidabashi, Chiyoda-ku,
Tokyo, 102-0073 Japan
Tel: +81-(0)3-3238-0676
Fax: +81-(0)3-3238-0996
E-mail: ips03@nippan-ips.co.jp

Distributed Exclusively in North America by
Digital Manga Distribution
1123 Dominguez St., Unit "K"
Carson, CA 90746, U.S.A.
Tel: (310) 604-9701
Fax: (310) 604-1134
E-mail: distribution@emanga.com
URL:http://www.emanga.com/dmd/

First printing: March 2002

ISBN: 4-7661-1240-7
Printed and bound in China by Everbest Printing Co., Ltd.

Chapter 1
Approaches to Drawing the Male Form

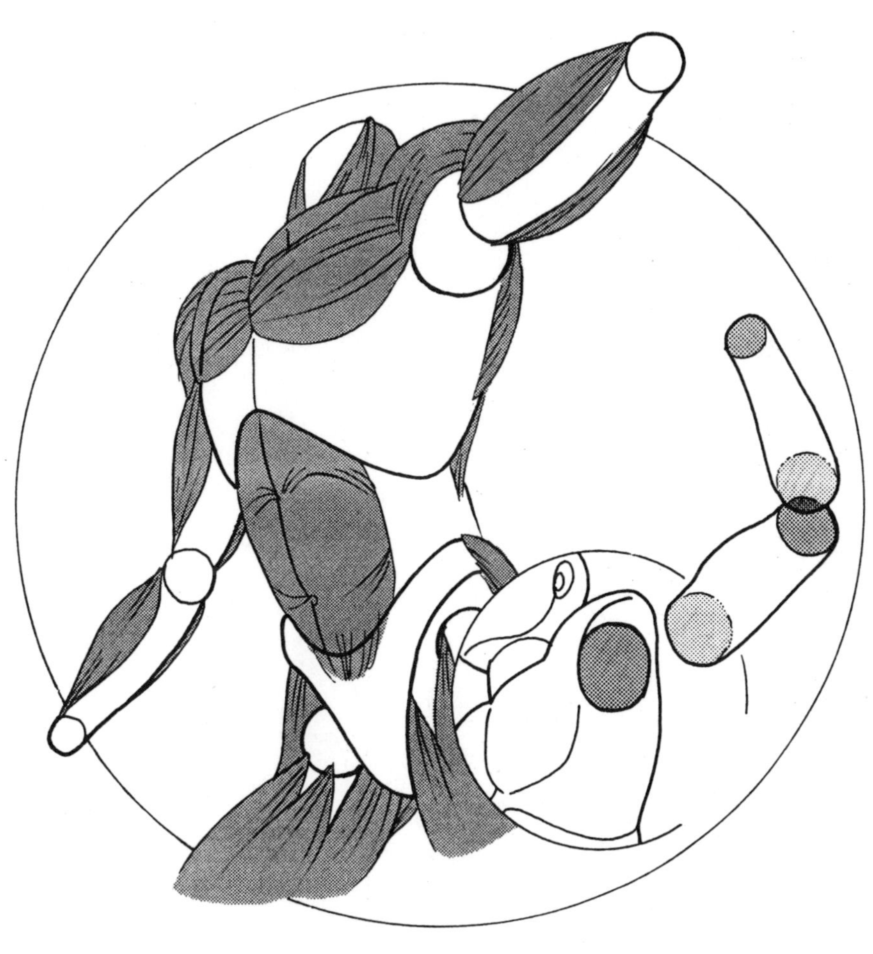

3 Approaches to Drawing the Male Form

1. The Body as a Triangle

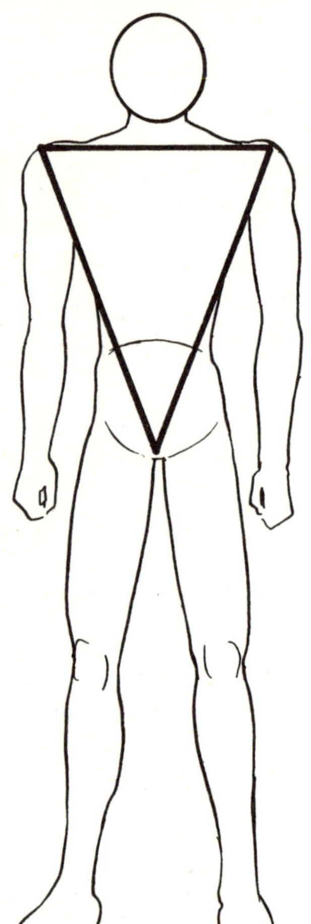

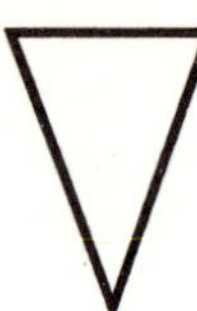

The distinguishing features of this approach are wide shoulders, a broad chest, and slim hips.

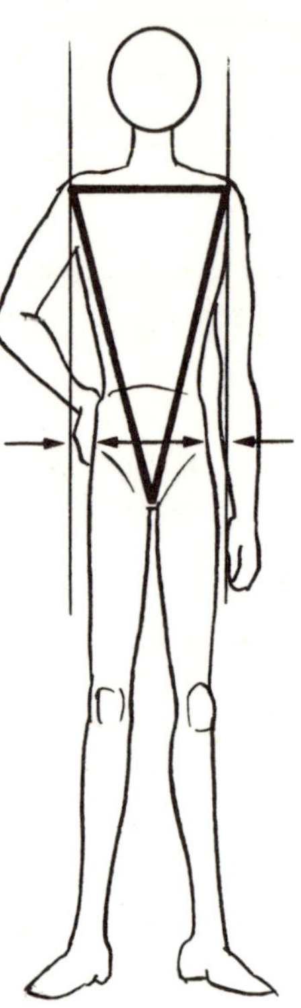

Even for a slimmer figure with narrow shoulders, drawing the hips at a width less than that of the shoulders creates the image of a male character.

2. Rigid Lines

Muscles have a firmness that allows a man's body to appear frail and yet still be strong. Use straighter lines to suggest this firmness.

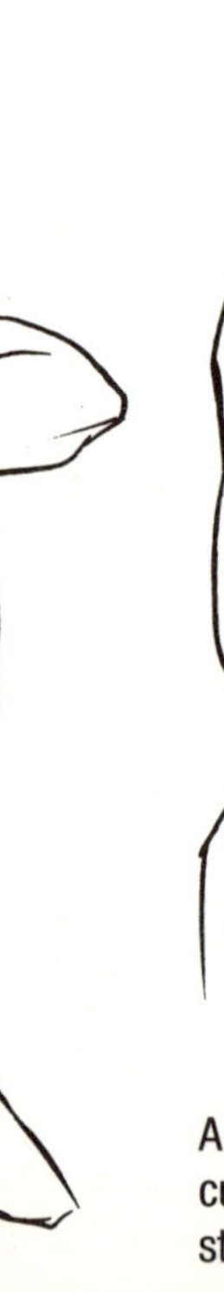

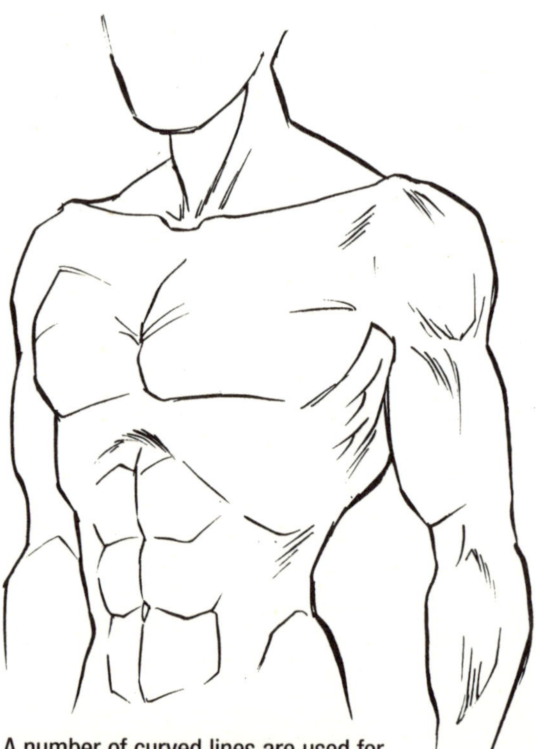

A number of curved lines are used for cut, well-toned muscles, but sharp, straight lines suggest hardness.

3. The Body as a Martini Glass

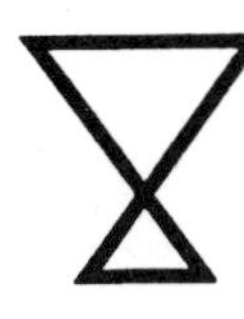

The distinguishing features of this approach are wide shoulders and slim hips. An abstraction of this form yields a "martini glass" shape.

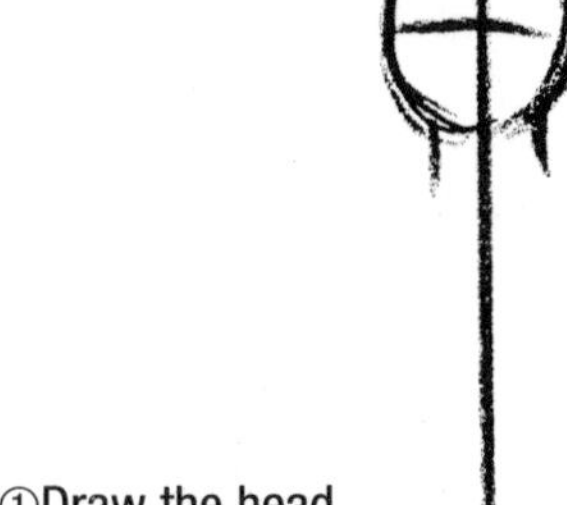

①Draw the head.
- Include the neck
- Drawing an axial line helps maintain balance.

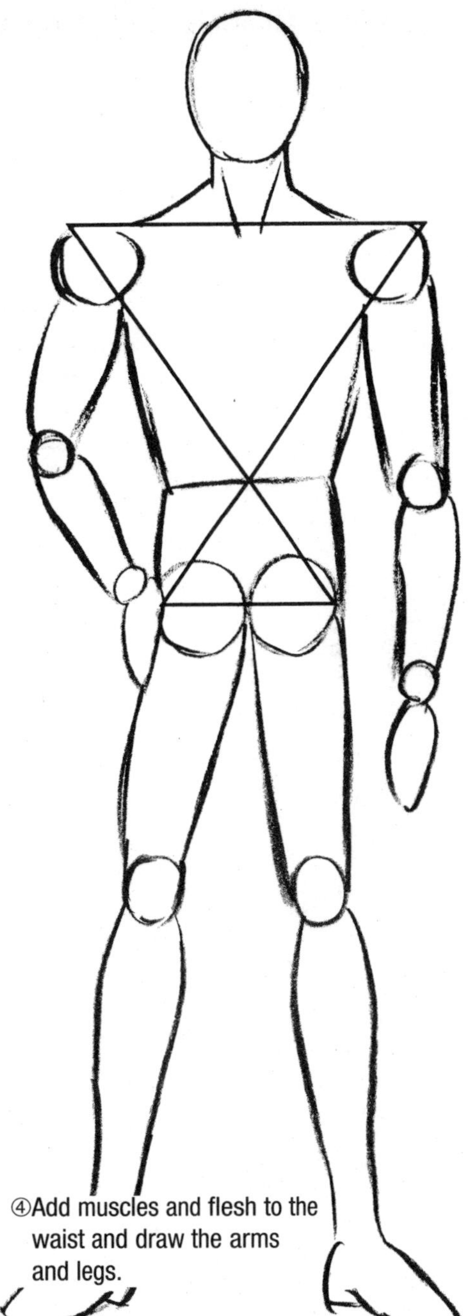

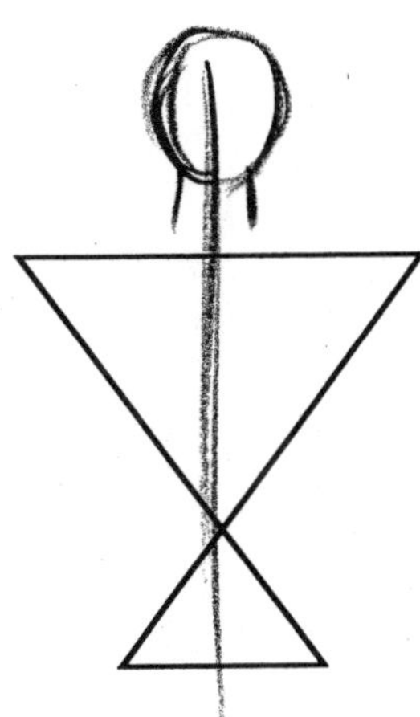

②Draw a martini glass shape for the body.

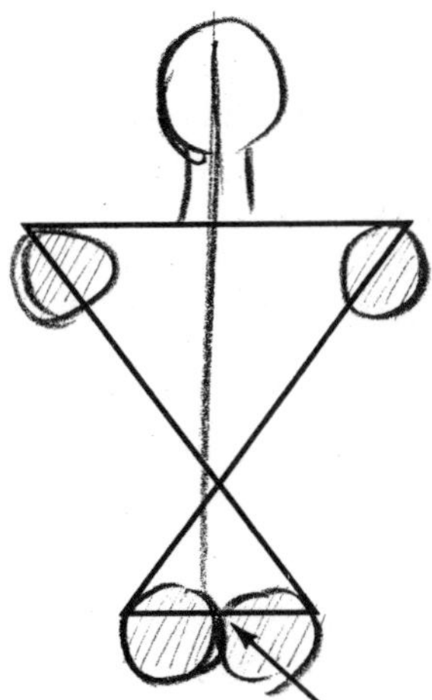

③Draw the areas from where the arms and legs originate (the joints). Draw the joints for the legs touching one another.

④Add muscles and flesh to the waist and draw the arms and legs.

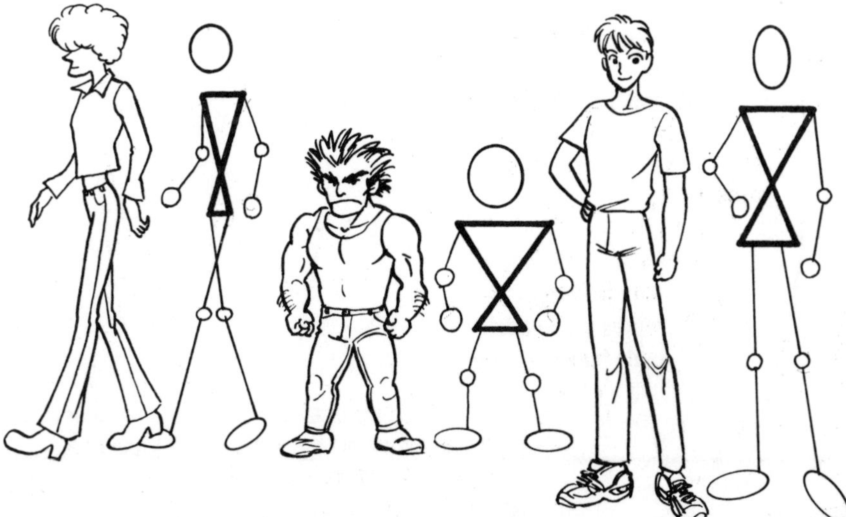

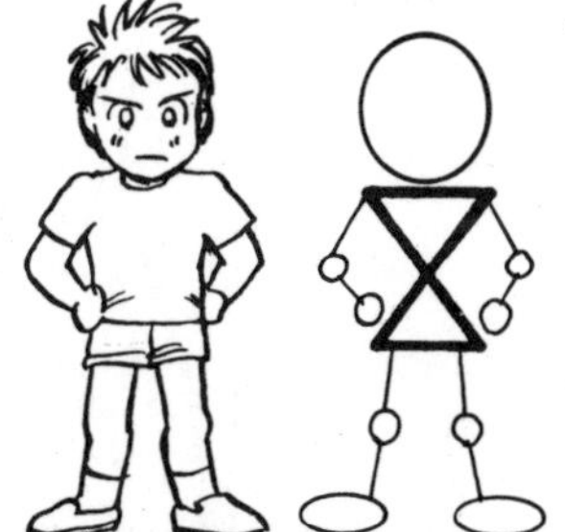

The character's body type depends on:
1. The proportion of the size of the character's head with the width of the shoulders.
2. Whether to use a long, thin martini glass or a short, stocky martini glass.

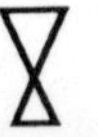

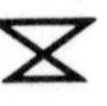

Distinguishing Features of the Male Form

The distinguishing features of the male form are a developed chest, a taught waist, and firm musculature spanning the entire body.

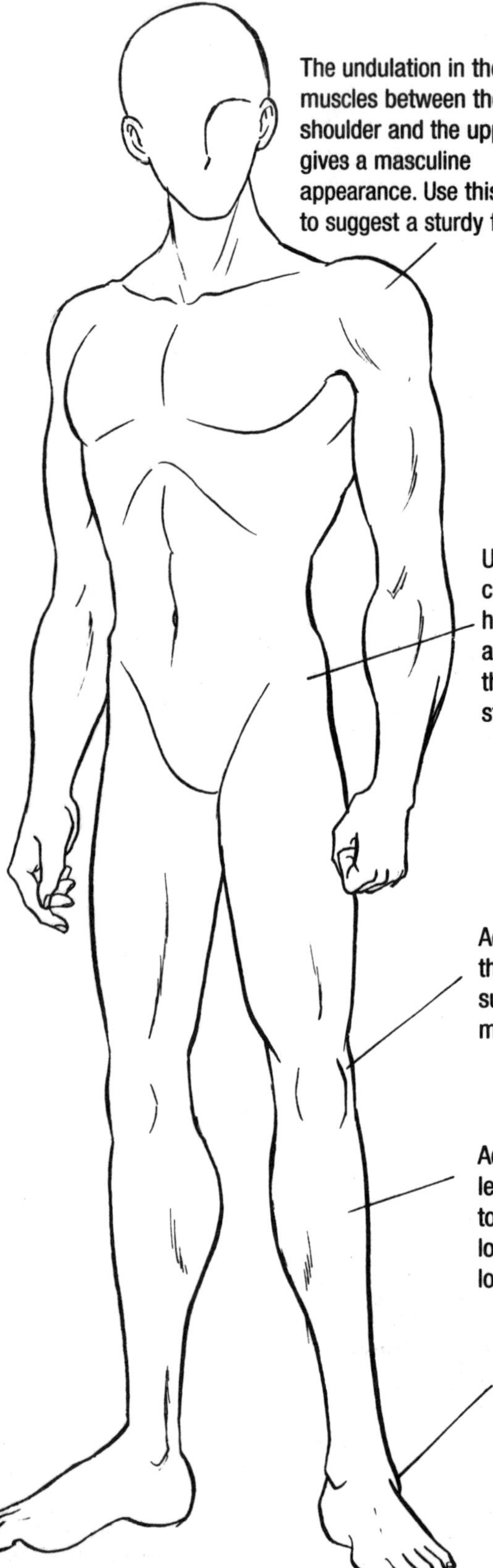

The undulation in the muscles between the shoulder and the upper arm gives a masculine appearance. Use this point to suggest a sturdy frame.

Use a very slight curve to define the hip. The figure will appear feminine if this line is not kept straight.

Adding shadow to the knee or shin suggests a masculine leg.

Adding hair to the leg is an easy way to make the figure look "male" but loses in aesthetics.

Clearly delineate the ankle to represent an adult male figure.

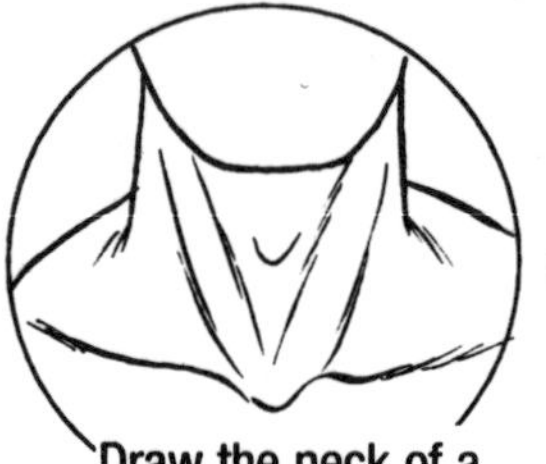

Draw the neck of a brawnier figure shorter and thicker.

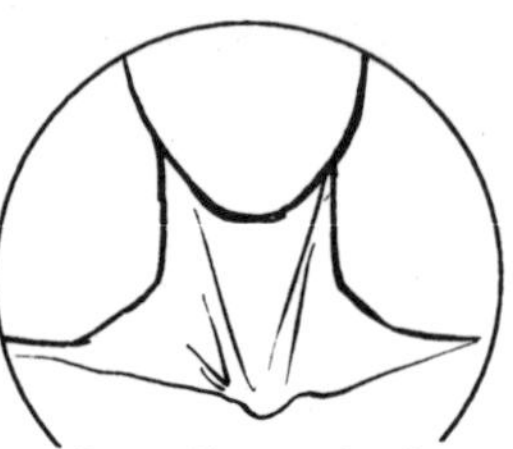

Draw the neck of a lean male figure more slender and longer.

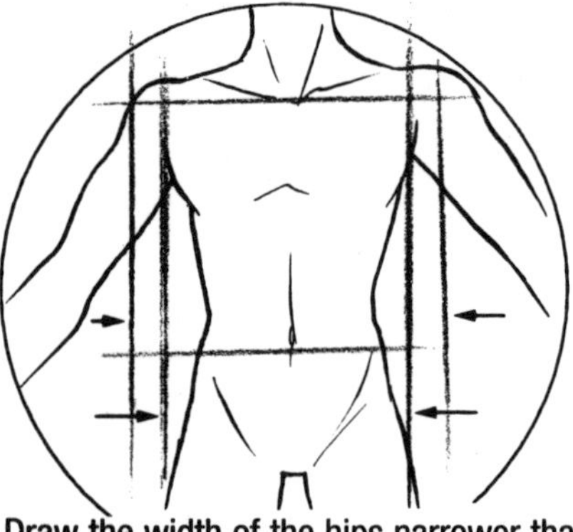

Draw the width of the hips narrower than that of the shoulders (underarms).

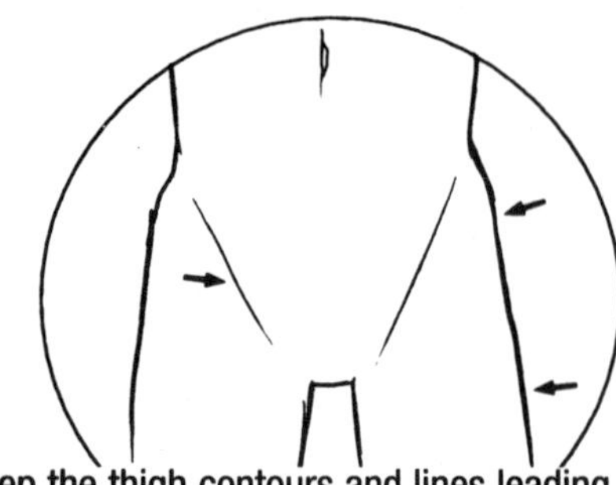

Keep the thigh contours and lines leading to the groin on the straight side, or the figure will appear feminine.

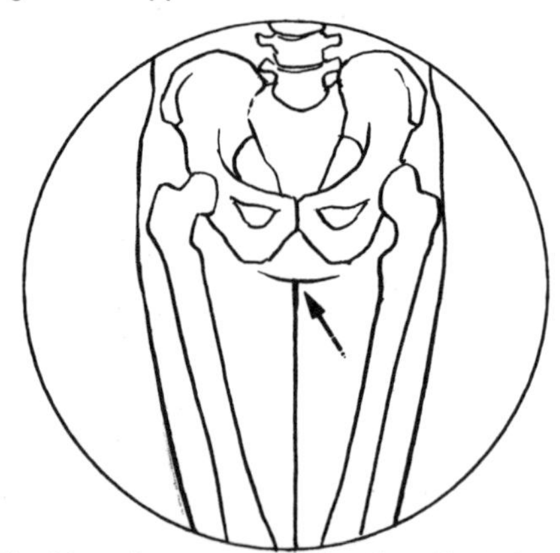

The hips of a man are taller than that of a woman, so the joints at the groin of a male figure touch when standing.

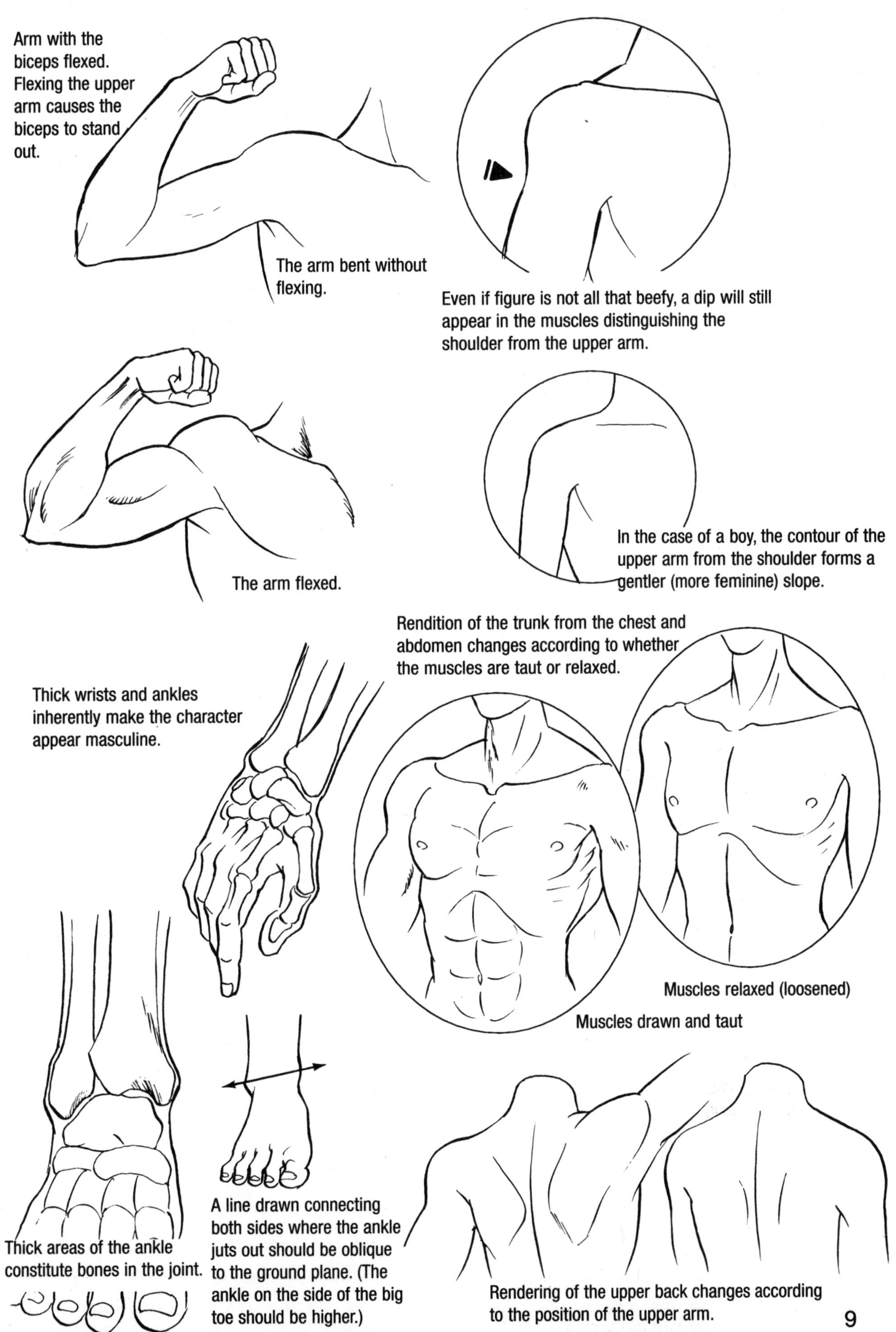
Arm with the biceps flexed. Flexing the upper arm causes the biceps to stand out.
The arm bent without flexing.
Even if figure is not all that beefy, a dip will still appear in the muscles distinguishing the shoulder from the upper arm.
The arm flexed.
In the case of a boy, the contour of the upper arm from the shoulder forms a gentler (more feminine) slope.
Rendition of the trunk from the chest and abdomen changes according to whether the muscles are taut or relaxed.
Thick wrists and ankles inherently make the character appear masculine.
Muscles relaxed (loosened)
Muscles drawn and taut
Thick areas of the ankle constitute bones in the joint.
A line drawn connecting both sides where the ankle juts out should be oblique to the ground plane. (The ankle on the side of the big toe should be higher.)
Rendering of the upper back changes according to the position of the upper arm.

Male and Female Skeletal Differences

Use the following as guidelines for drawing male and female figures: The chest area of the male should be around 1.5 times larger than that of the female while the hip area should be around 2/3 the size of the female.

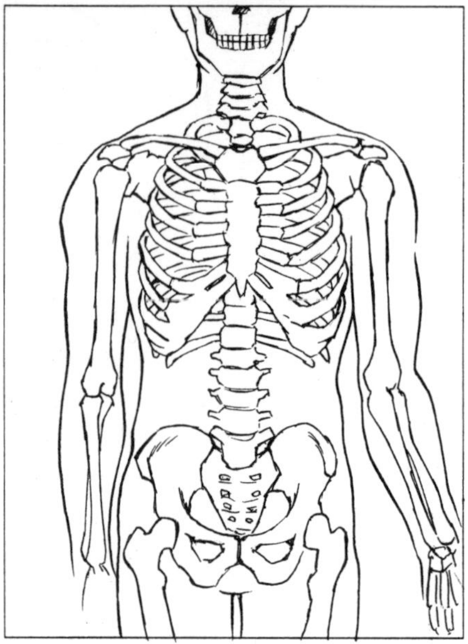

Male Figure

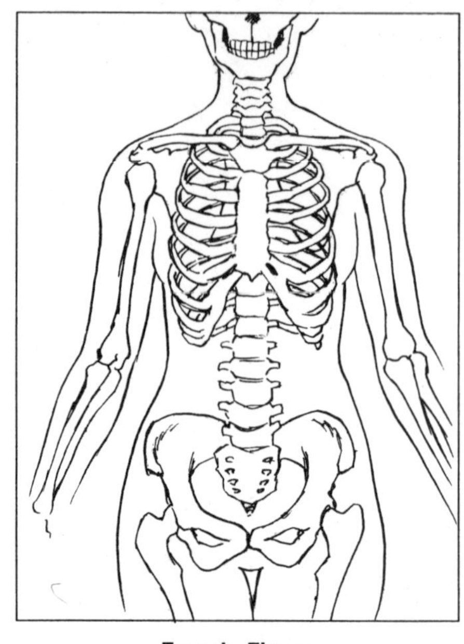

Female Figure

The shoulders extend beyond the widest point of the ribcage.

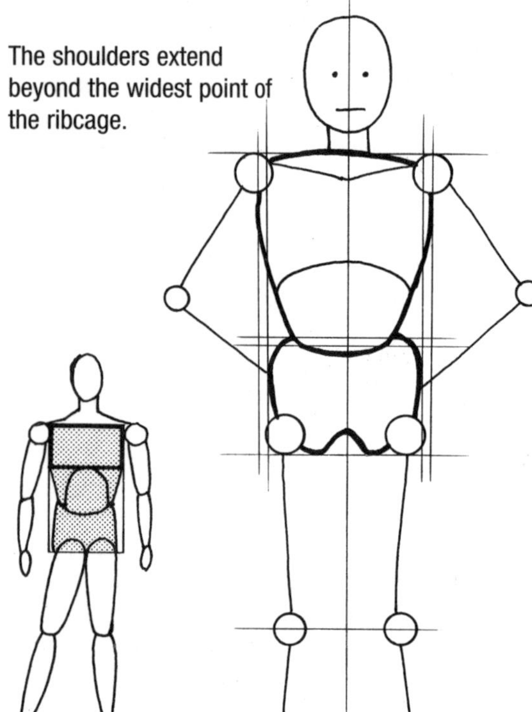

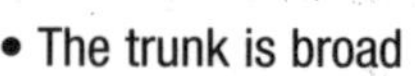

- The trunk is broad

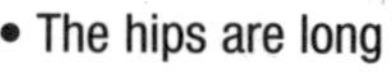

- The hips are long

The widest point of the hips is equal to the width of the shoulders.

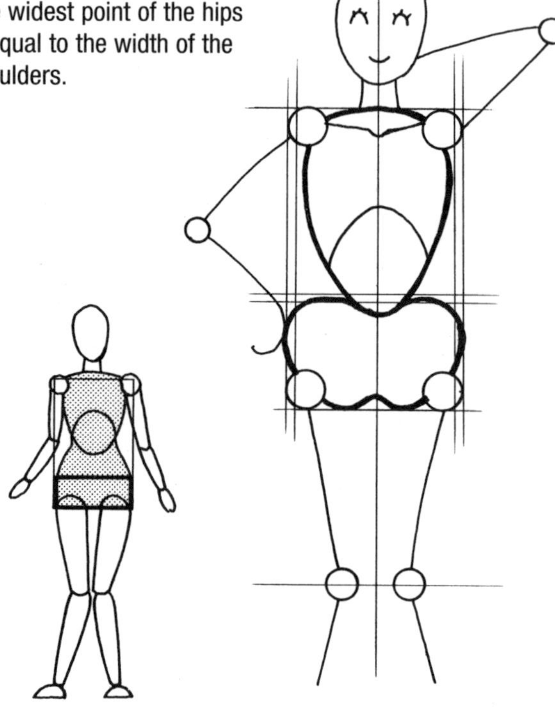

- The body is long
- The hips are wide

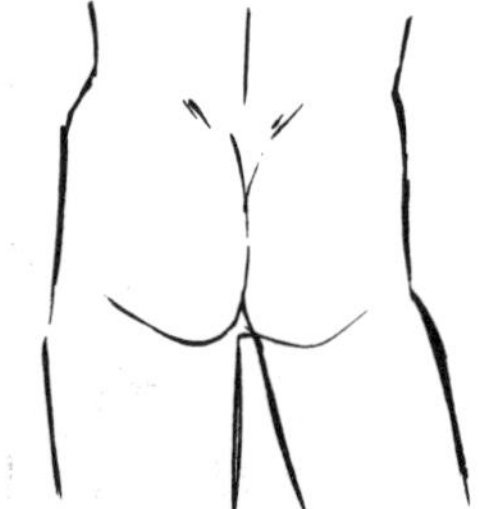

Lines are straighter in the male figure and curvature kept to a minimum.

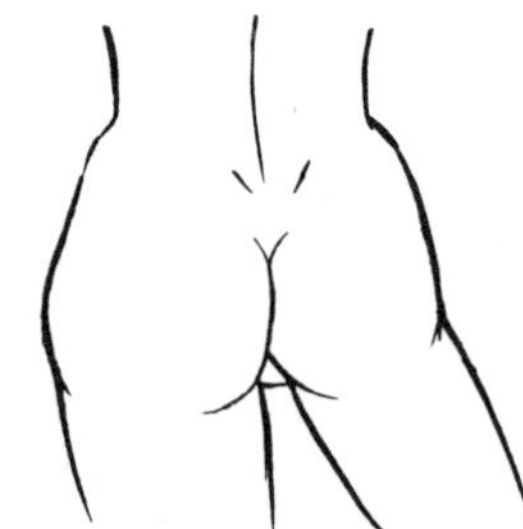

Lines from the waist to the hips in a female figure are rounder and curvature maximized.

Male Figure

The male figure's chest area is thick and hips slender.

Female Figure

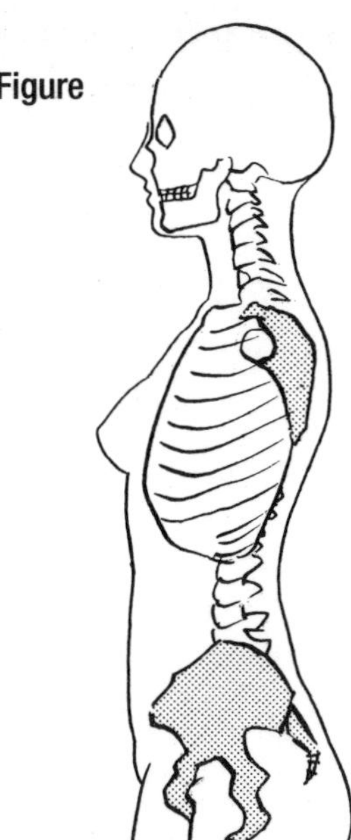

The female figure's chest area is shallow and hips expansive.

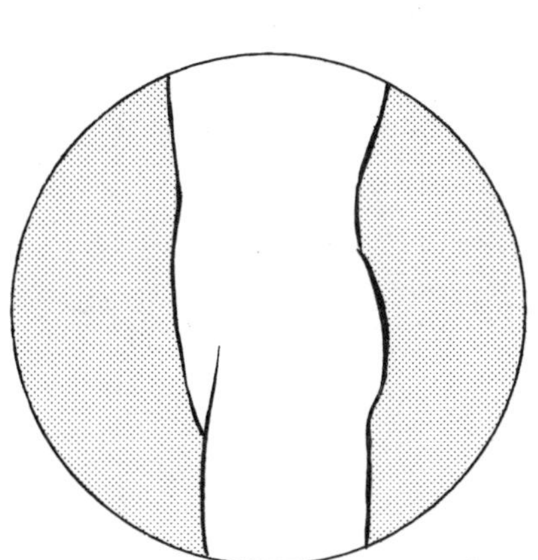

Masculine hips have a gentle slope.

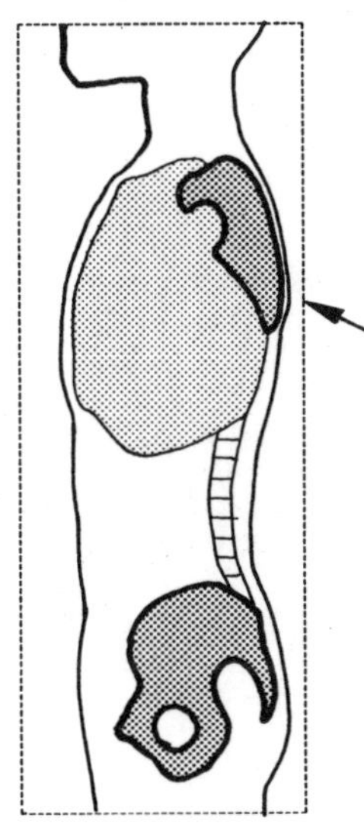

When standing erect, the posterior of a male figure does not extend beyond his upper back.

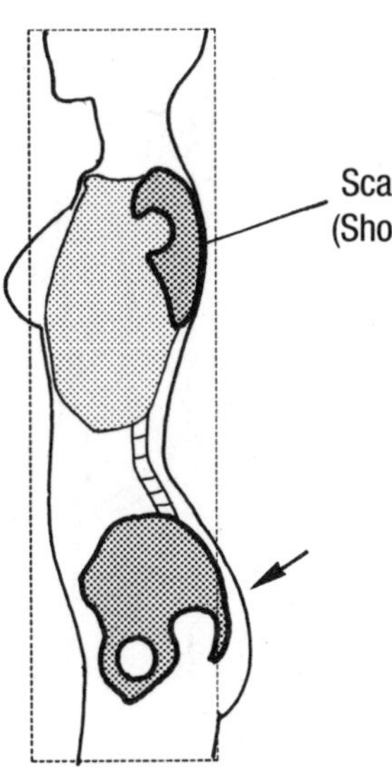

The posterior of a female figure extends beyond her shoulder blades even when standing.

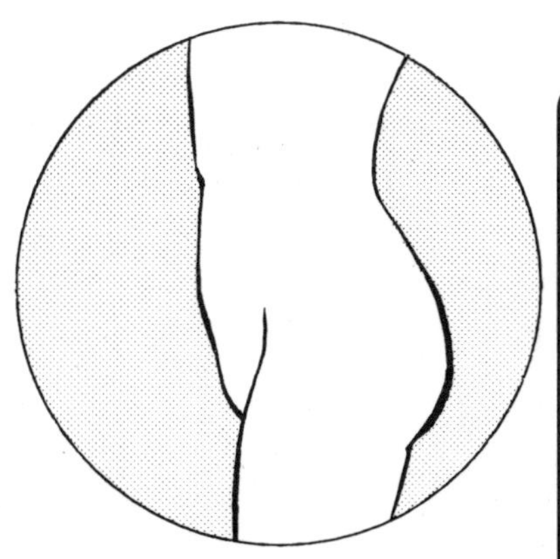

Feminine hips have a dramatic slope.

Male and Female Muscular Differences

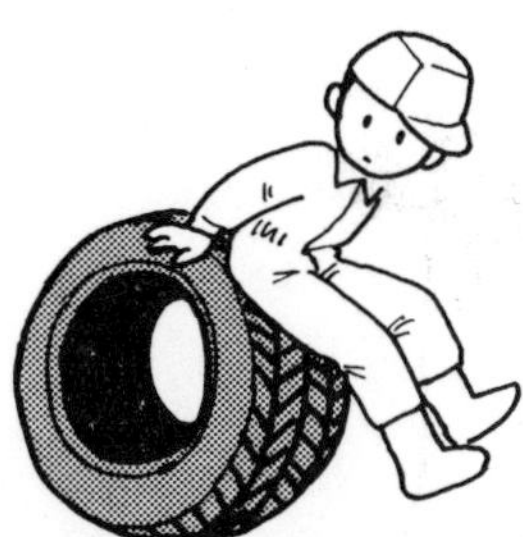

The substance of a male character's body is like a car tire.

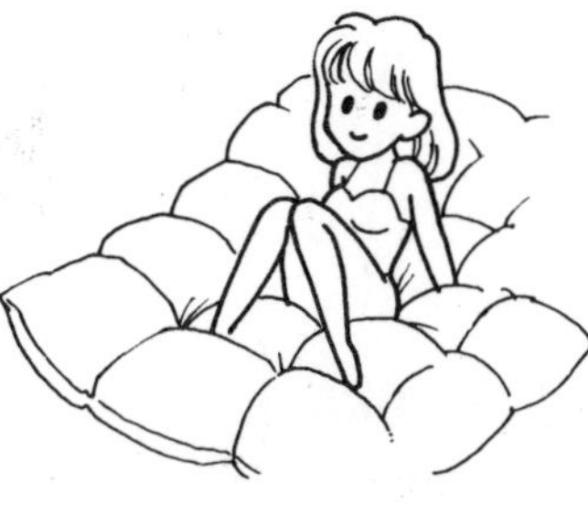

The substance of a female character's body is like a down quilt.

The textures of a man and a woman's muscles are completely different. When drawing a male character, remember that he is a fundamentally different creature from that of a woman.

Giving the Body a 3-Dimensional Feel (Skeletal and Muscular Structure Evident from under the Flesh)

The male character's body is like a board. However, knowing where the curves and crevices form will help you draw a convincing male character and give your character presence.

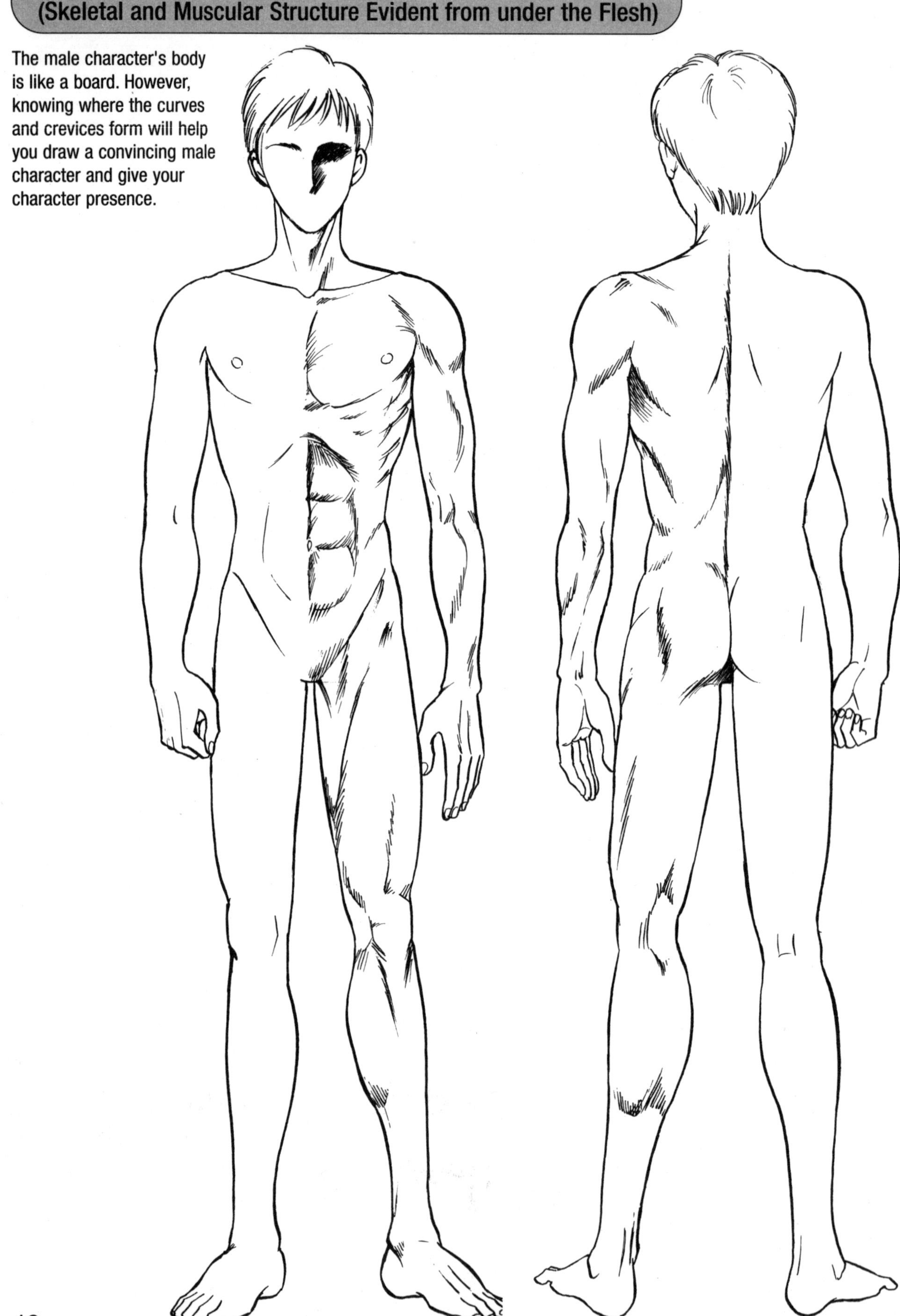

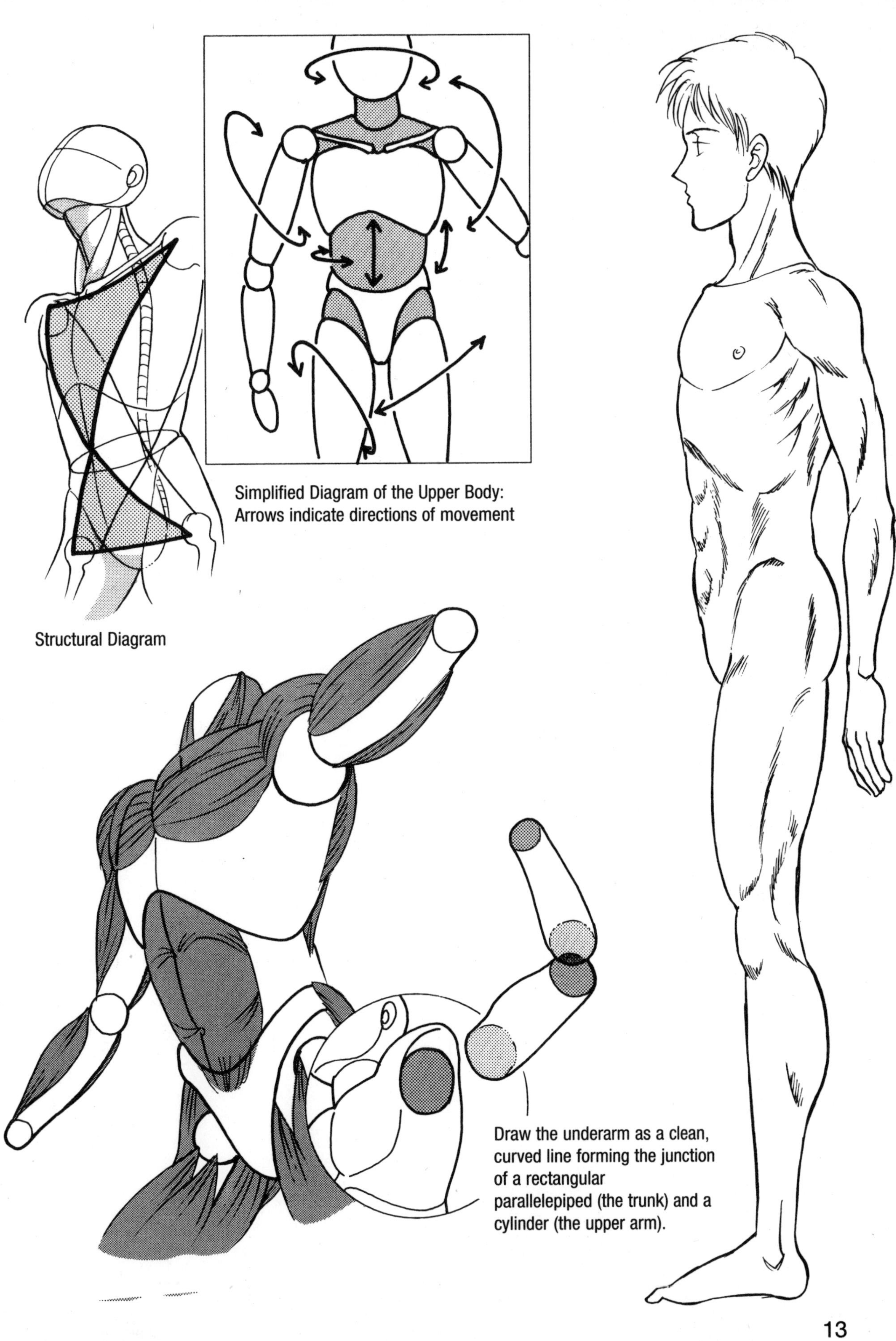

Simplified Diagram of the Upper Body: Arrows indicate directions of movement

Structural Diagram

Draw the underarm as a clean, curved line forming the junction of a rectangular parallelepiped (the trunk) and a cylinder (the upper arm).

Expressing Musculature

The most common areas for exaggerating muscles in drawings are the arms, the chest, and the legs.

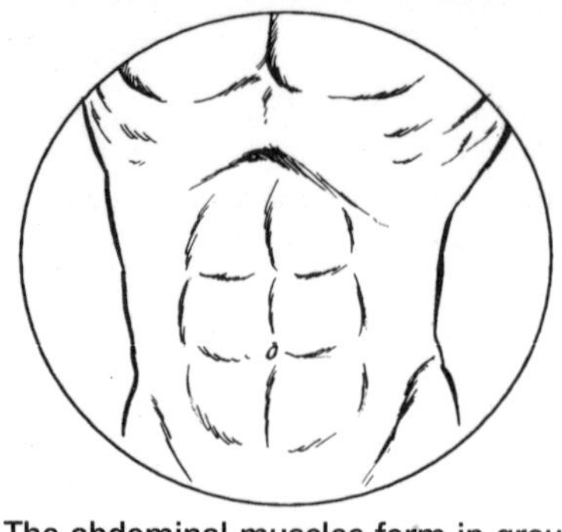

The abdominal muscles form in groups of 2 rows horizontally and 3 rows vertically. Use a washboard stomach only when suggesting a well-defined, cut abdomen.

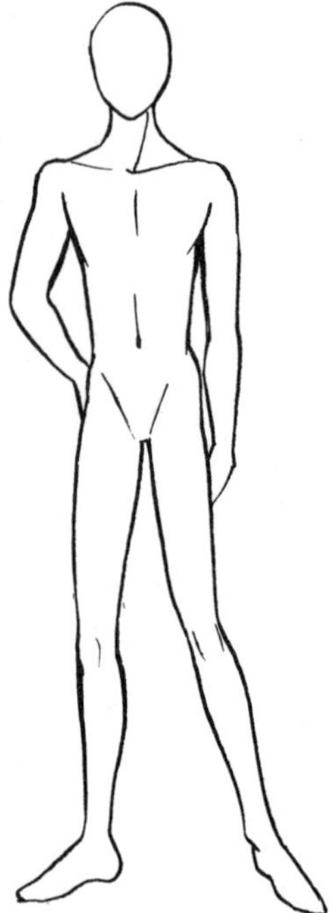

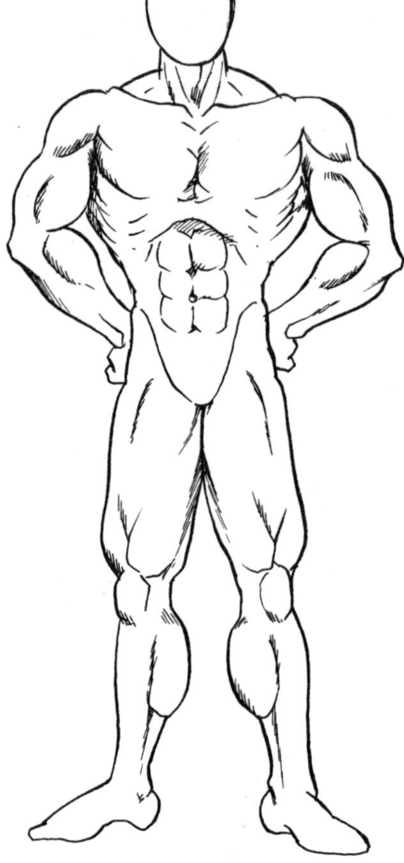

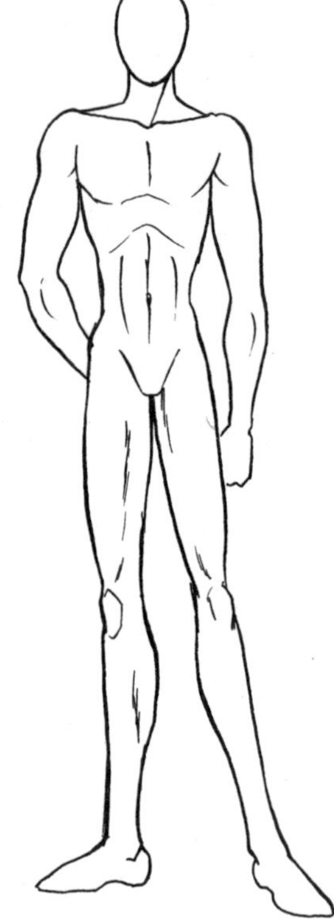

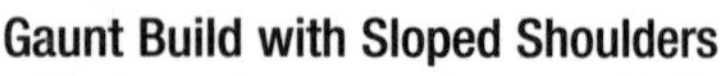

Gaunt Build with Sloped Shoulders

- To downplay musculature, add dips and curves at the joints.
- When drawing a slender neck and shoulders, downsize the hips to about the same degree.
- Eliminate rendering of almost all muscles between the chest and abdomen.

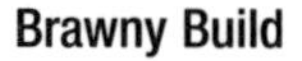

Brawny Build

- Draw the neck short and thick and the shoulders and clavicle, burly
- Make the chest and shoulders expansive and muscular. Keep the waist slim-about the same width as the head.
- Exaggerate the undulation of muscles in the arms and legs and draw the areas around the joints narrow.

Lean Build

- Draw firm shoulders.
- Use clean lines in the chest and abdomen.
- Add moderate undulation to the muscles in the arms and legs to give the character a sturdy appearance.

The extent of muscular conditioning and skeletal structure affect how the body looks from the lower back to the posterior. Use the position of lines in the posterior and curves in the thighs to distinguish the characters' body types.

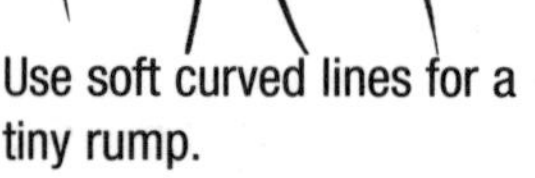

Use soft curved lines for a tiny rump.

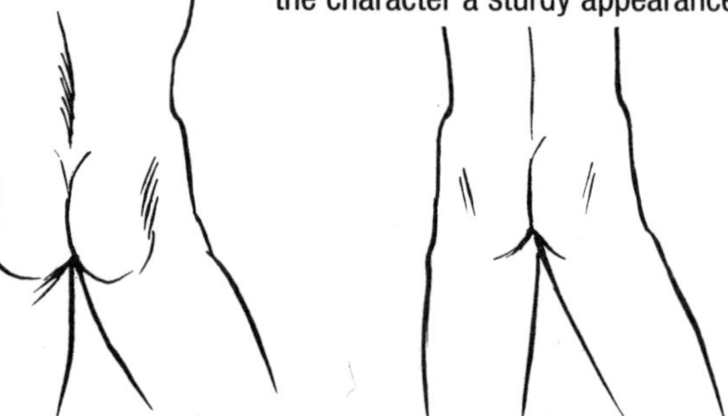

Use a combination of straight and curved lines for firm, athletic posterior.

Use primarily straight lines for a typically male posterior with prominent bone definition.

The back of a thin male character is similar to that of a woman. Make the character's back appear more masculine by keeping the posterior small, using straighter lines, and minimizing the jutting of the pelvis.

Rear View of a Thin Male Character

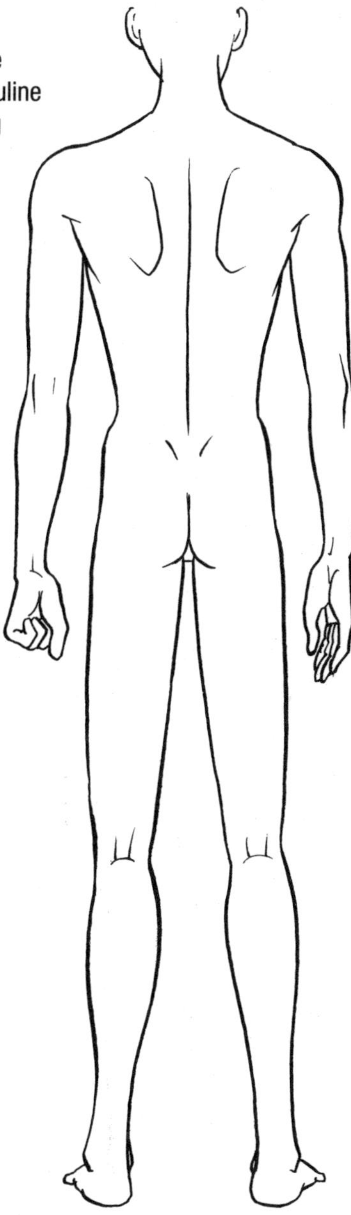

Rear View of a Muscular Male Character

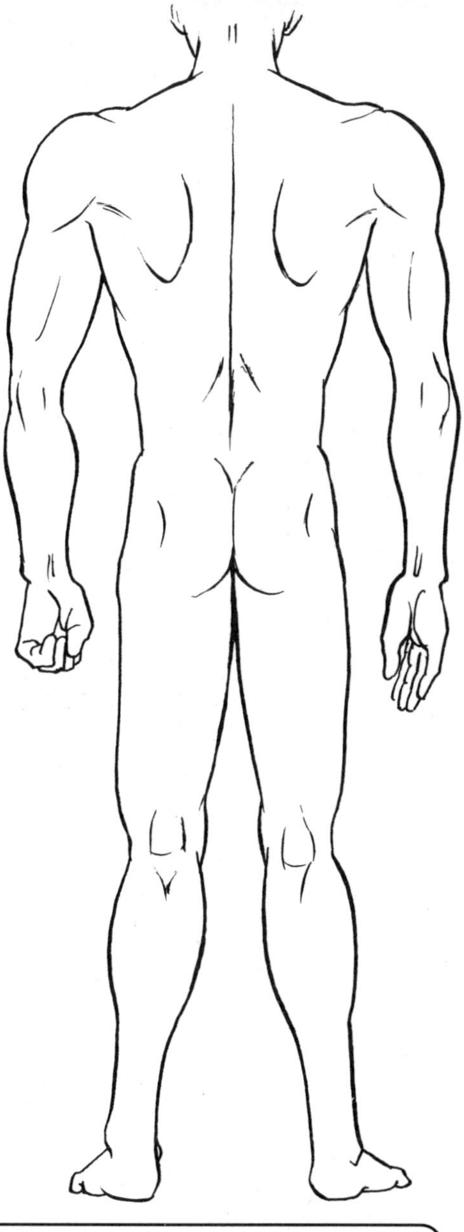

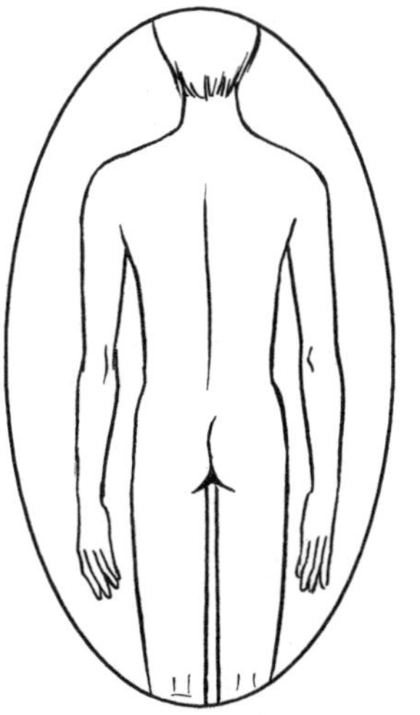

Back of a Boy
Since a boy is still in the growing stage, do not include lines suggesting skeletal structure or muscle contours.

Sloped vs. Squared Shoulders

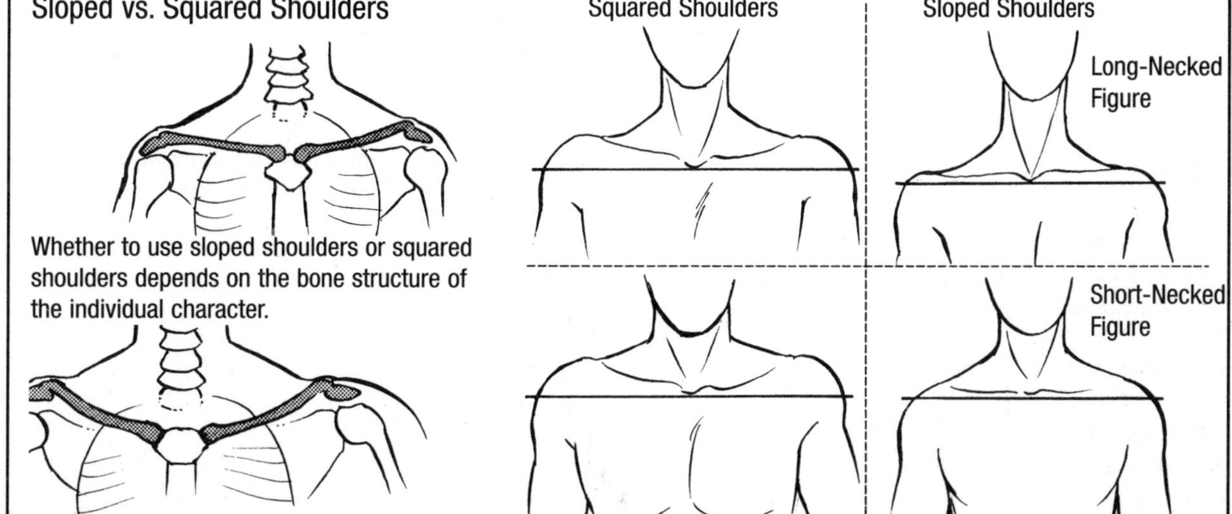

Whether to use sloped shoulders or squared shoulders depends on the bone structure of the individual character.

Note that individuals with developed muscles connecting the neck and shoulders (trapezius) appear to have short necks and sloped shoulders.

Assorted Body Types

3 body types are used in drawings: an average build, a slim build, and a muscular build. In the case of male characters, depending on the muscular conditioning of the figure, the same character can take on an entirely different appearance.

1. Average Build

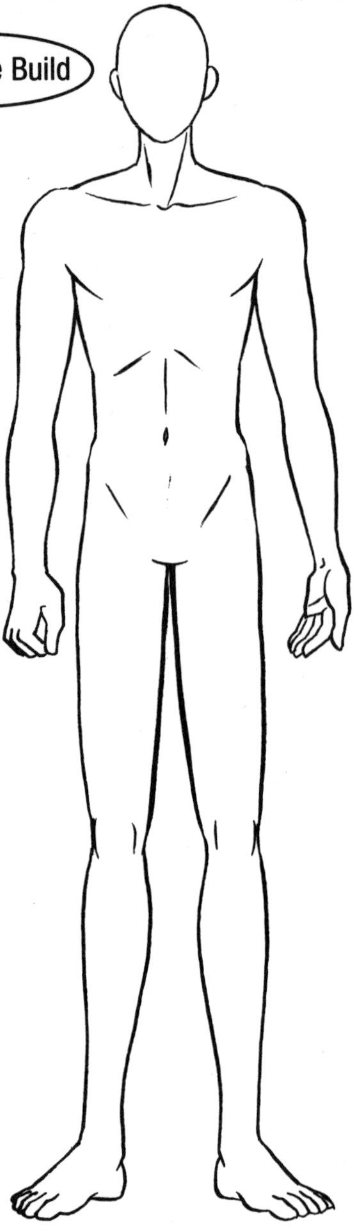

Typical Build

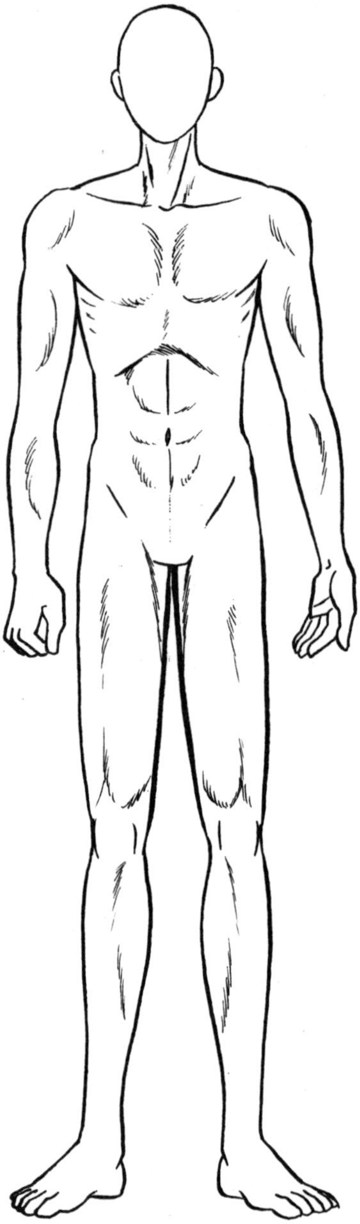

Muscular Build

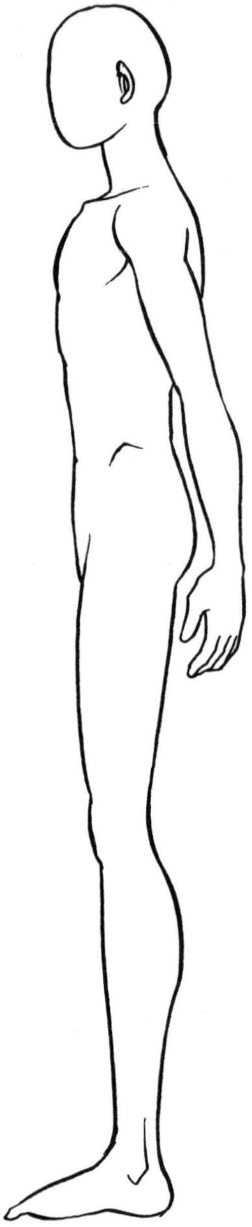

Typical Build: Side View

Addition of Muscles

- Causes the chest area to expand and the chest to stick out.
- Requires the arms and legs not to be drawn only with straight lines, but instead with curves and dips to suggest muscles.
- Causes the wrists and ankles to appear thinner and joints to appear thicker, brawnier.
- Causes the neck and shoulders to become thicker.

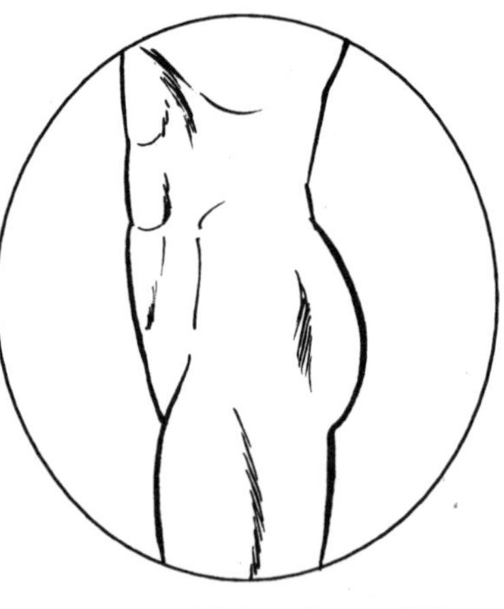

Muscular Build: Side View of Hips

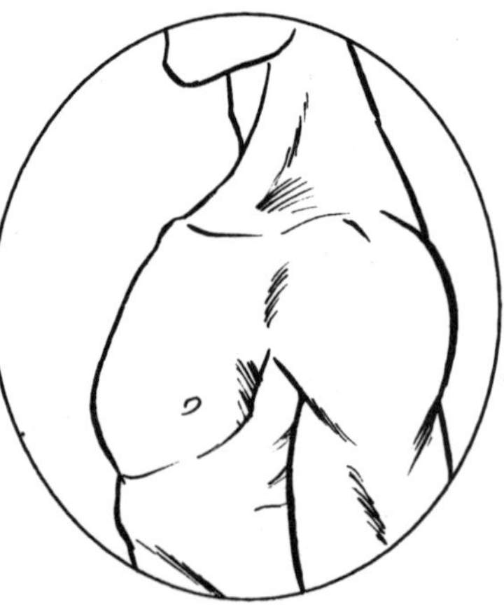

Muscular Build: Side View of Chest

2. Slim Build

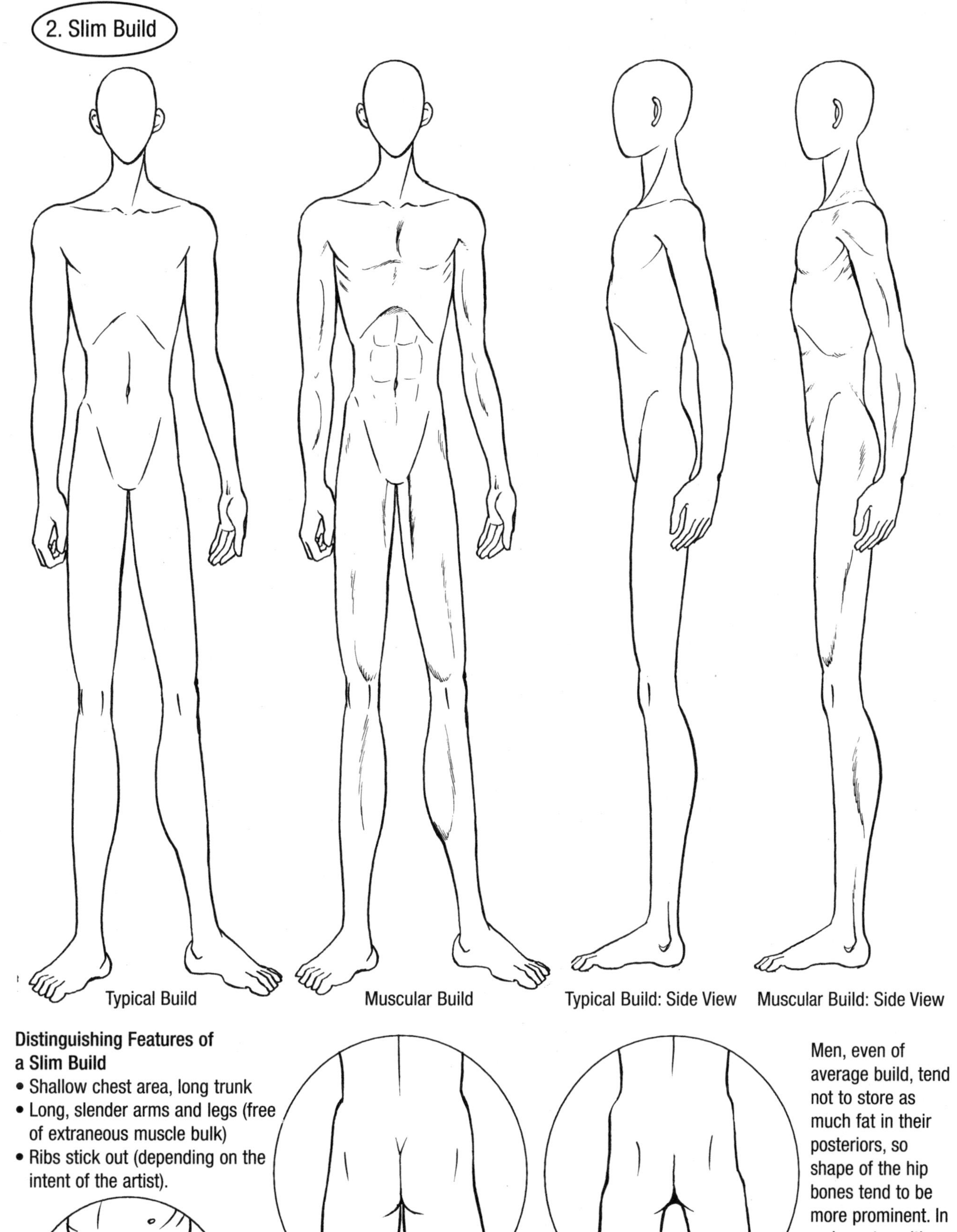

Typical Build

Muscular Build

Typical Build: Side View

Muscular Build: Side View

Distinguishing Features of a Slim Build

- Shallow chest area, long trunk
- Long, slender arms and legs (free of extraneous muscle bulk)
- Ribs stick out (depending on the intent of the artist).

Posterior of a Character with an Average Build

Posterior of a Character with a Slim Build

Men, even of average build, tend not to store as much fat in their posteriors, so shape of the hip bones tend to be more prominent. In a character with a slim build, the bones tend to stand out even more.

Masculine Face Types

Male character face types tend to be divided into two general categories: faces for women's manga and faces for men's manga.

Traditional Male Characters in Women's Manga

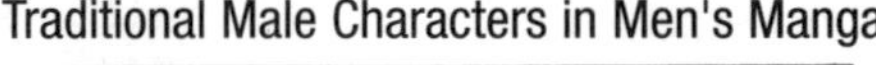

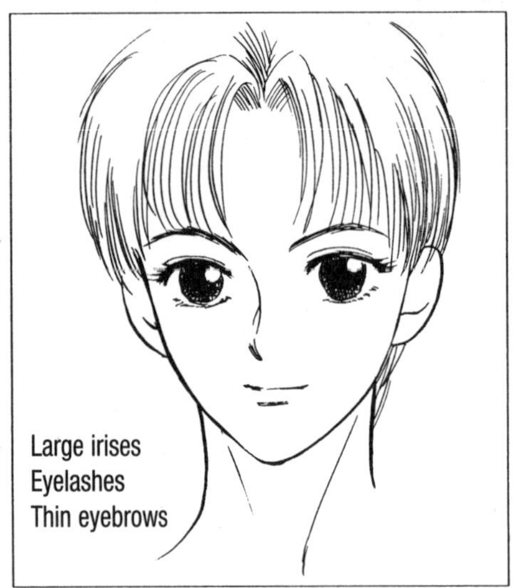

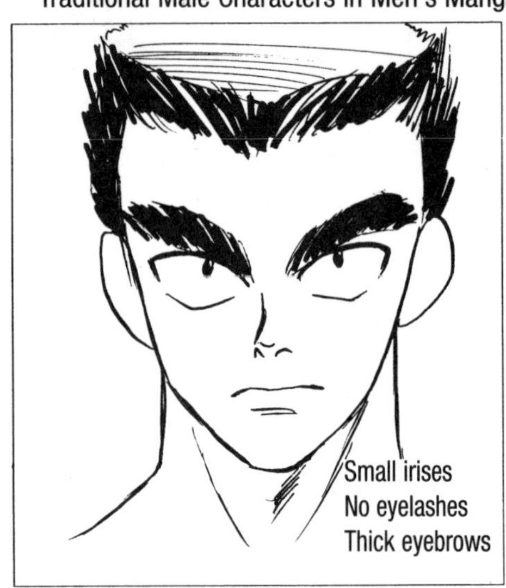

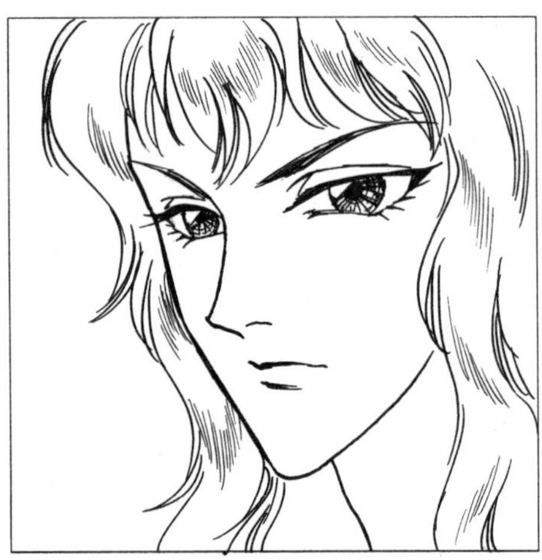

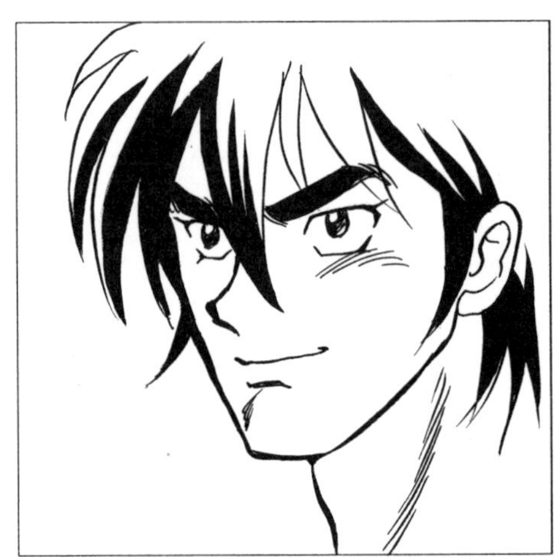

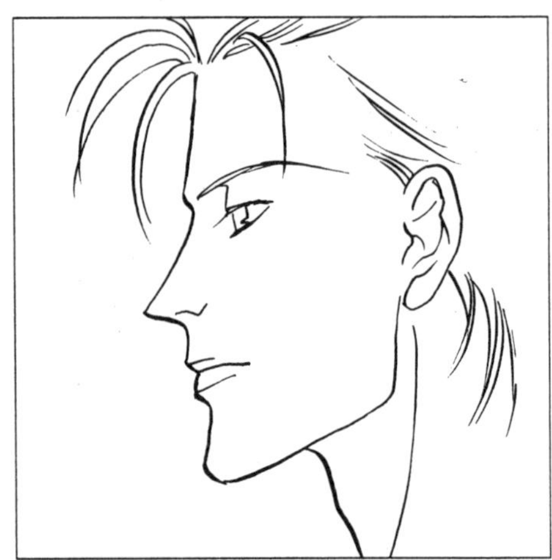

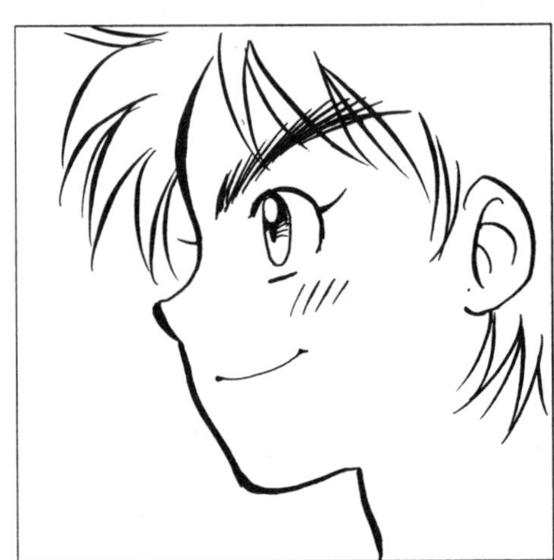

Male Characters in Women's Manga
The classic male character in women's manga is a dashing love interest designed according to women's ideals and desires. The variety of male characters echoes those of their female counterparts.

Male Characters in Men's Manga
Traditionally, the majority of these characters were conceived of as "strong," "good-looking," and "men of action" when they were rendered by the artists. Recently, however, men's manga has seen an increase in character variety, particularly with more timid, feminine male characters.

Drawing a Masculine Face

There are two approaches to drawing male characters. The first is to start right off the bat drawing a male character, while the other is to draw a female character's face and then add to it a male body.

1. Starting with a Male Face

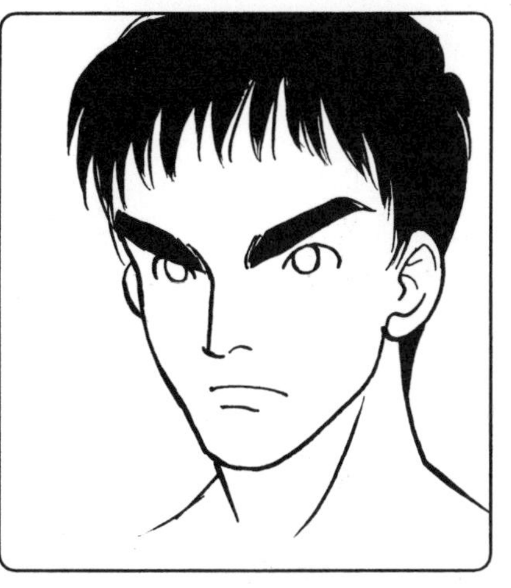

Character with typically male facial features
Thick eyebrows, small irises, lacking eyelashes, thick neck, large mouth, square jaw, and a down-turned nose

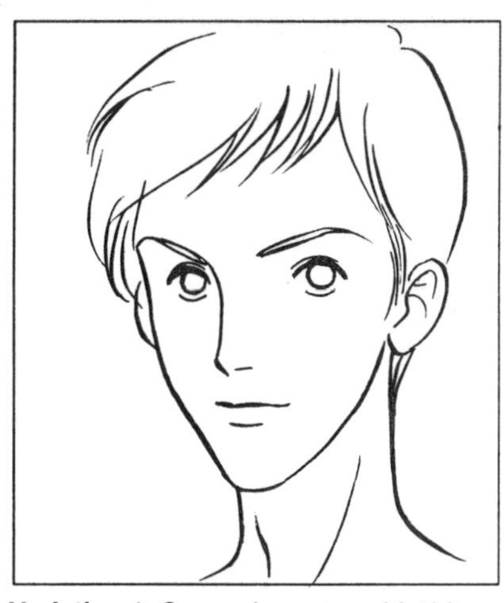

Variation 1: Same character with thin eyebrows and a slender neck

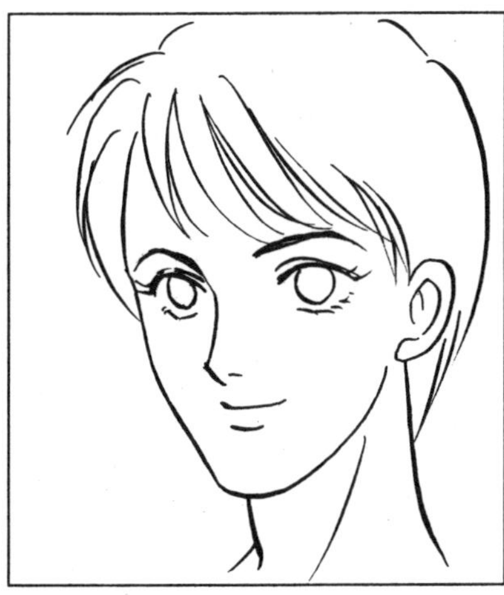

Variation 2: The character's neck and eyebrows are kept thin, while the eyes are enlarged and eyelashes are added.

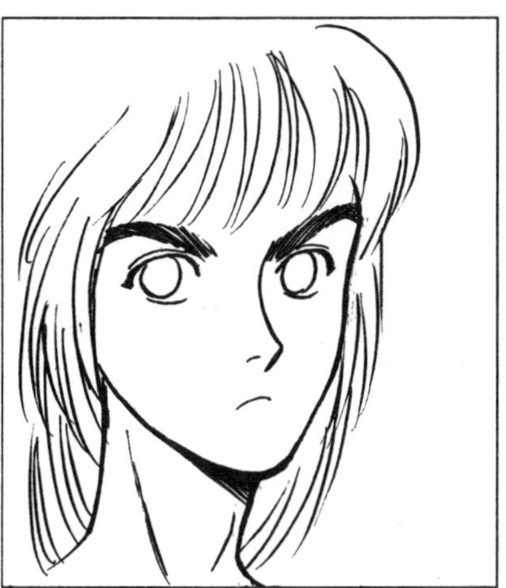

Variation 3: Character with female facial features, using thick eyebrows and lack of eyelashes to indicate the character's real gender

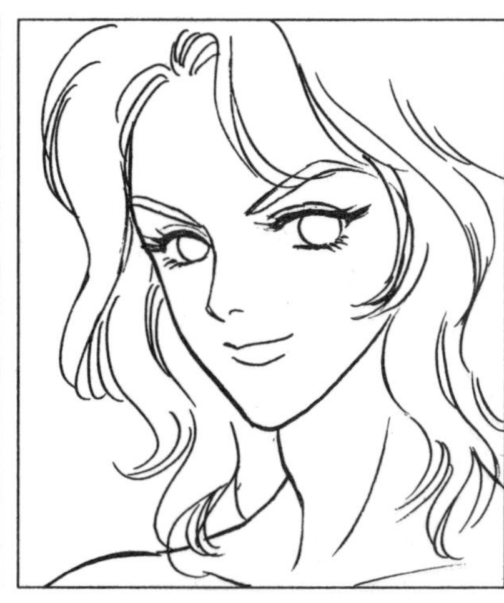

Variation 4: Character with total female facial features, with the exception of thick eyebrows
The neck contour is used to define the Adam's apple.

2. Adding a Male Body to a Female Face

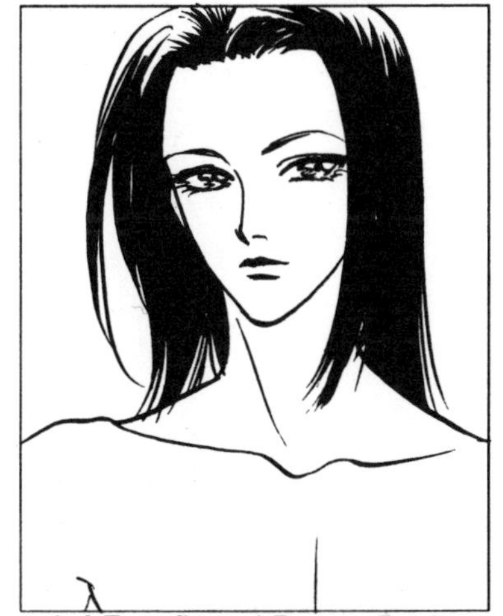

Type 1: A Transfigured Femme Fatale.
The character is converted through the rendering of the body, using the neck and shoulder contours and shoulder width.

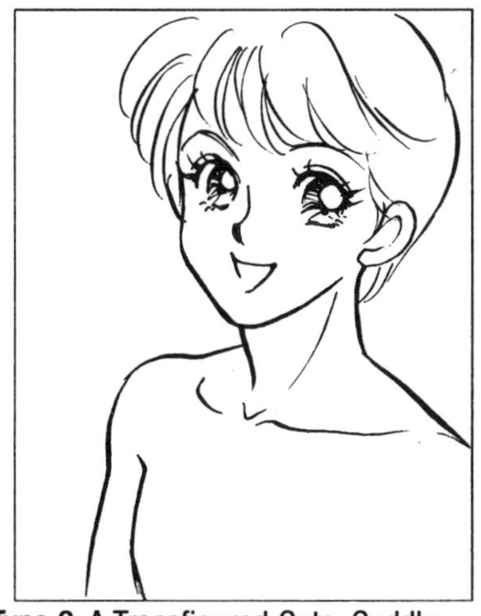

Type 2: A Transfigured Cute, Cuddly Bobbysoxer.
The character is converted through use of a shorter, thicker neck.

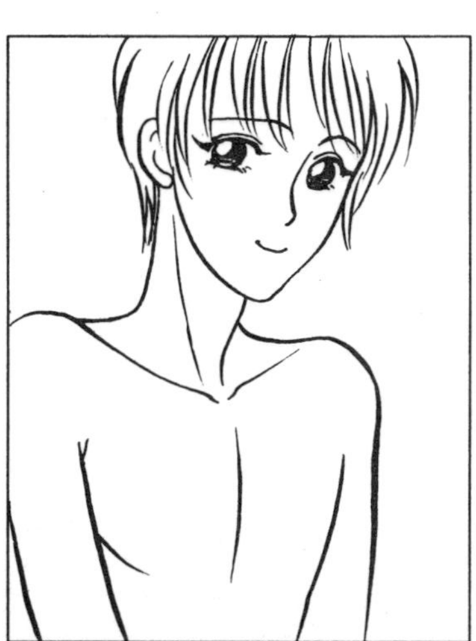

Note that a male character's gender can be suggested by not drawing areolas, even if the character still has a slender neck and shoulders.

Differences between Adults and Children

Draw the height of an adult (young) male at 7 or more heads in length, while using a length of 5 to 6 heads for a preadolescent boy.

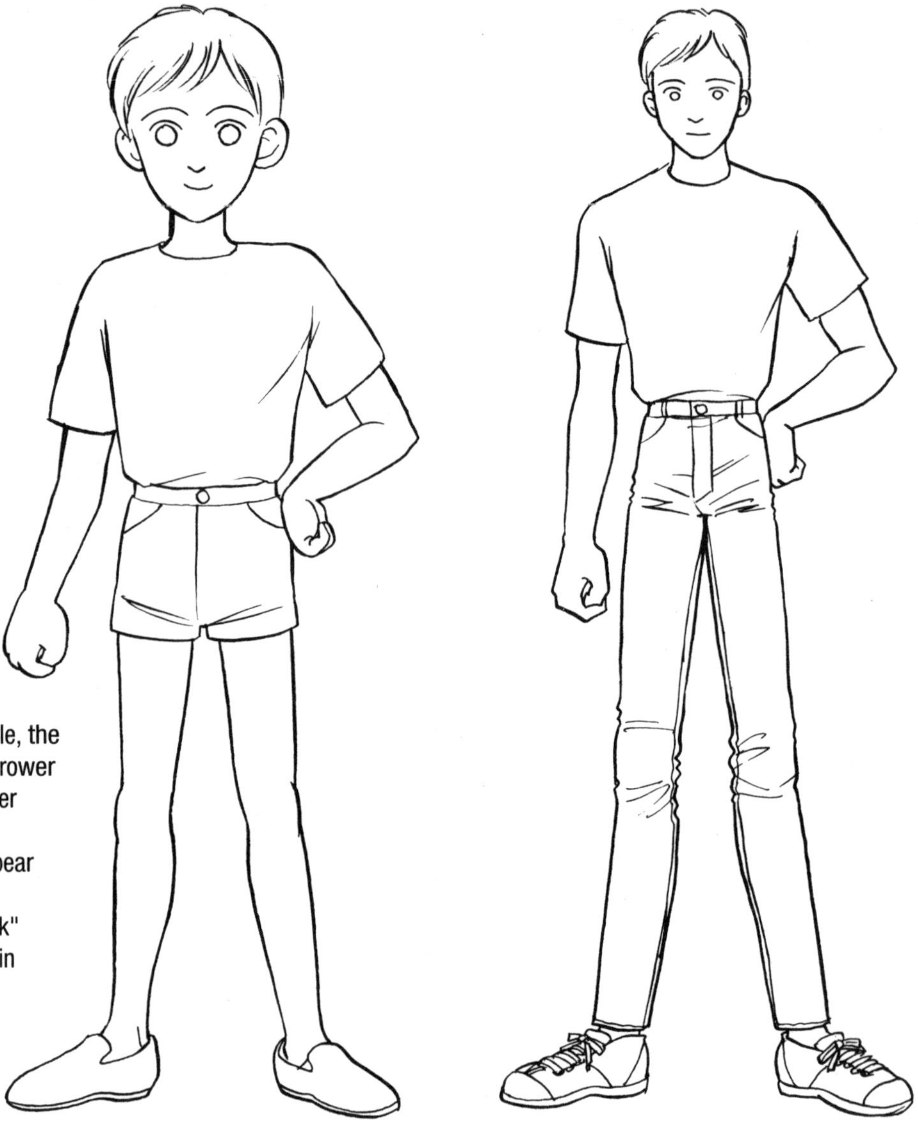

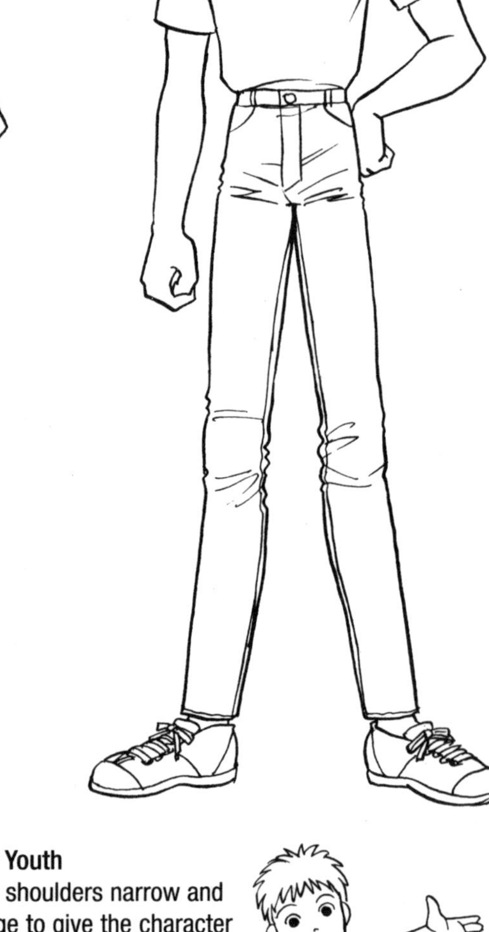

In contrast to the adult male, the preadolescent boy has narrower shoulders (a relatively larger head) and a shorter trunk.
To make the character appear more like a "boy" than a "child," use a simple "stick" shape to give the figure thin rather than pudgy arms.

A Chubby Preadolescent Boy
Keep the hands and legs pudgy and short.

A child's fingers are short.

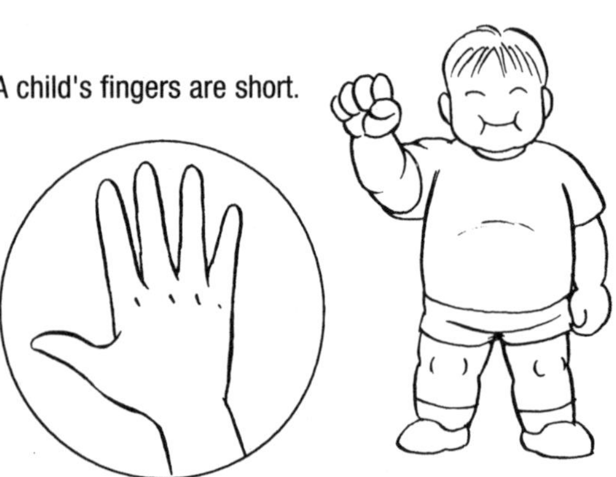

A Gangly Youth
Draw the shoulders narrow and head, large to give the character a childlike appearance.

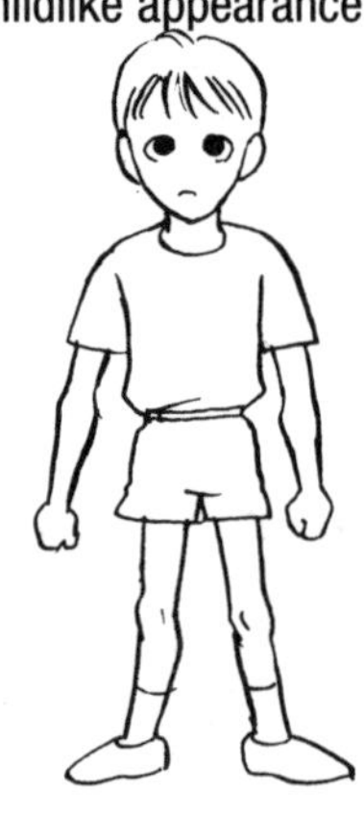

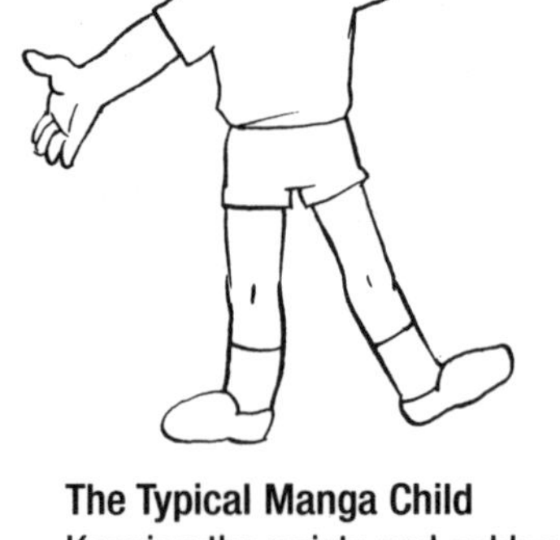

The Typical Manga Child
Keeping the wrists and ankles on the thick side makes the character appear childlike..

Chapter 2
The Male Body
Parts and Connectives

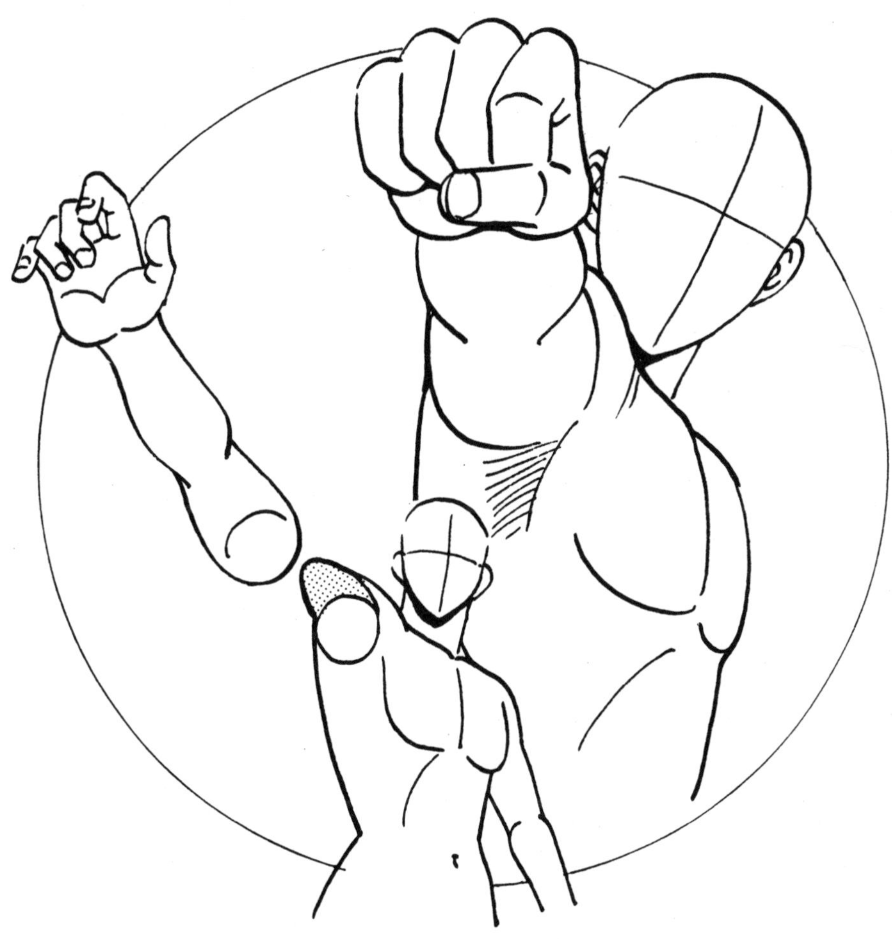

The Head and Neck (The Skull and Neck Vertebrae)

The neck does not stem from directly underneath the head, but rather from the back of the head.

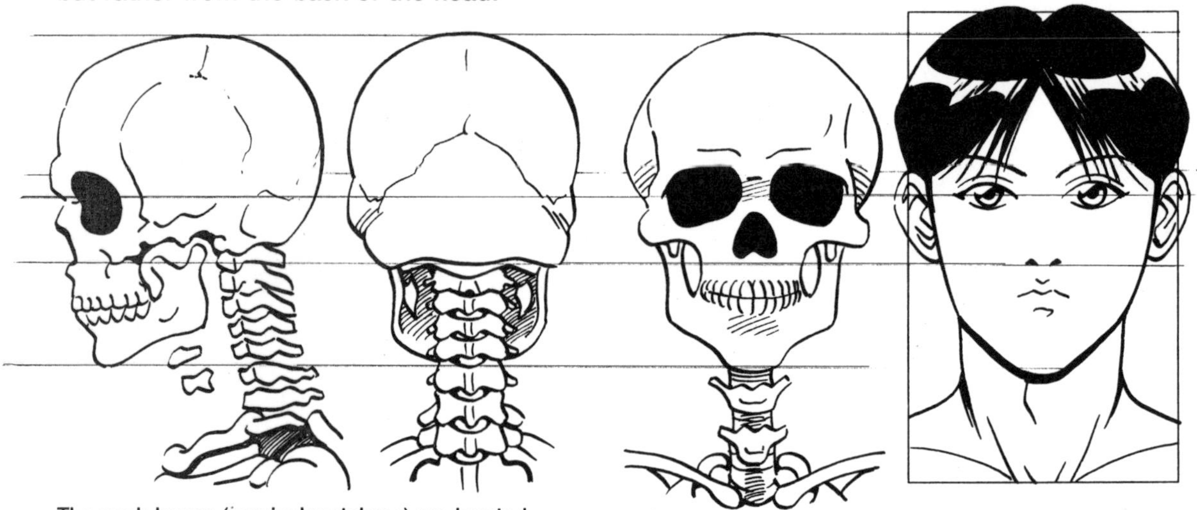

The neck bones (cervical vertebrae) are located behind the jaw.

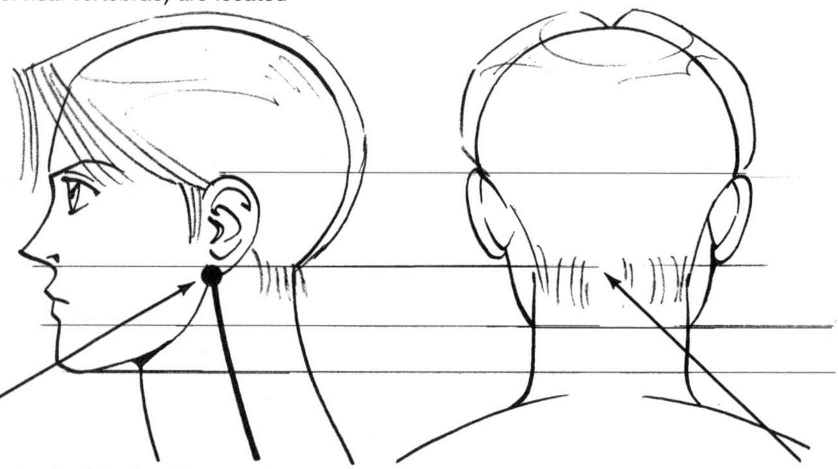

The area where the back of the head meets the neck is about the same height as a horizontal line connecting the bottom of the nose with the mouth.

The hairline starts where the back of the head meets the neck.

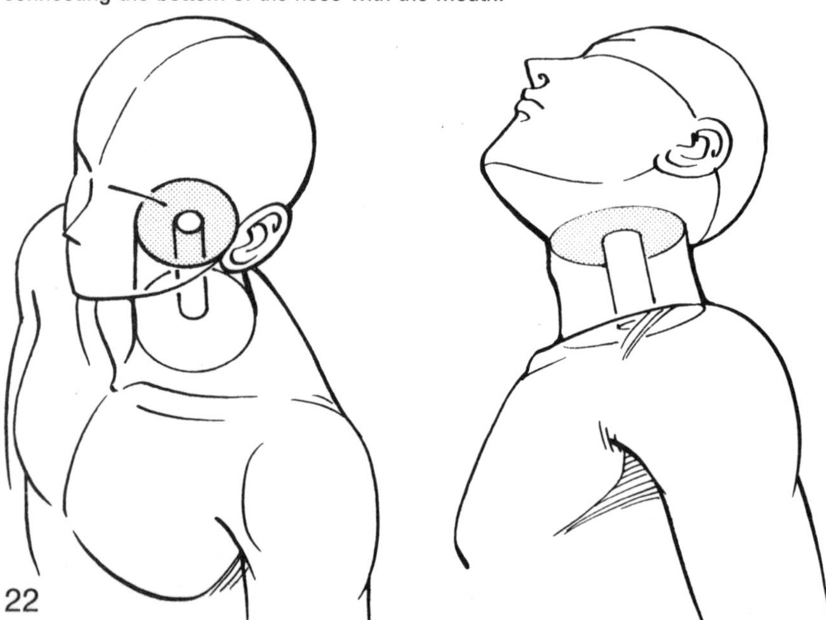

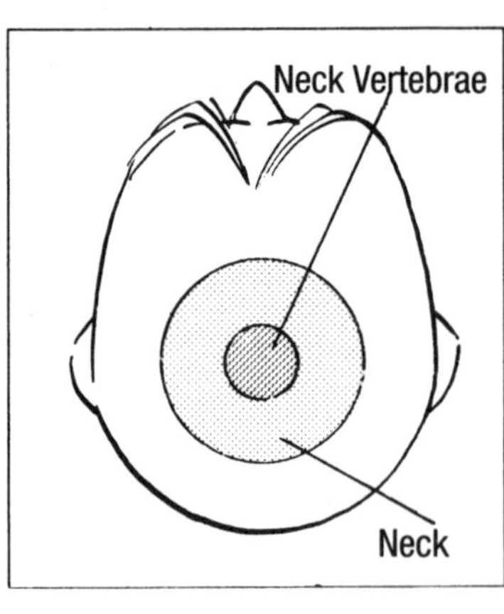

Direct Overhead View of the Head

Parts of the Head and Proportions

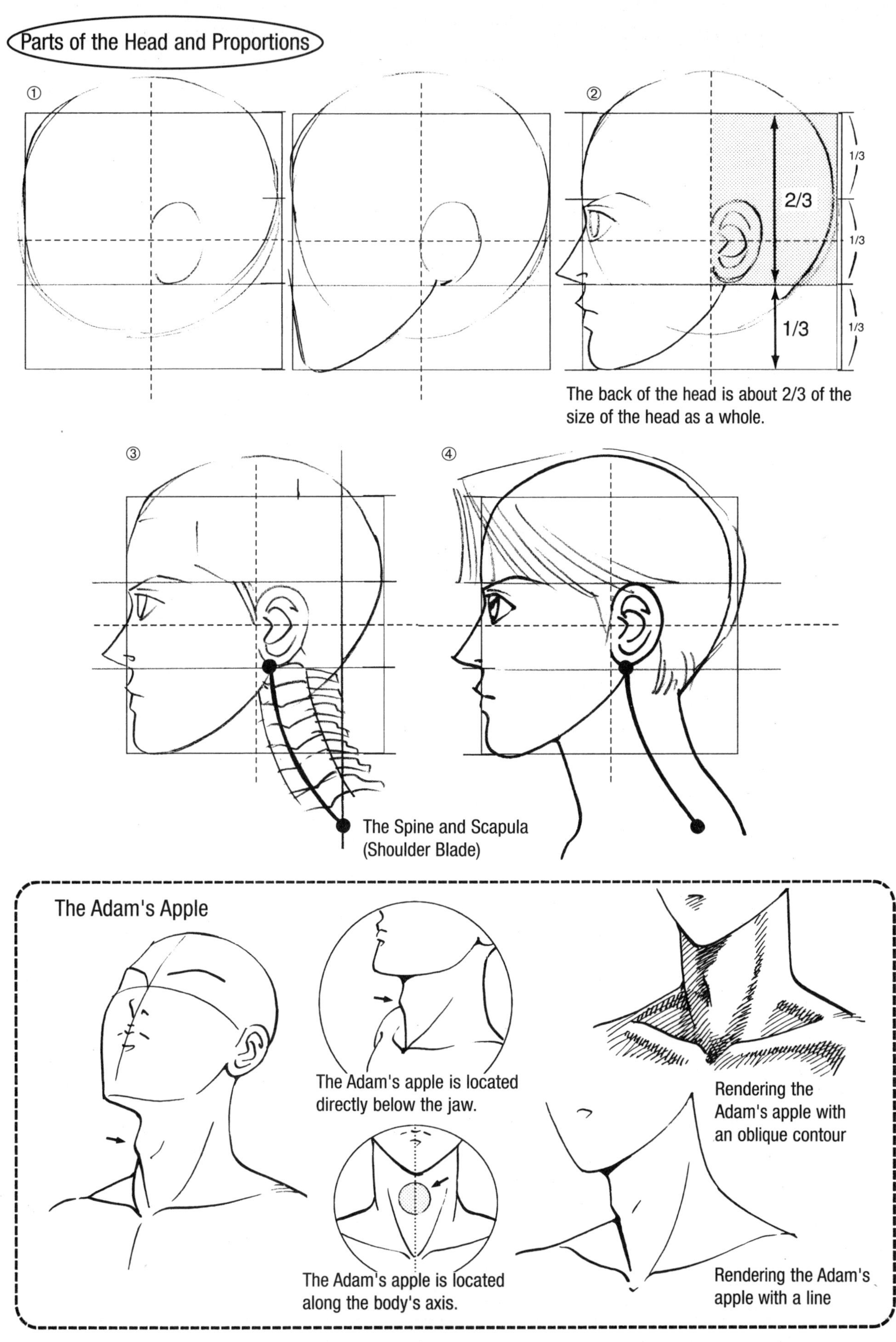

Relationship between the Neck and Shoulders

The key to a convincing character is to give the head, neck, and trunk depth. Practice the relationship between these parts using a simplified figure.

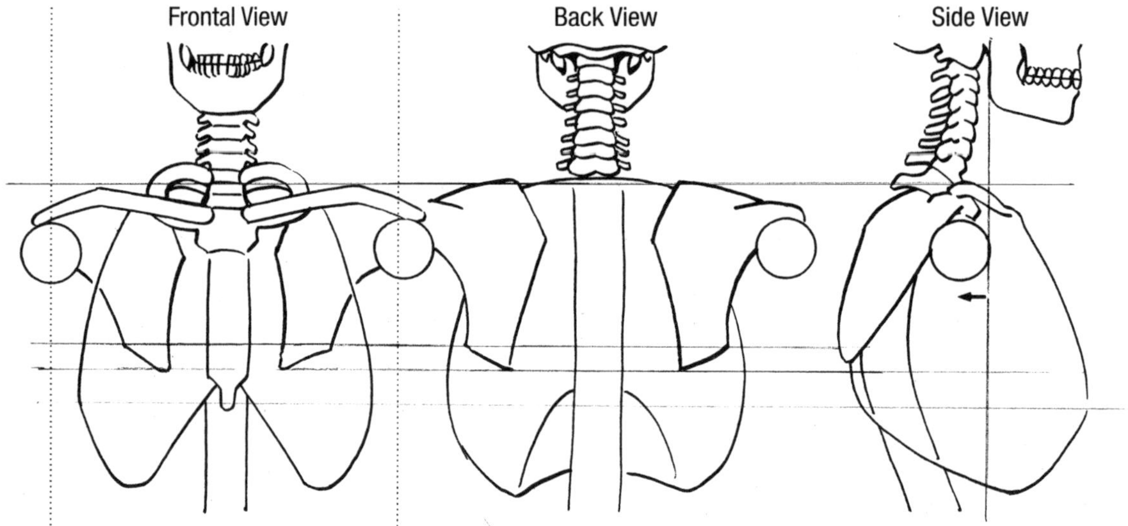

Frontal View

Back View

Side View

The shoulders are located behind the axial line.

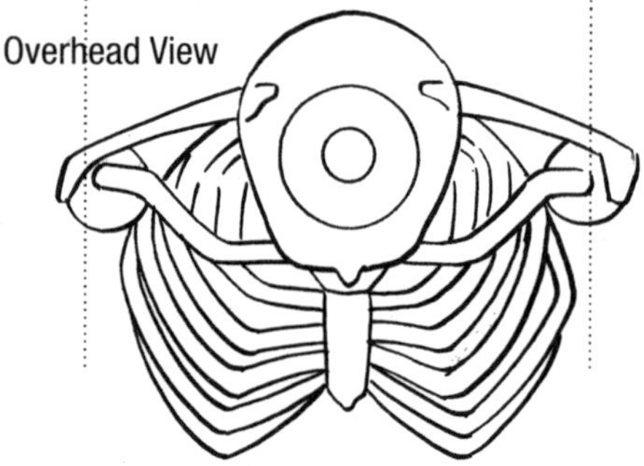

Overhead View

Proportion of the Head to the Trunk

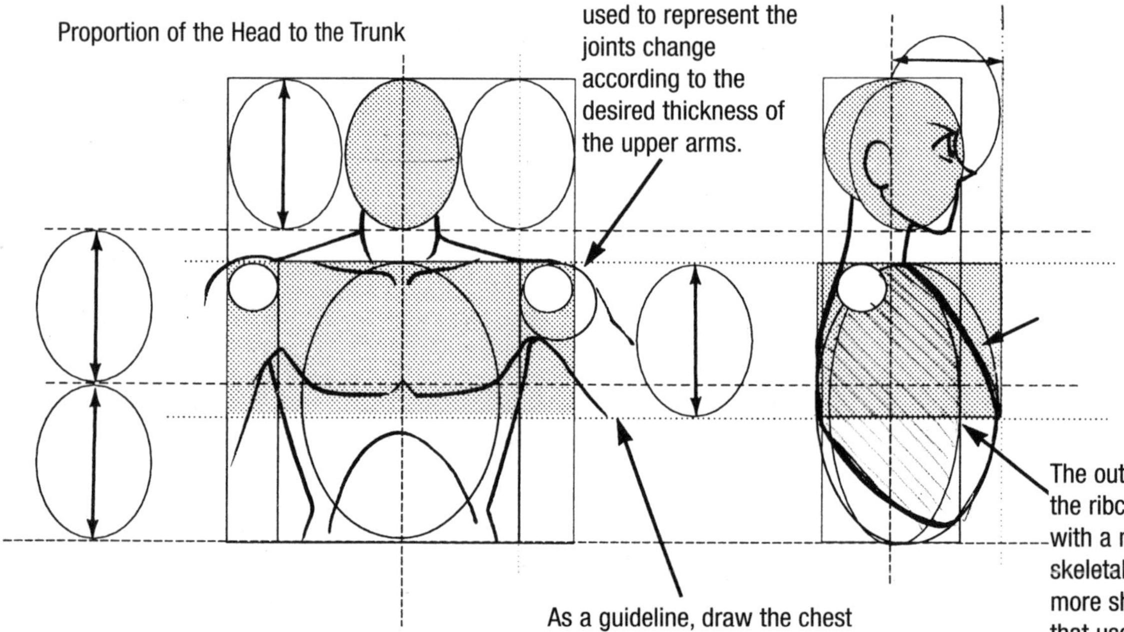

The sizes of the circles used to represent the joints change according to the desired thickness of the upper arms.

As a guideline, draw the chest below the neck at about the height of one head.

The outer contour for the ribcage of a figure with a more realistic skeletal structure is more shallow than that used for manga, where it is drawn puffed out boldly.

Study the relationship between the head and the chest using box figures.

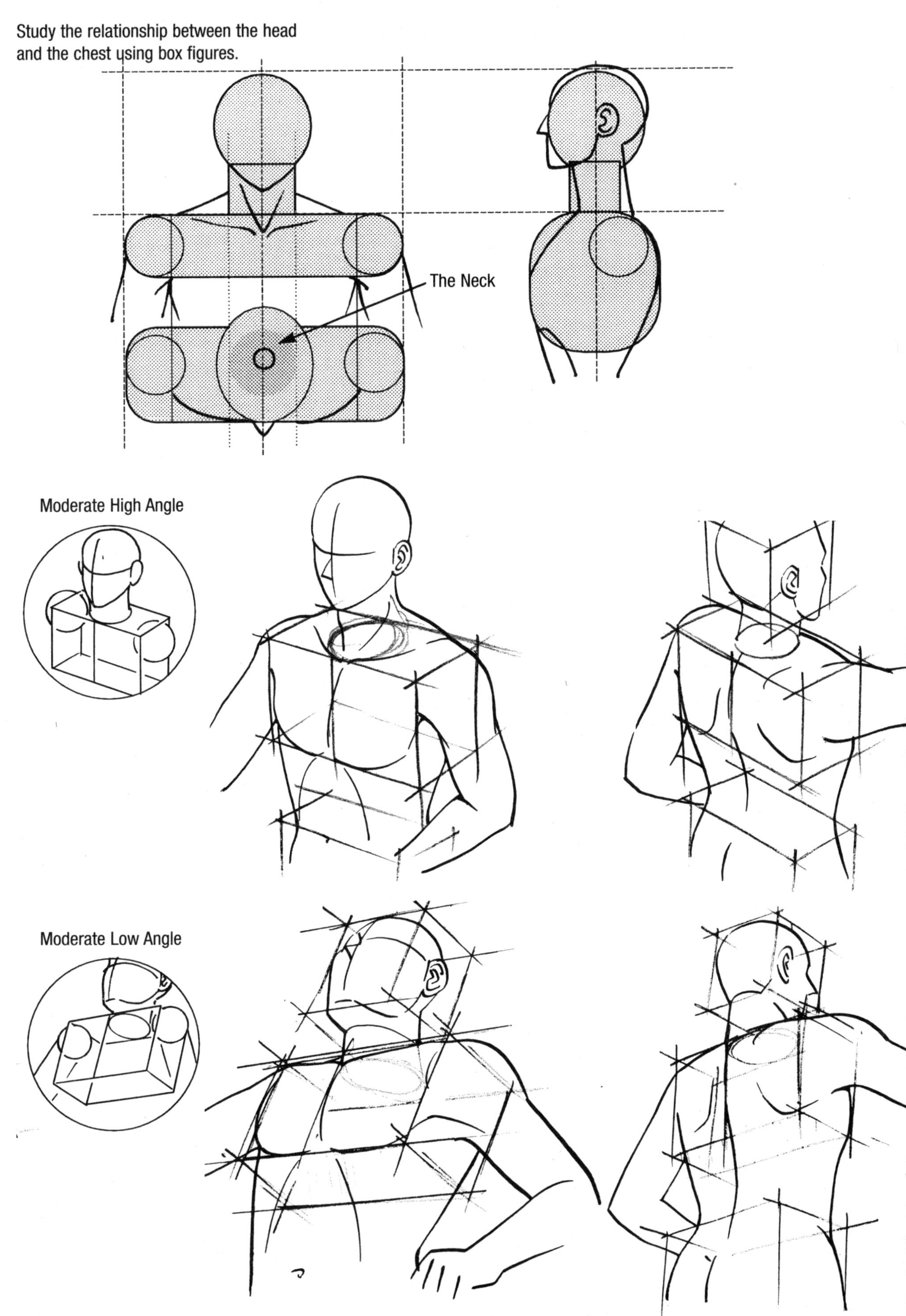

The Shoulders

How the Shoulder is Attached (The Underarm)

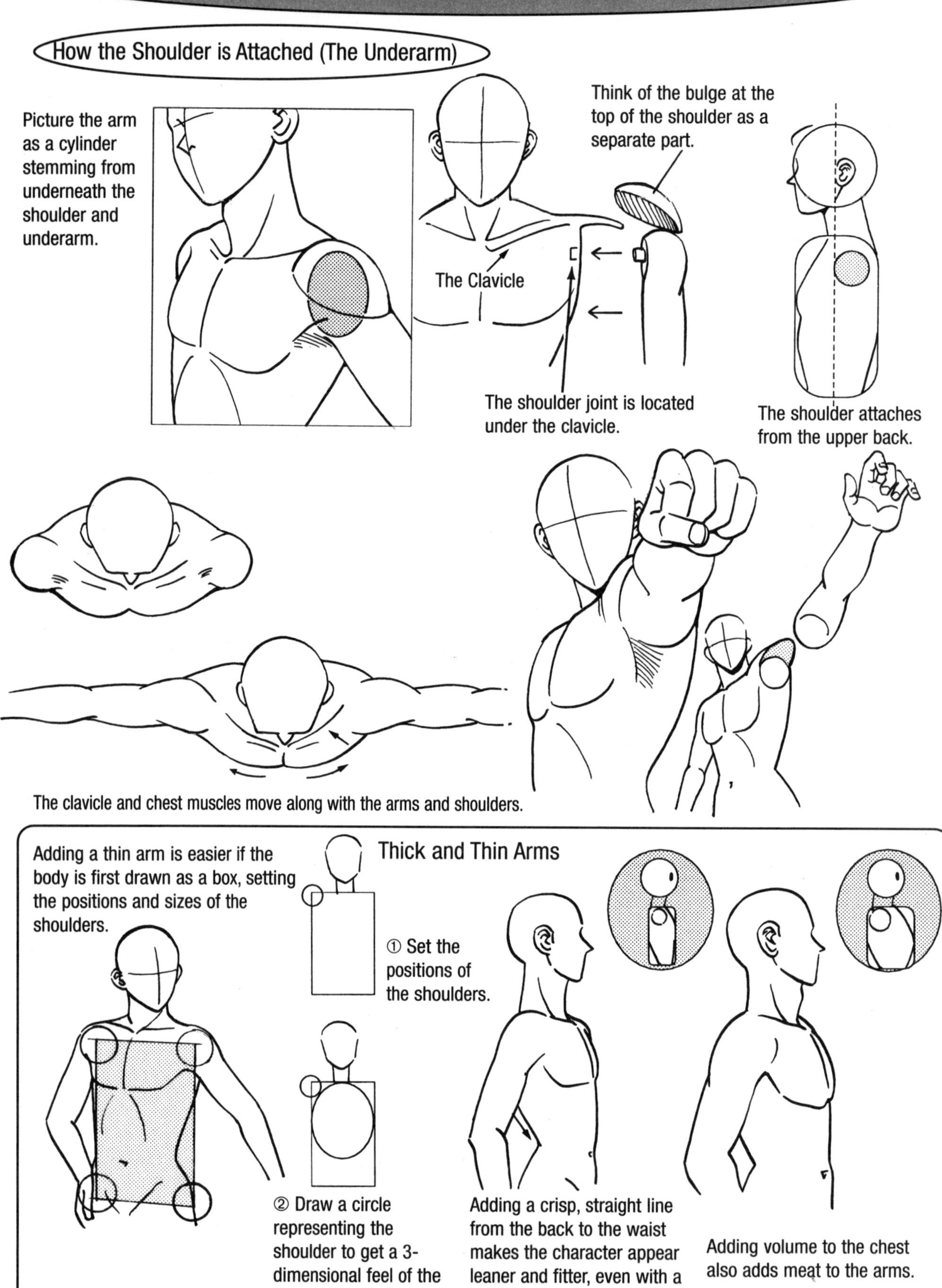

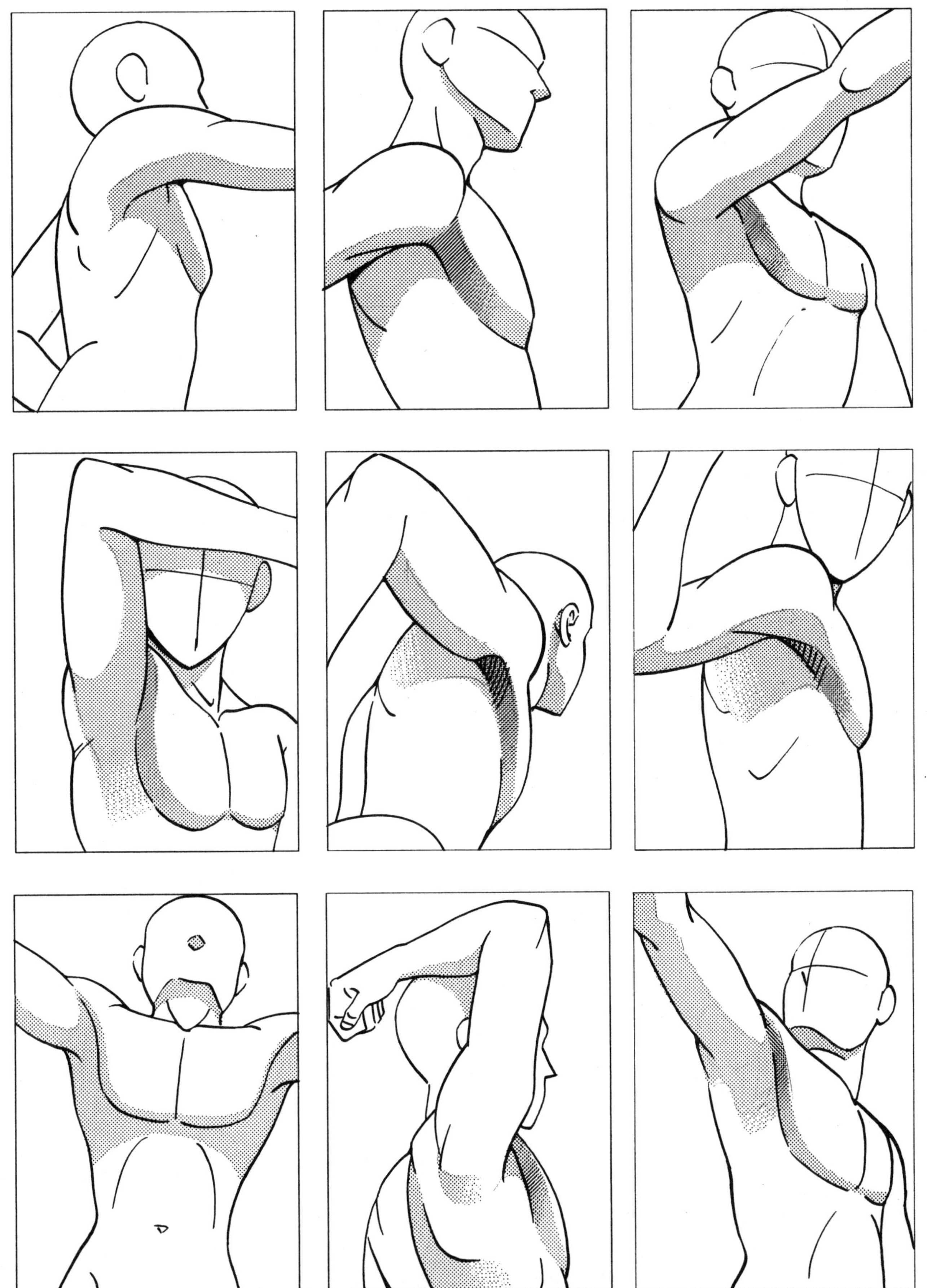

The Shoulders and Upper Back

Because the shoulder blade is connected to the shoulder joint, the appearance of the back changes according to the movement of the shoulders and arms above the chest.

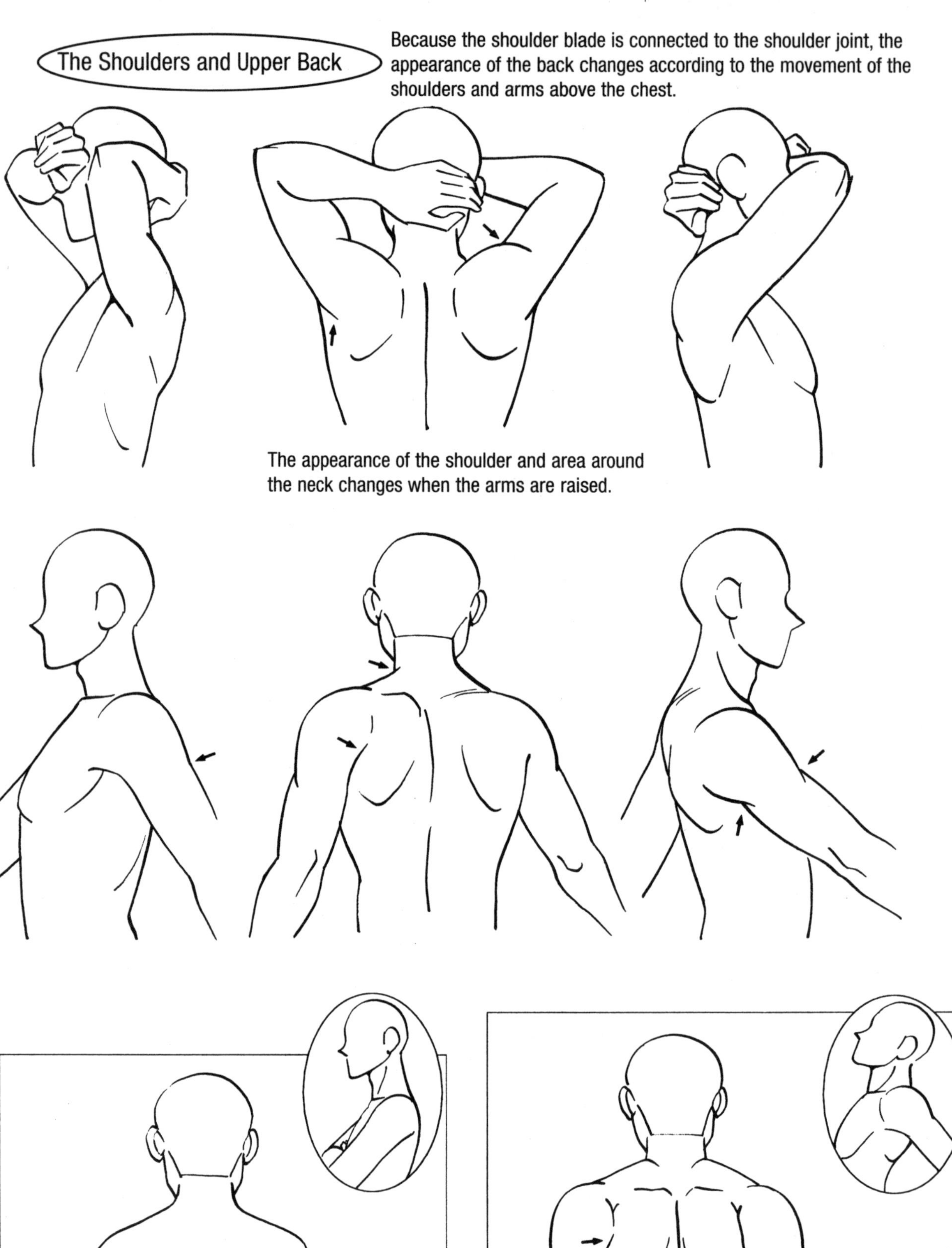

The appearance of the shoulder and area around the neck changes when the arms are raised.

Note how the underarms change when the arms rotate to the back, causing the underarms to move forward.

The Shoulders and Chest

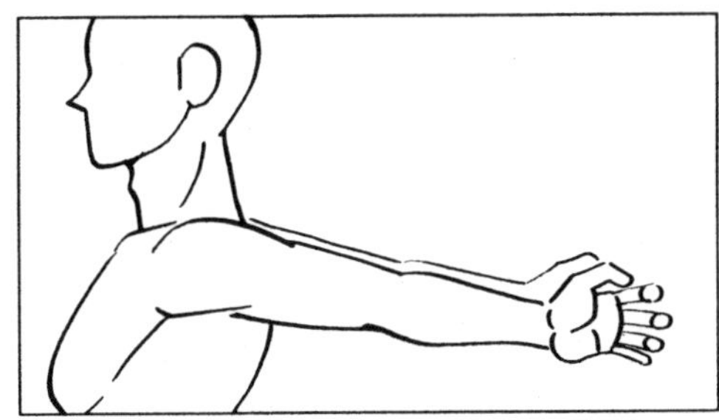

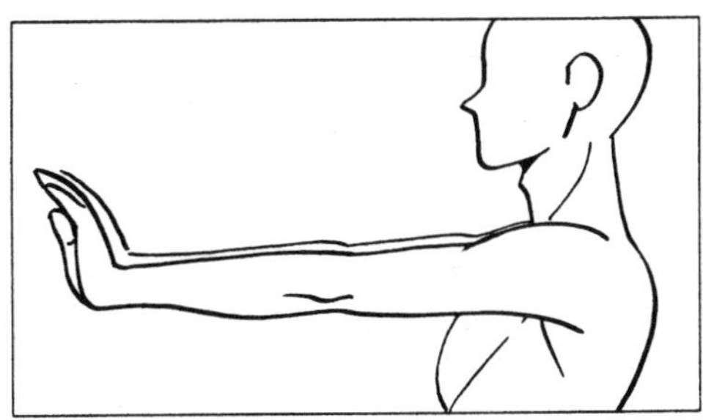

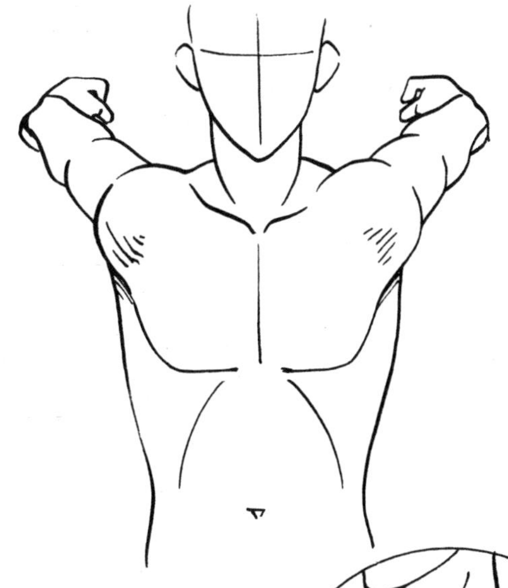

Extending the arms straight outward from behind pulls back the chest muscles.

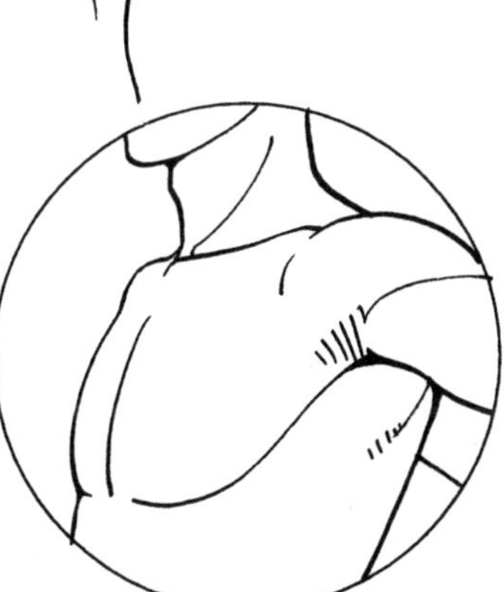

Extending the arms straight outward in front causes the chest muscles to bunch together in the front.

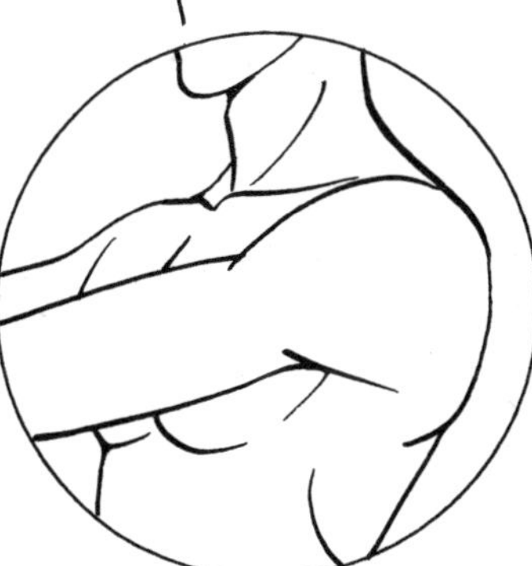

Raising the Arms in a Relaxed Position

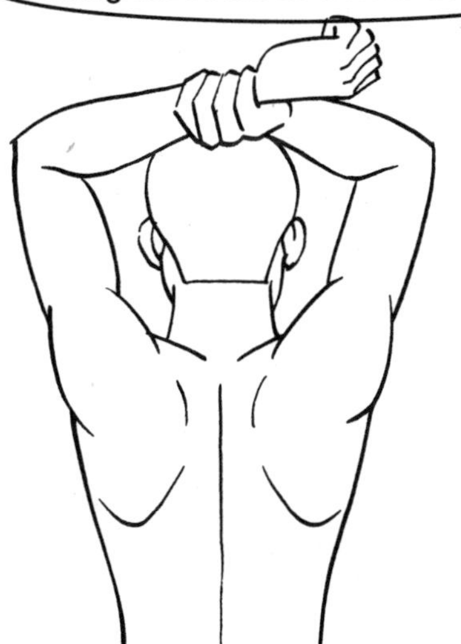

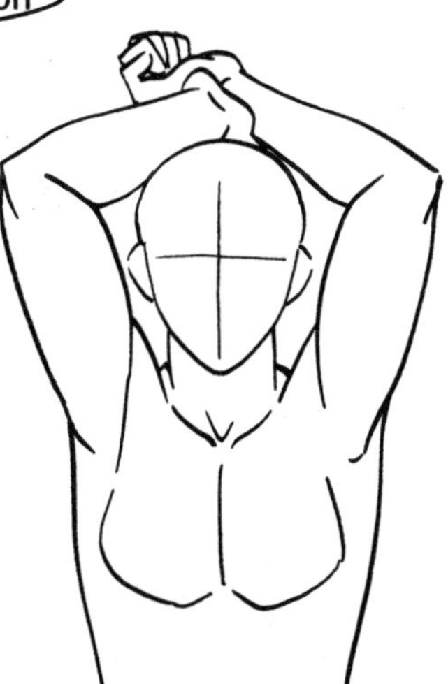

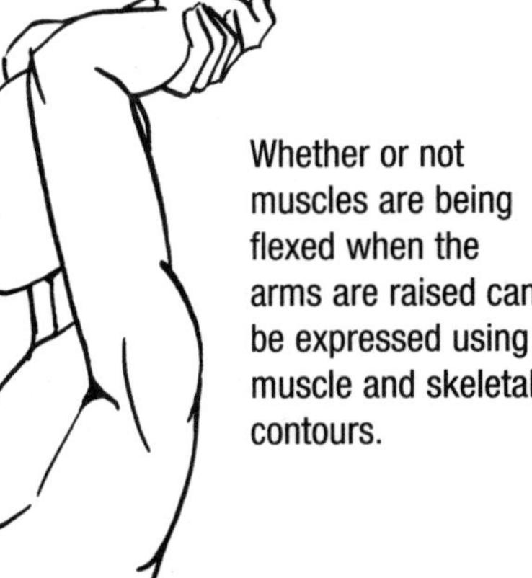

Whether or not muscles are being flexed when the arms are raised can be expressed using muscle and skeletal contours.

The Arms and Elbows

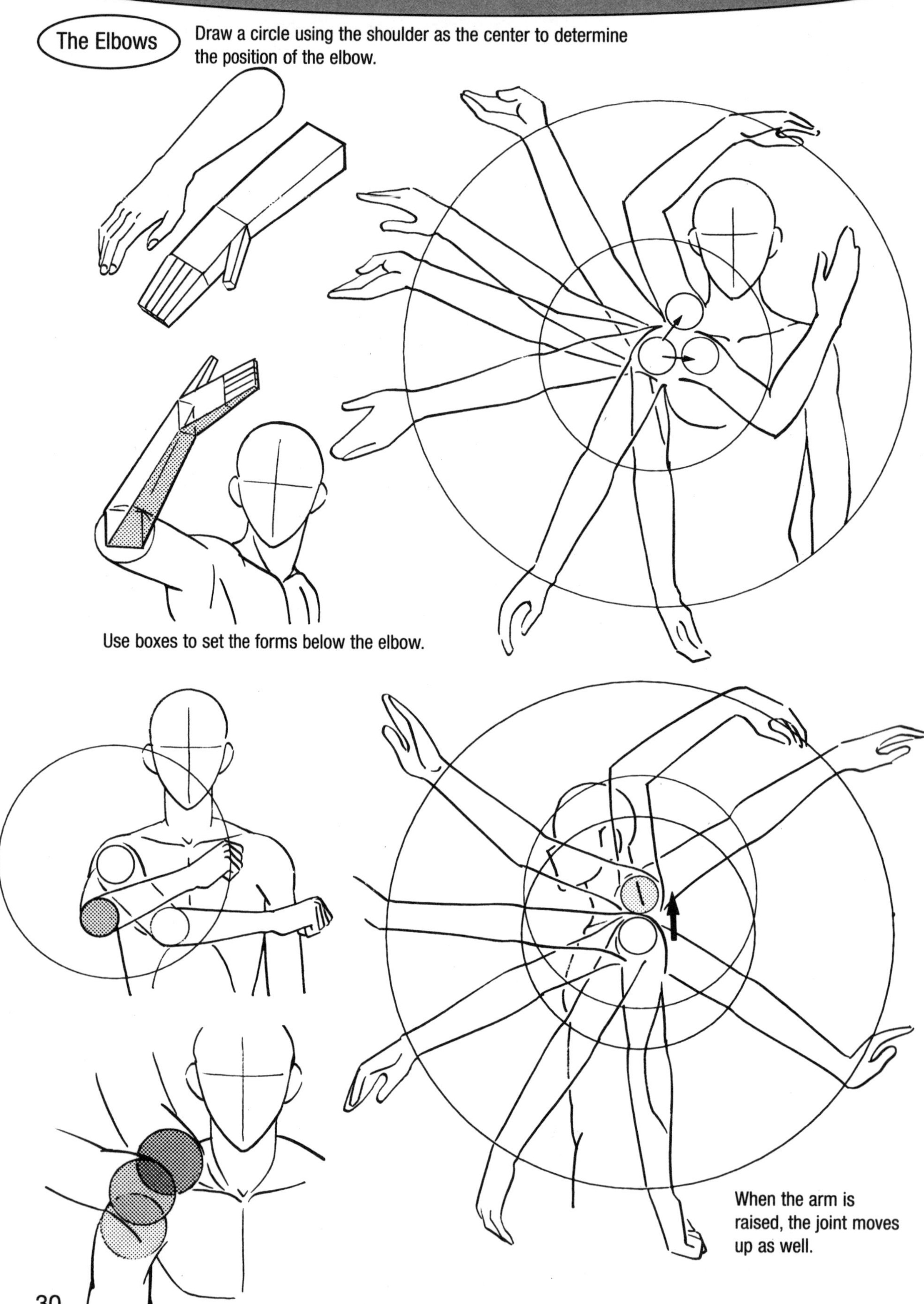

The Elbows

Draw a circle using the shoulder as the center to determine the position of the elbow.

Use boxes to set the forms below the elbow.

When the arm is raised, the joint moves up as well.

Assorted Representations of the Elbow

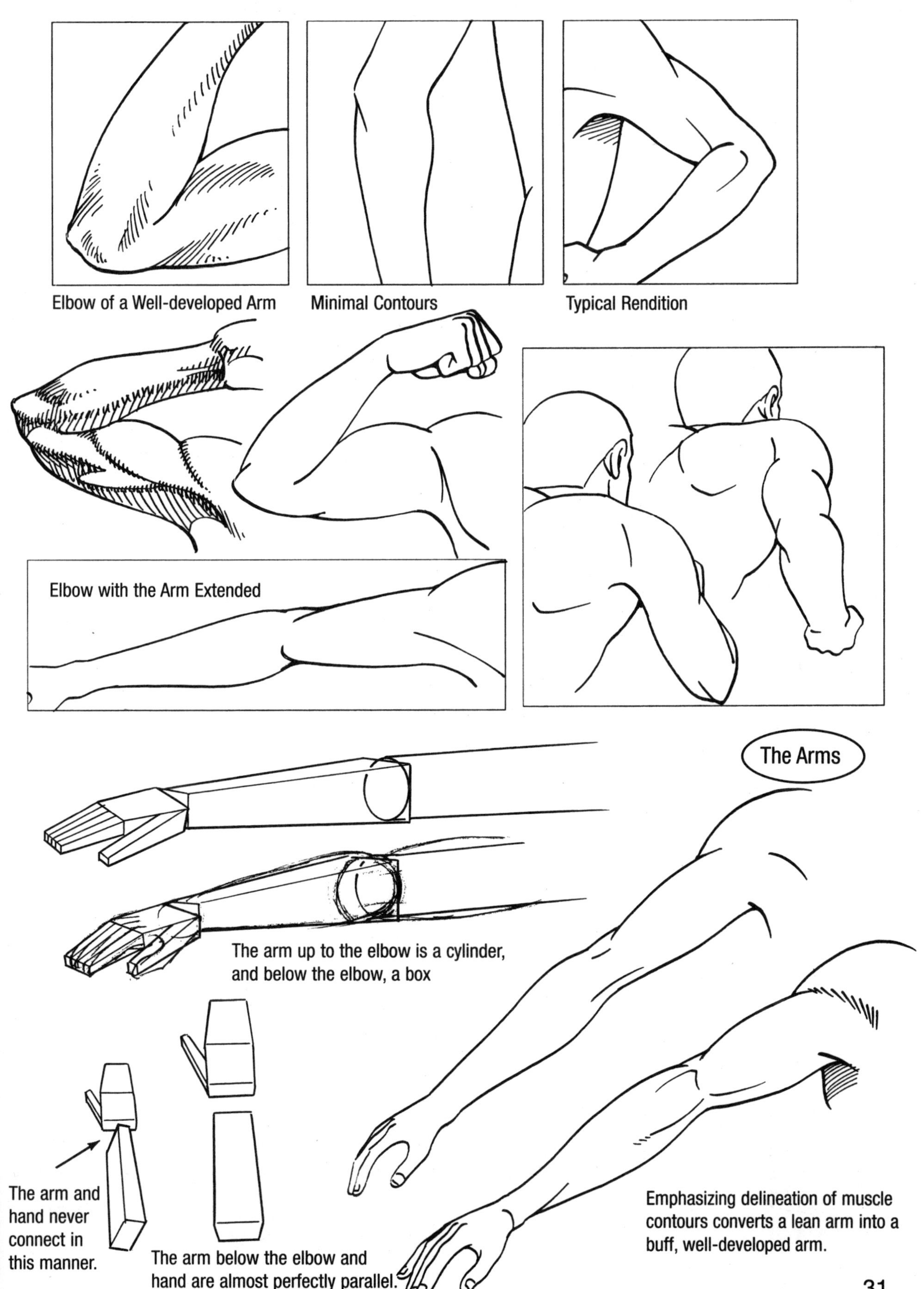

Representing the Chest and Trunk

There are 4 general body types popularly used in manga: the average build, the lean build, the gaunt build, and the muscular build. Depending on the particular work, the body may be rendered either in a manga-esque or realistic (gekiga or manga with darker, more dramatic themes) style.

Figures in manga are basically abbreviated (less lines) versions of realistically rendered figures.

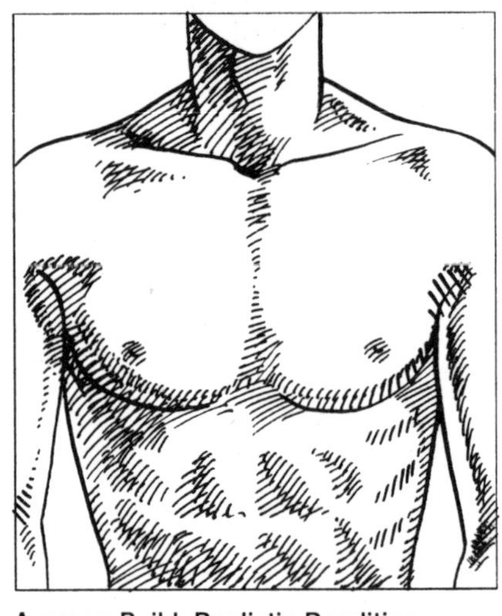

Average Build: Realistic Rendition

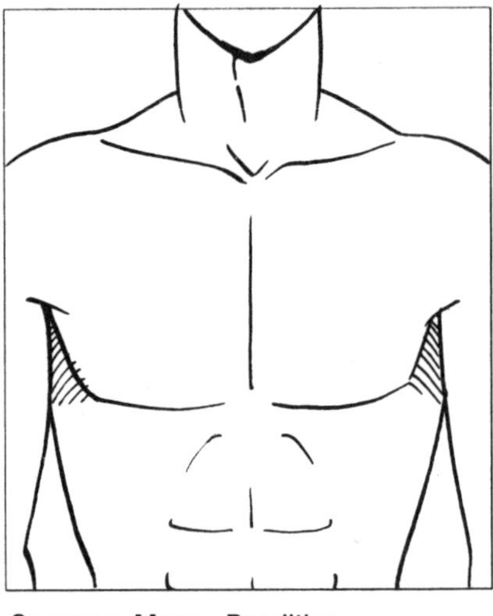

Common: Manga Rendition

Manga Renditions

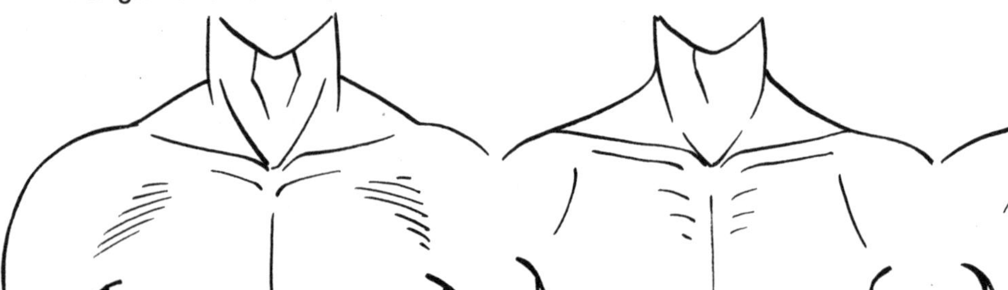

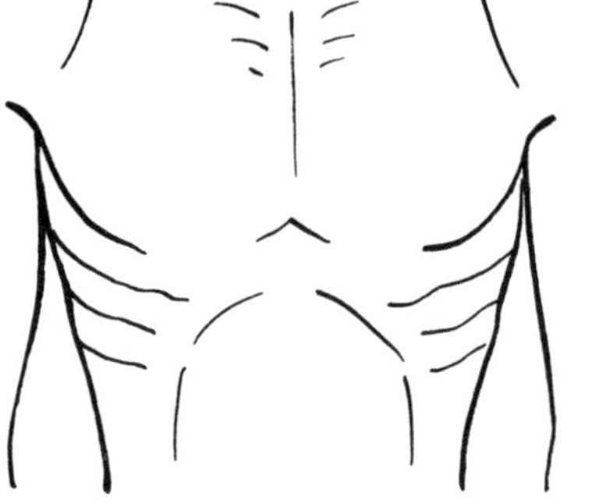

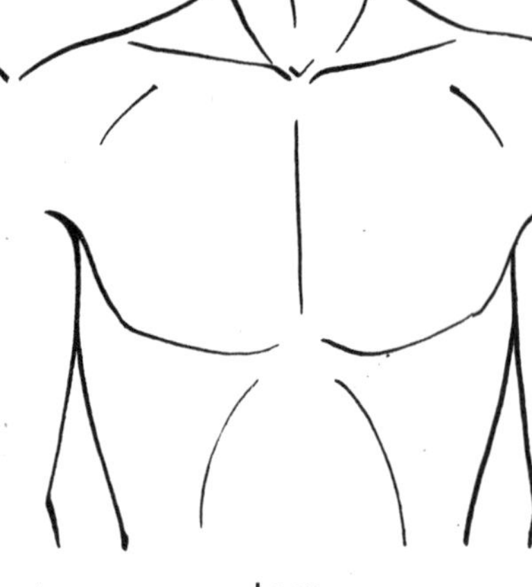

Muscular

Gaunt

Lean

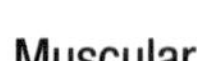

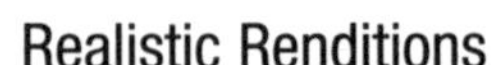

Realistic Renditions

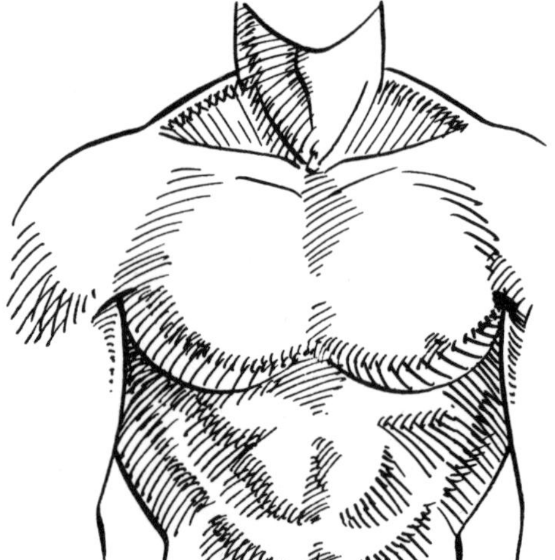

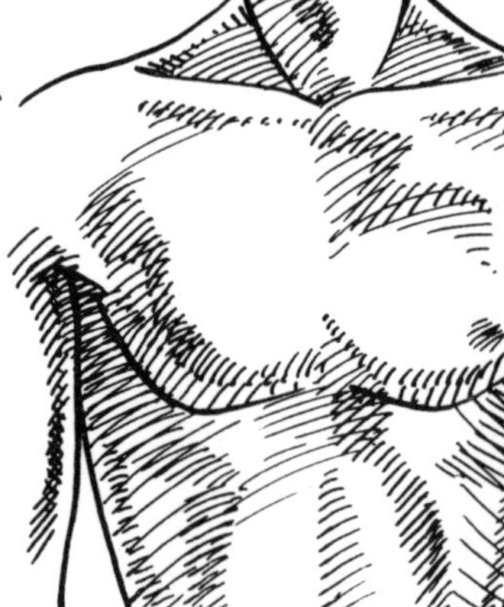

Muscular

Gaunt

Lean

In realistic renderings, a muscular body is typically handled using lines while other body types are rendered in sheet tone.

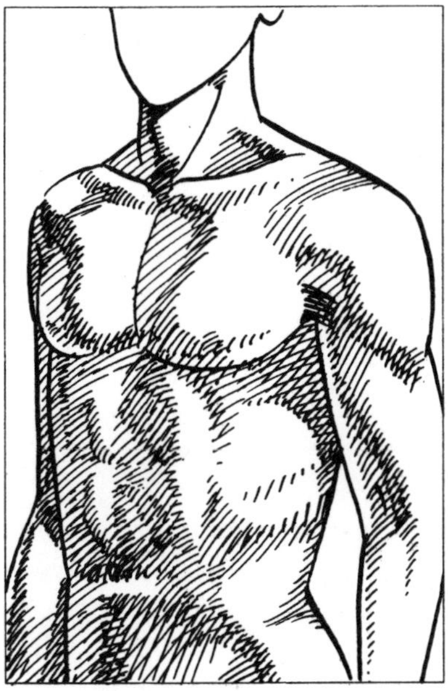

Average Build: Realistic Rendition

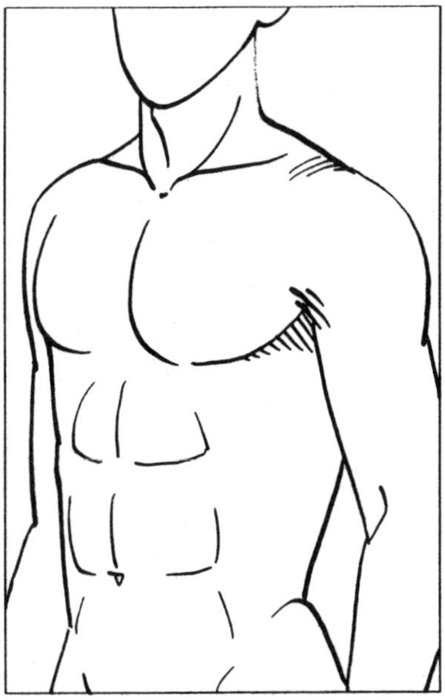

Average Build: Manga Rendition

Manga Renditions

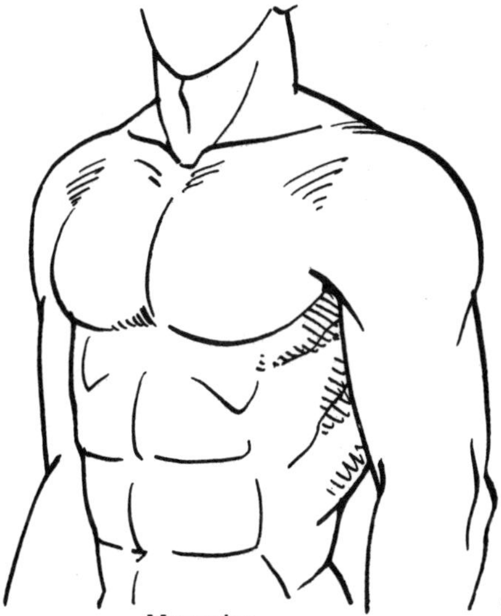

Muscular

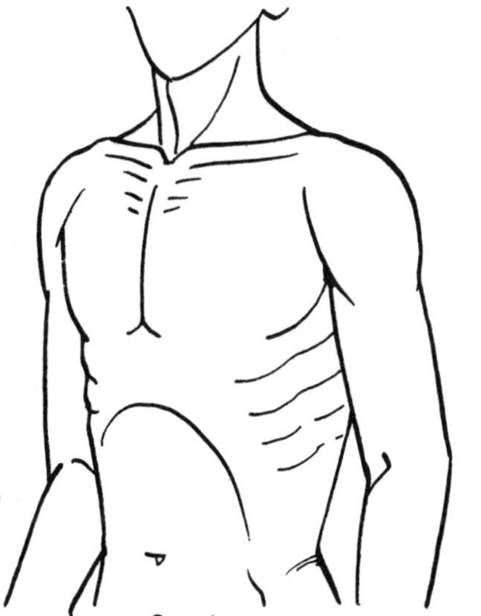

Gaunt

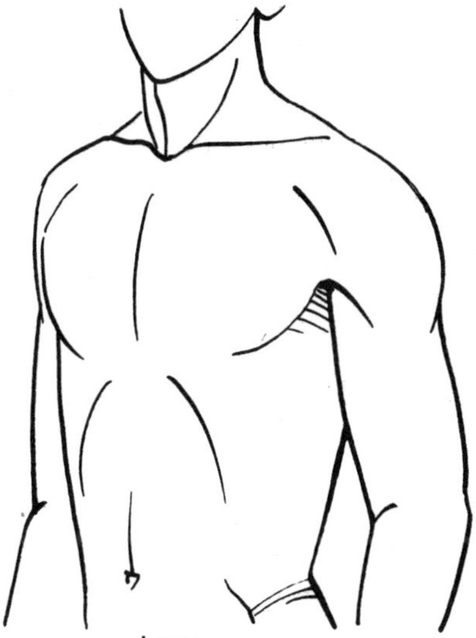

Lean

Realistic Renditions

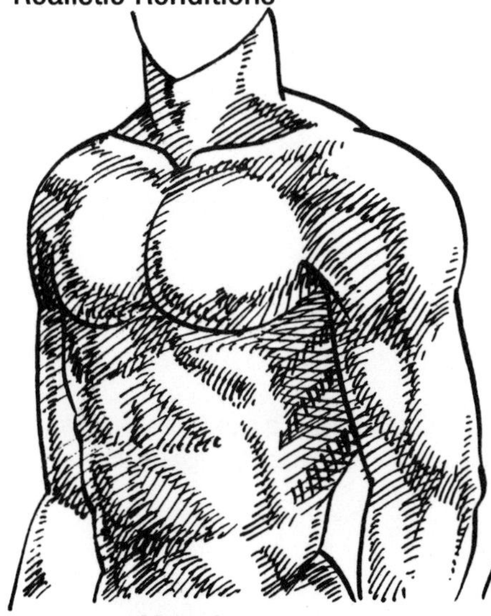

Muscular

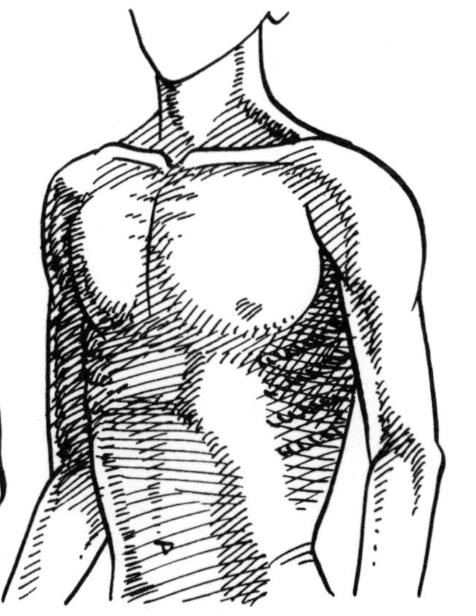

Gaunt

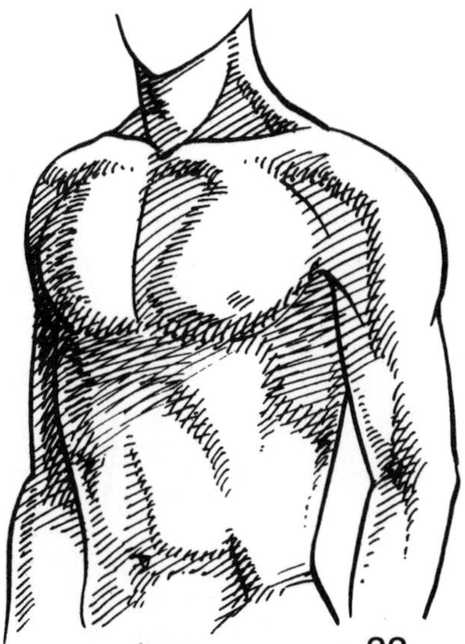

Lean

The Waist

Picture the abdominal/waist area as a contrast to the shoulders and the junction where the body's lower half attaches to the upper half.

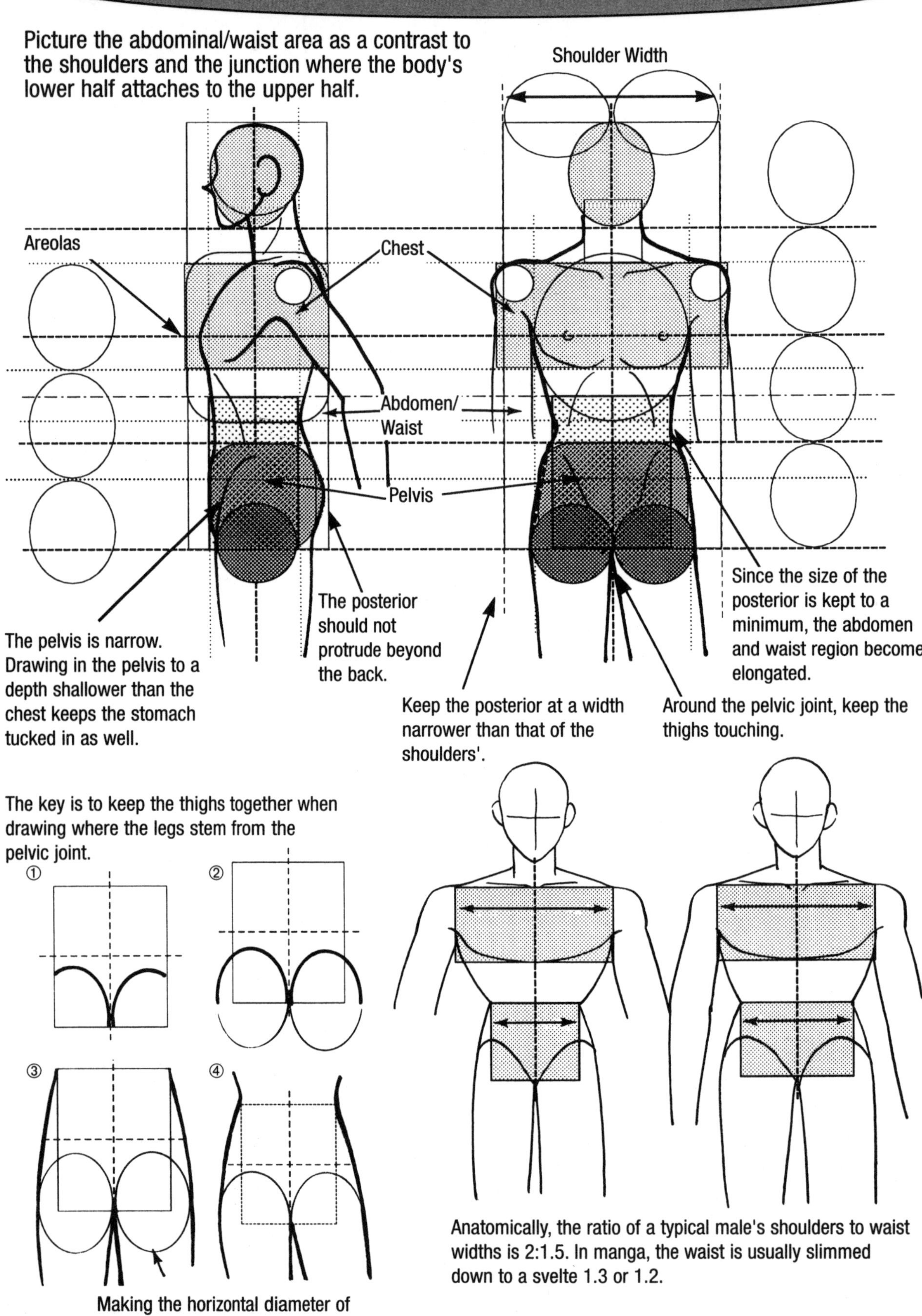

Drawing the Waist

Picture the waist and chest as boxes.

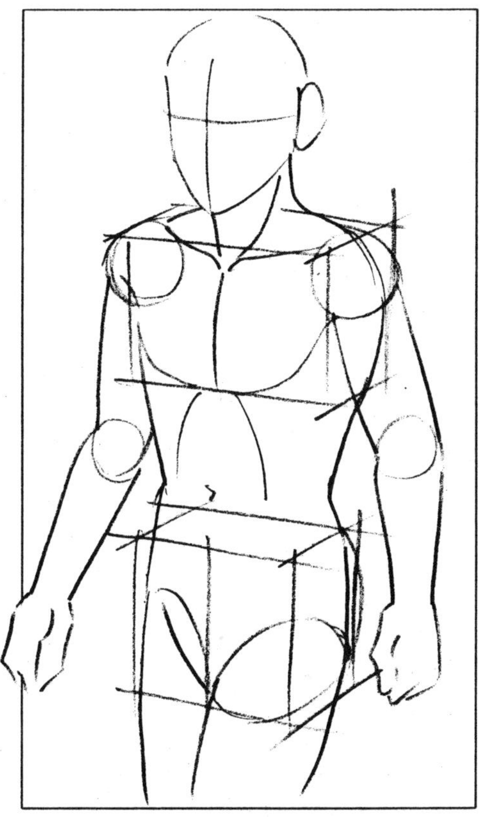

① Draw a rough sketch of the body as a whole to visualize the waist.

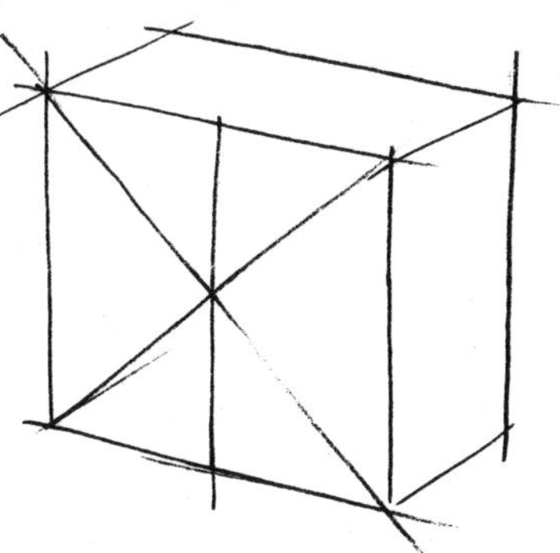

② Establish the pelvic area and the axis.

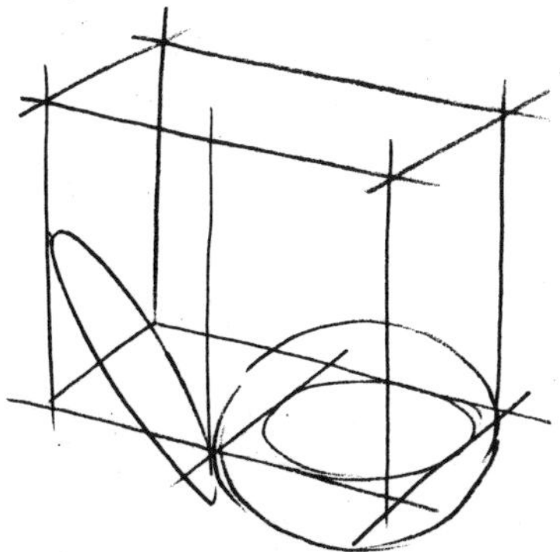

③ Draw ovals for the leg joints.

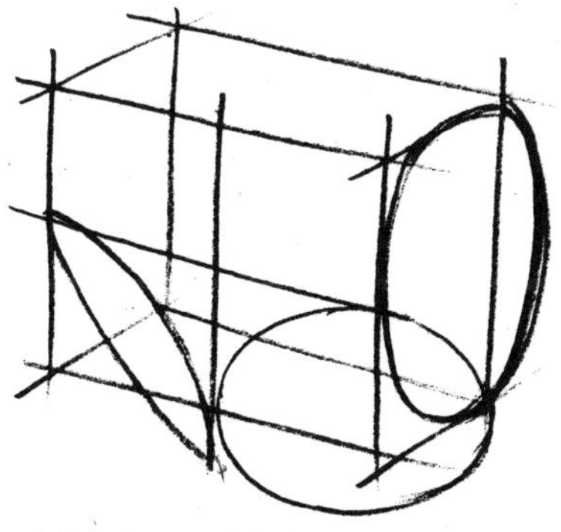

④ Establish the positioning and shape of the posterior.

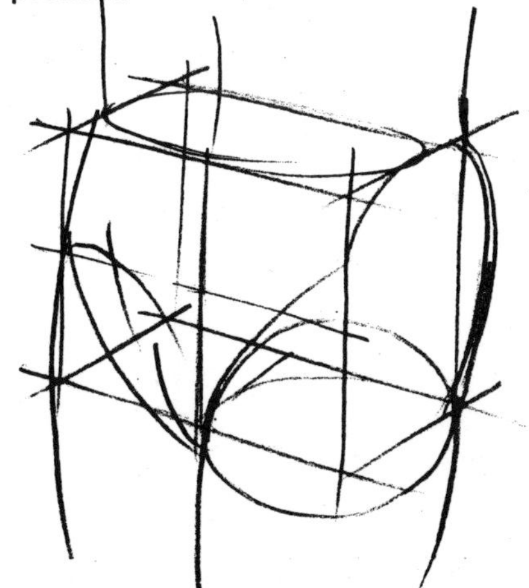

⑤ Draw the legs stemming from the pelvis.

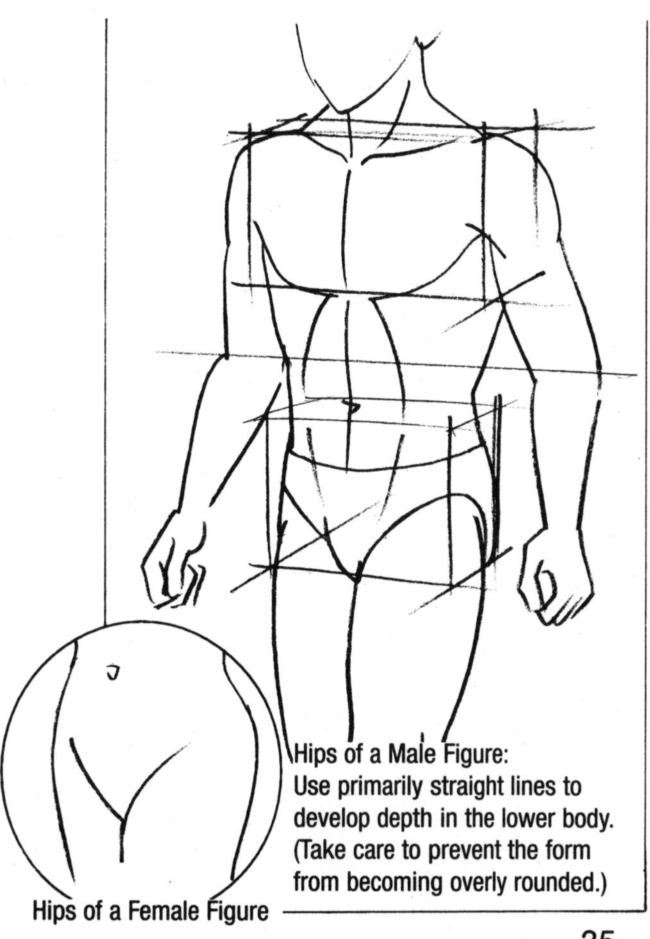

Hips of a Male Figure:
Use primarily straight lines to develop depth in the lower body. (Take care to prevent the form from becoming overly rounded.)

Hips of a Female Figure

The Legs

Skeletally, men tend to be bowlegged.

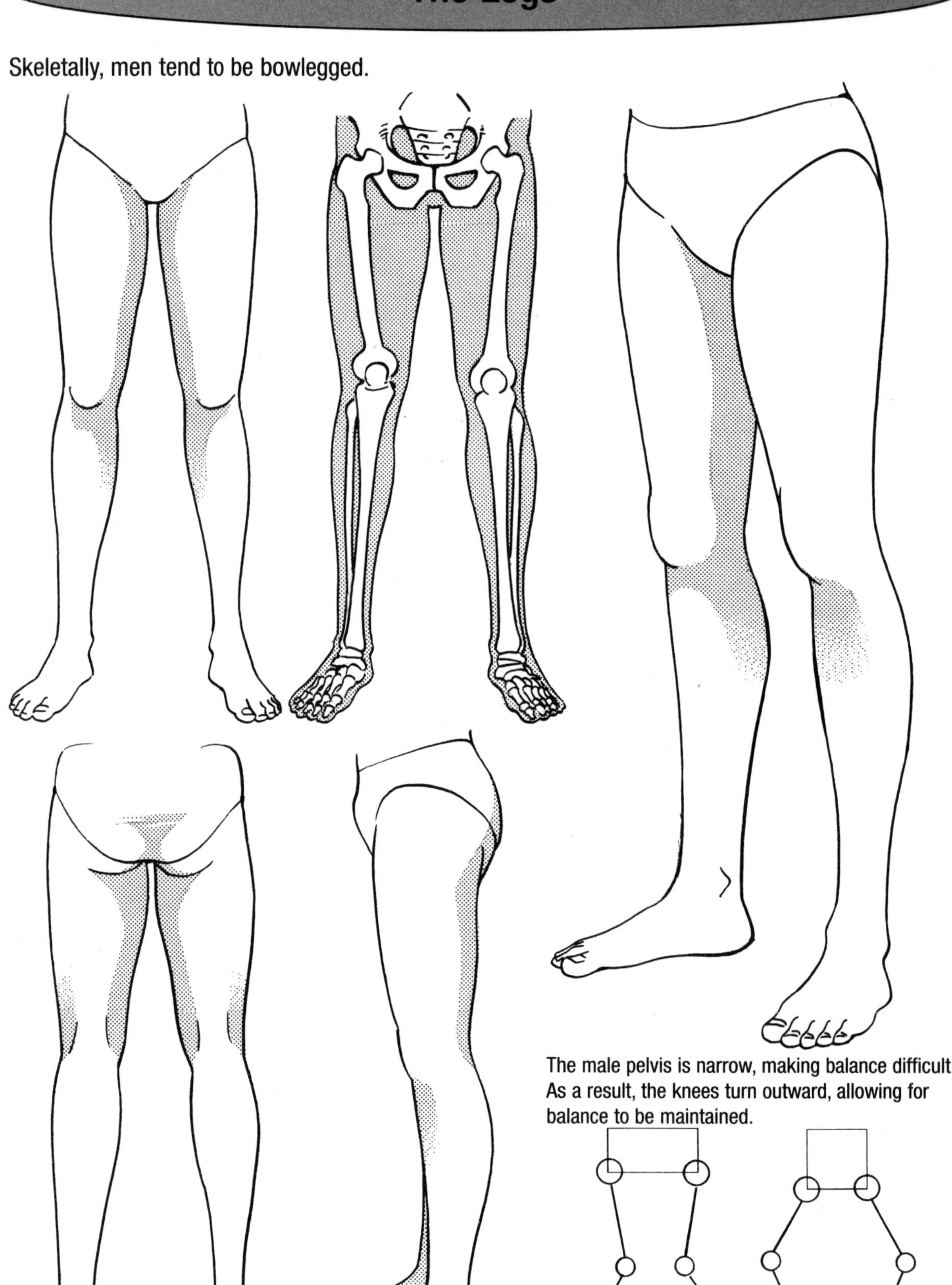

The female pelvis is wide, facilitating balance.

Legs of a Man

In order to de-emphasize bowleggedness, have the character stand at an angle or with legs spread.

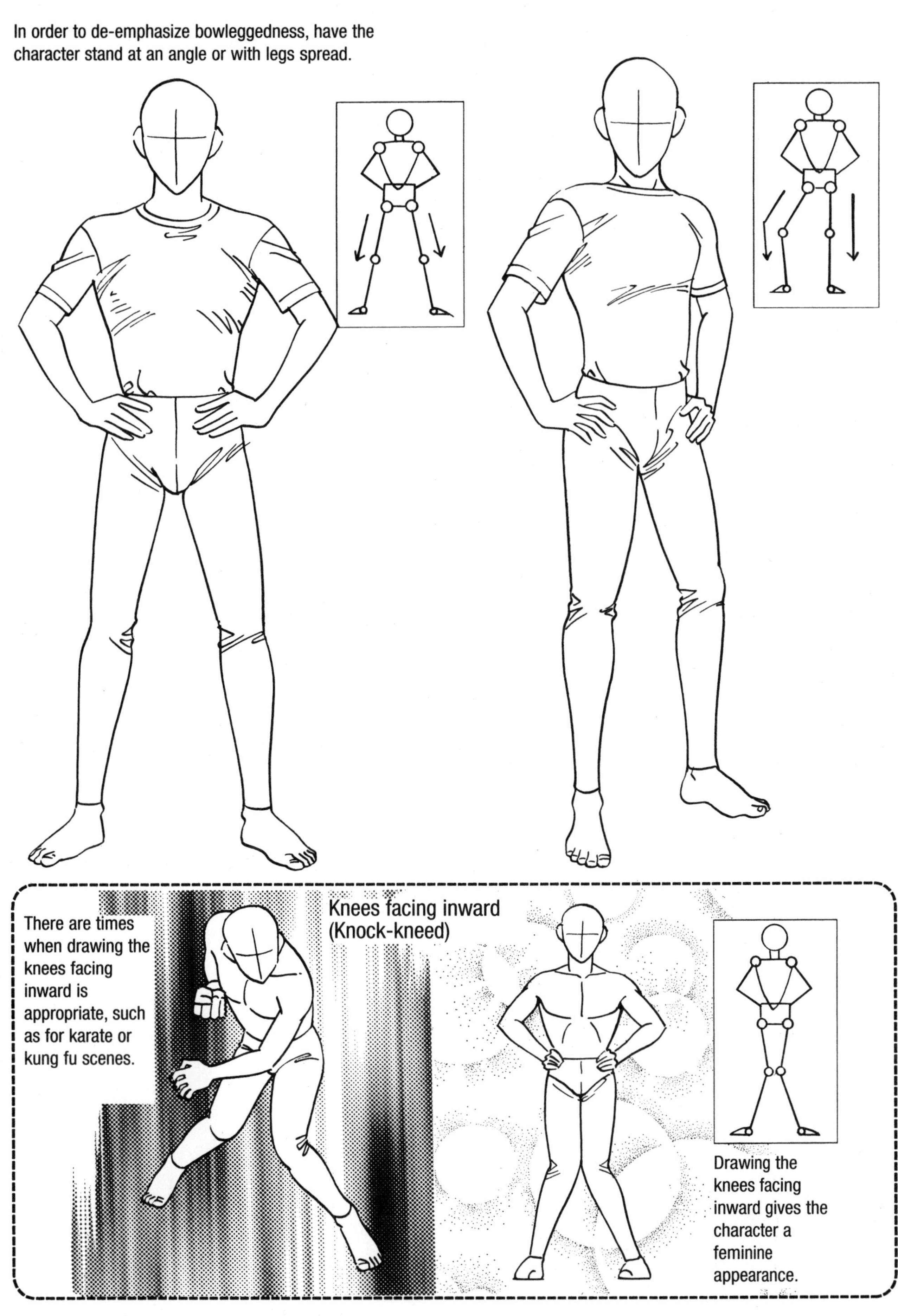

Leg Types

Lean Build

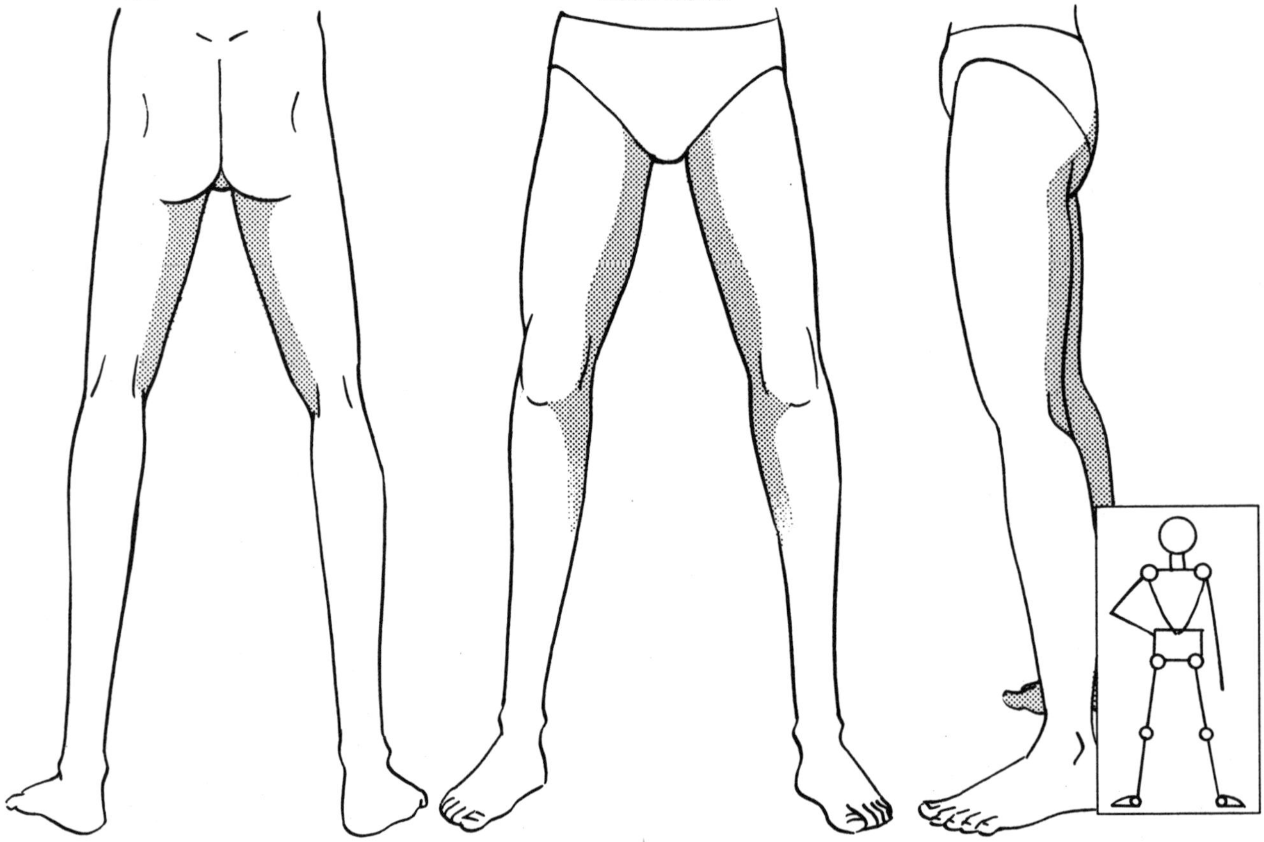

The thighs of a well-conditioned male can exceed 60 cm, about the circumference of a women's waist.

Muscular Build

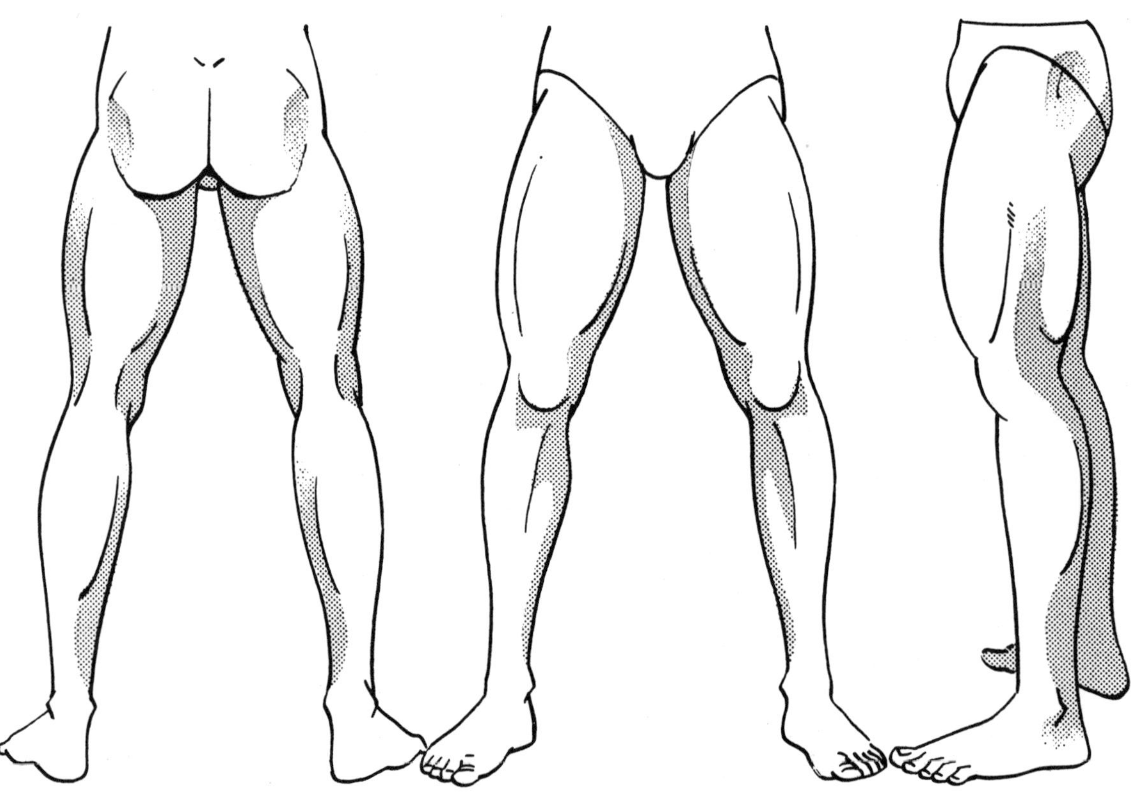

Muscles do not change inherently, whether the character's build be lean or brawny. The different body builds are distinguished by the delineation (emphasis) of the muscles.

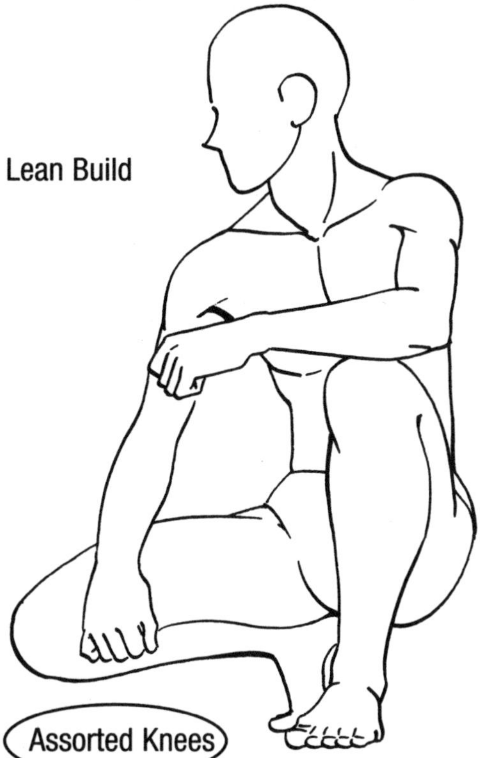

Lean Build

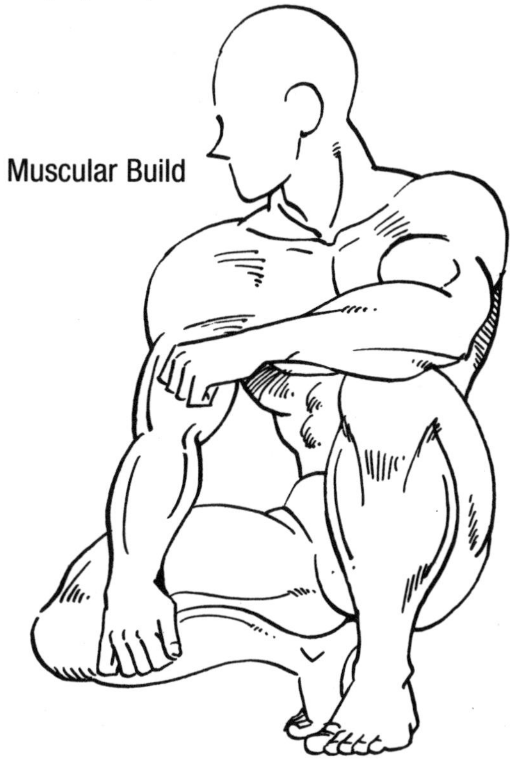

Muscular Build

Assorted Knees

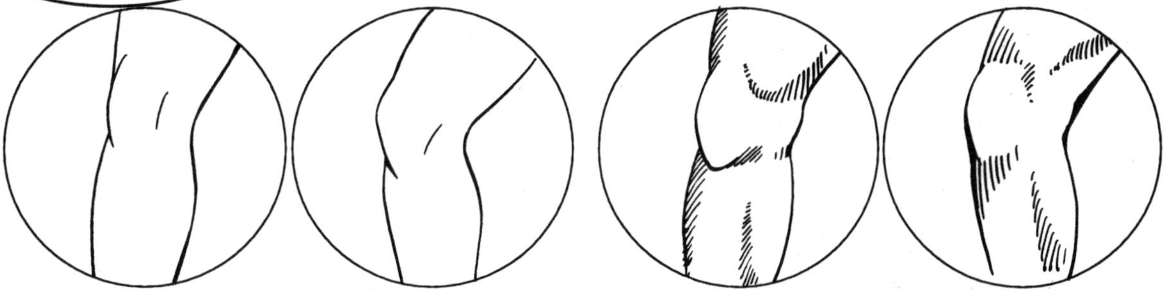

Minimal Lines

Realistic Rendition

The Legs of a Child vs. of an Adult

A child's legs lack the muscular bulges of an adult's. Realistically, the legs of a child tend to be thin and reedy, but in manga they are often rendered as thick staffs.

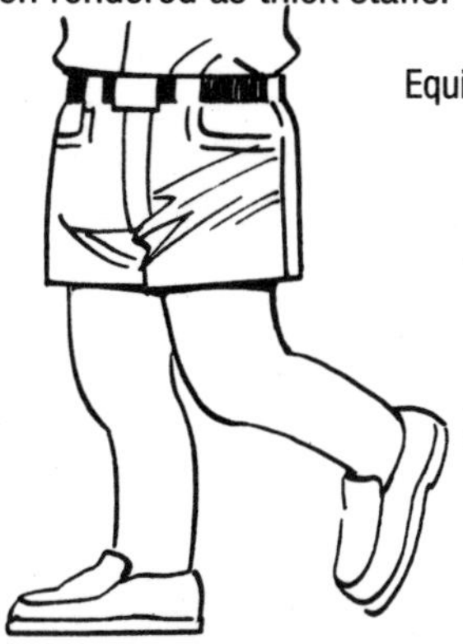

Equidistant

Equidistant

Short

Long

Legs of a Child: Manga Rendition

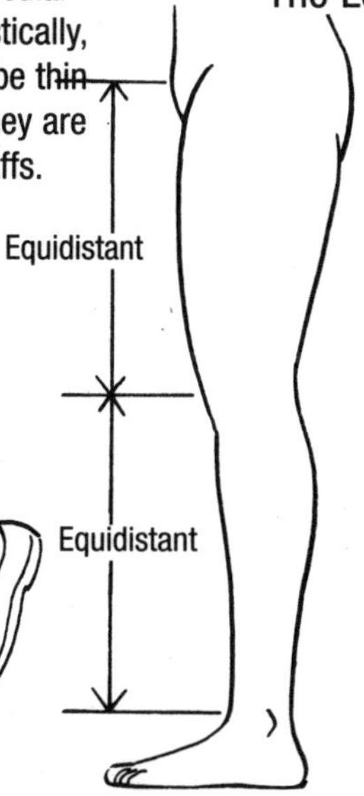

Legs of a Child: Realistic Rendition

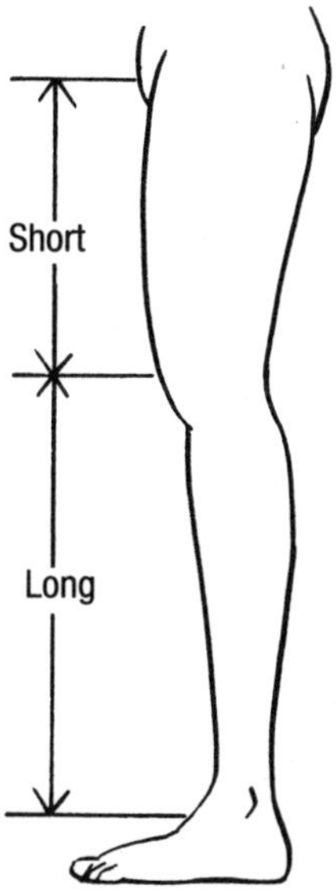

Legs of an Adult

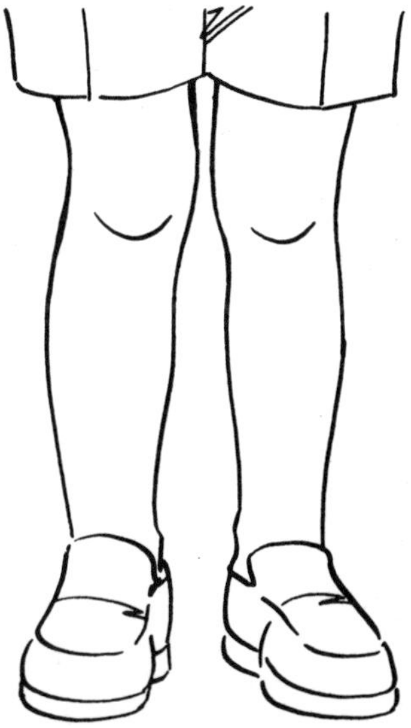

Children tend not to be bowlegged.

The Feet

The distinguishing features of the foot are that they lay almost flat on the ground and that thick layers of skin cover the toes, making them appear coarse.

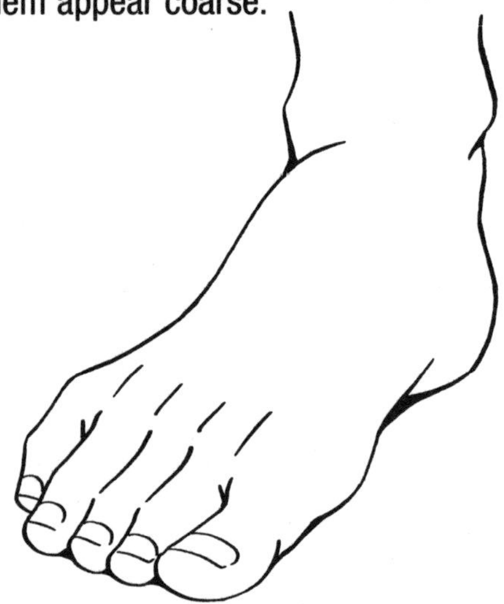

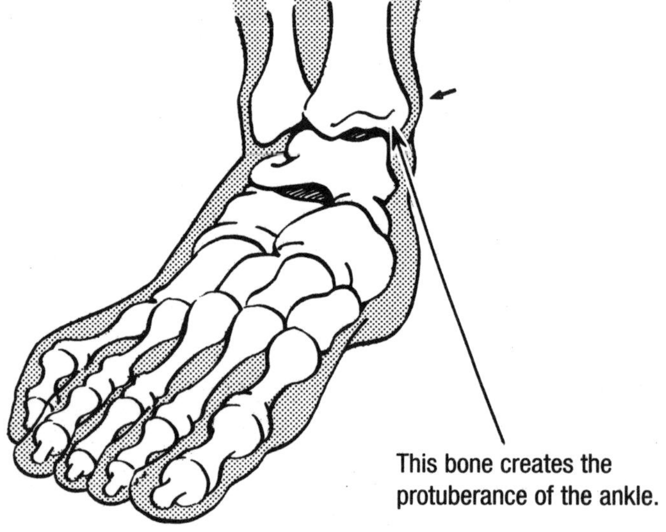

Inside View of the Right Foot

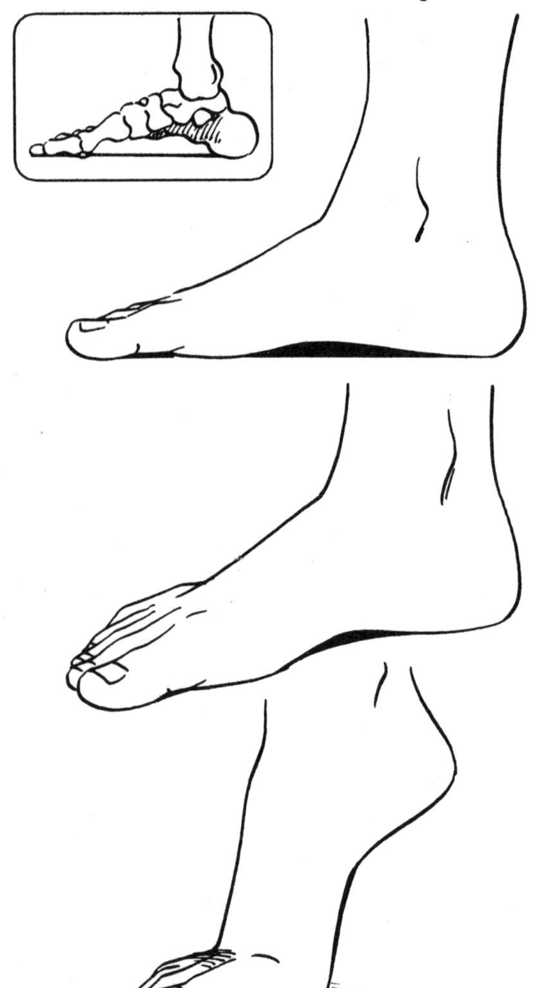

Outside View of the Right Foot

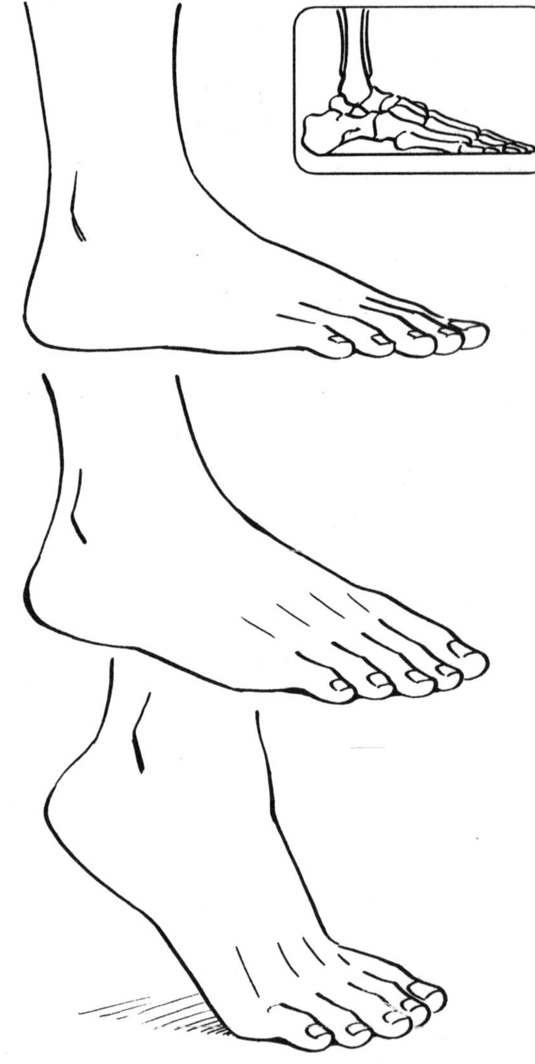

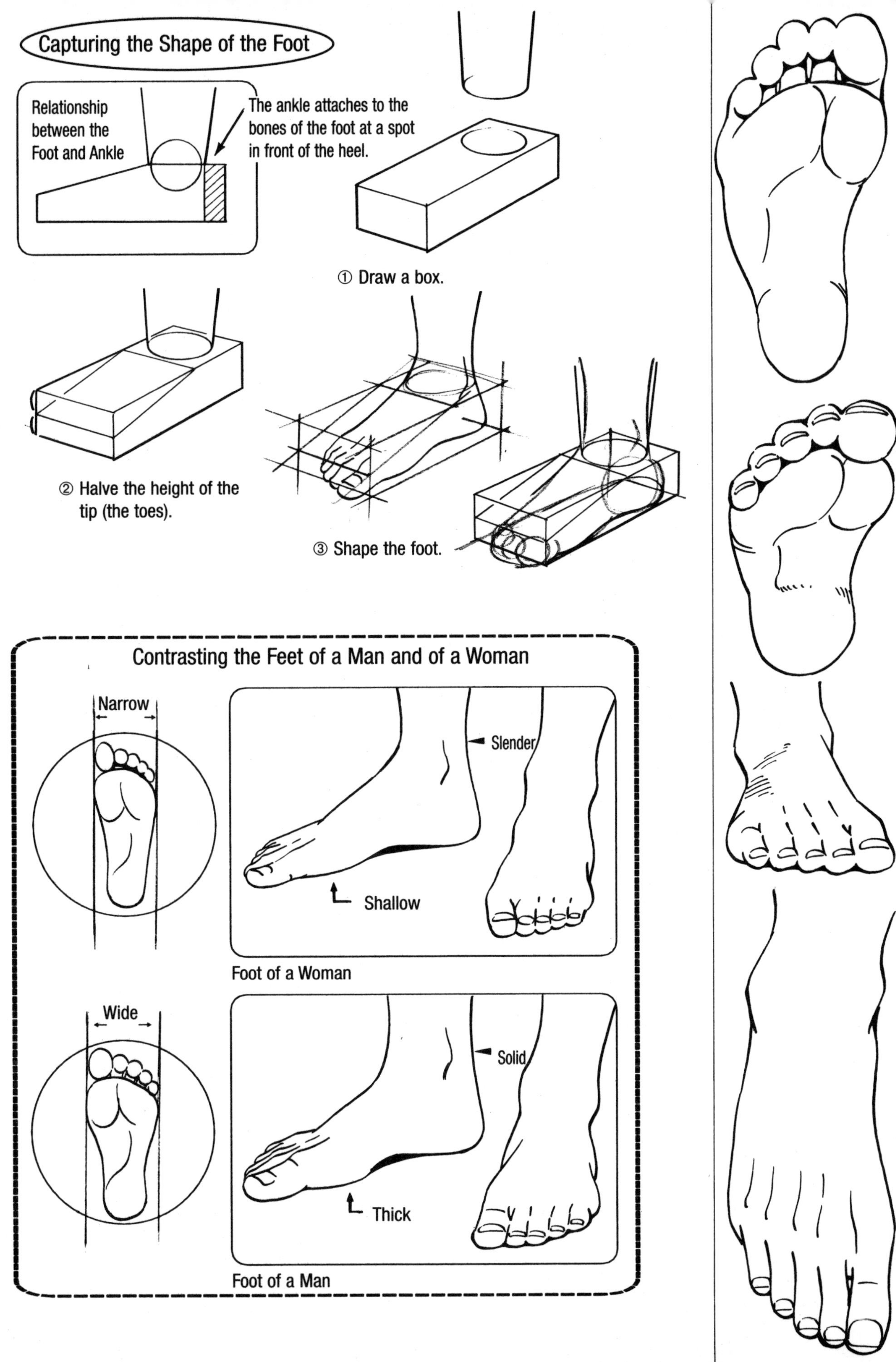
Capturing the Shape of the Foot
Relationship between the Foot and Ankle
The ankle attaches to the bones of the foot at a spot in front of the heel.
① Draw a box.
② Halve the height of the tip (the toes).
③ Shape the foot.
Contrasting the Feet of a Man and of a Woman
Narrow
Slender
Shallow
Foot of a Woman
Wide
Solid
Thick
Foot of a Man

Assorted Feet Standing and Walking

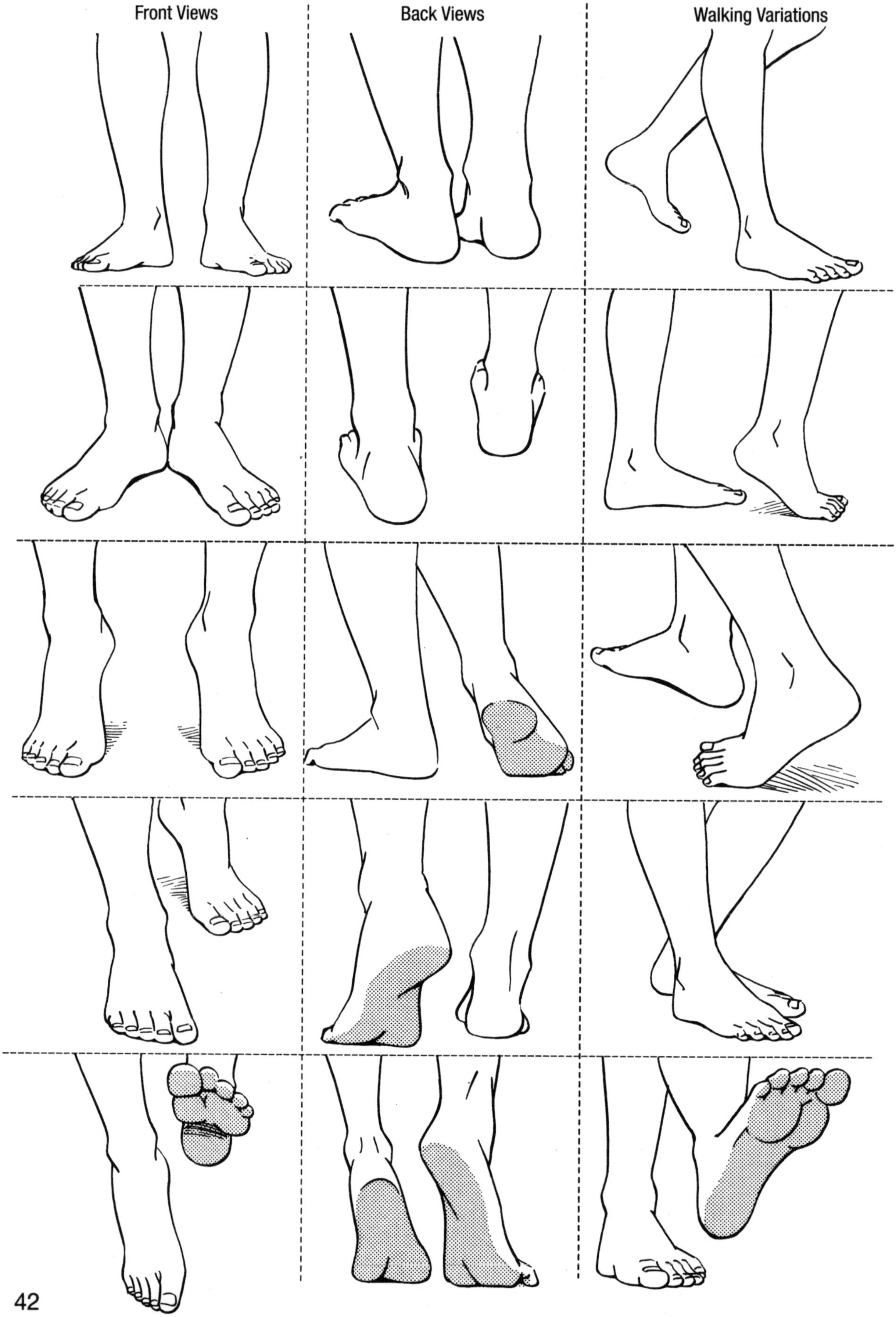

Front Views

Back Views

Walking Variations

The Hands

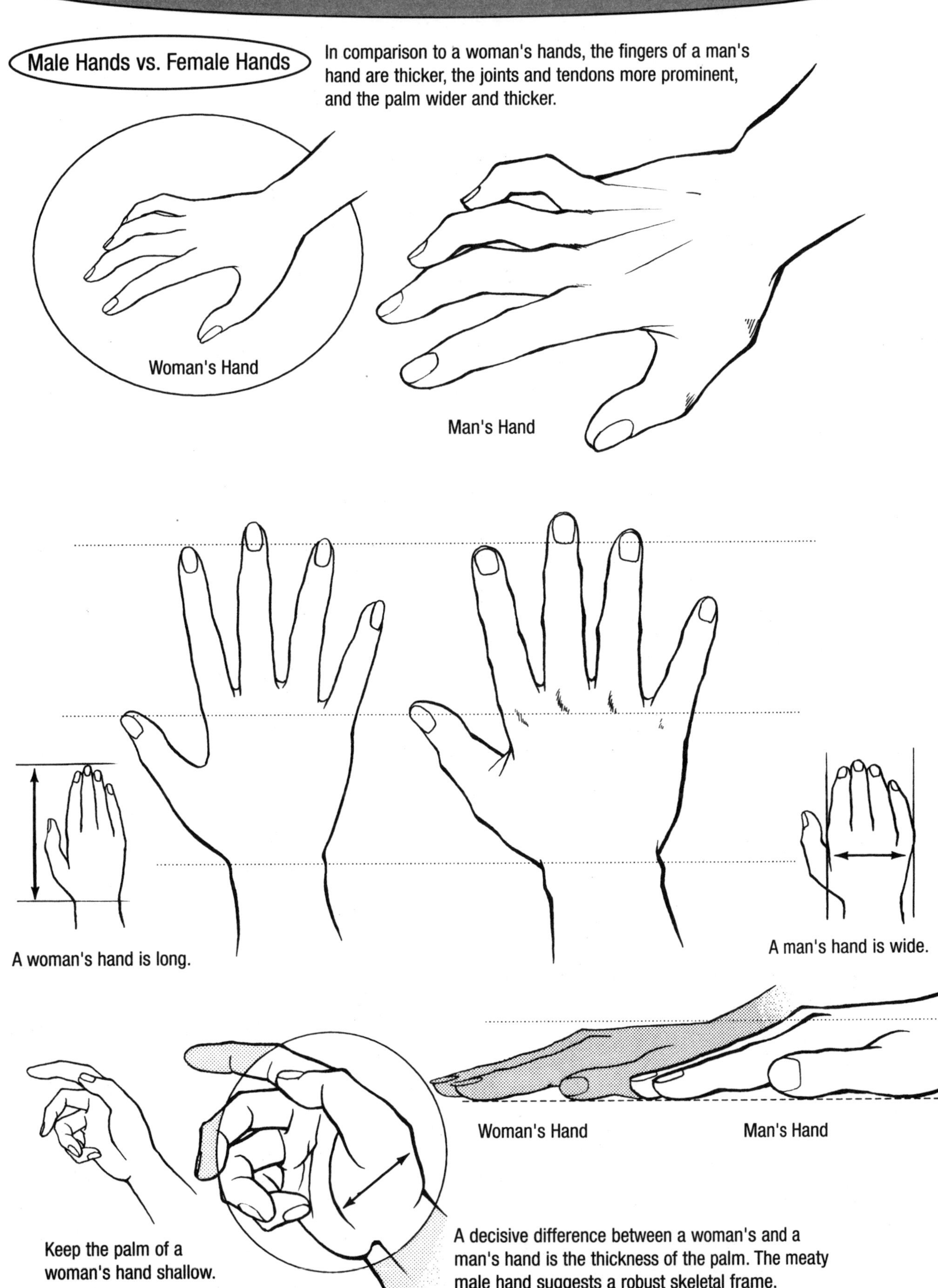

Male Hands vs. Female Hands
In comparison to a woman's hands, the fingers of a man's hand are thicker, the joints and tendons more prominent, and the palm wider and thicker.
Woman's Hand
Man's Hand
A woman's hand is long.
A man's hand is wide.
Woman's Hand
Man's Hand
Keep the palm of a woman's hand shallow.
A decisive difference between a woman's and a man's hand is the thickness of the palm. The meaty male hand suggests a robust skeletal frame.

Sinewy Hands vs. Slender Hands

The difference between the sinewy hand versus the slender hand becomes apparent in the length of the fingers and in the joints.

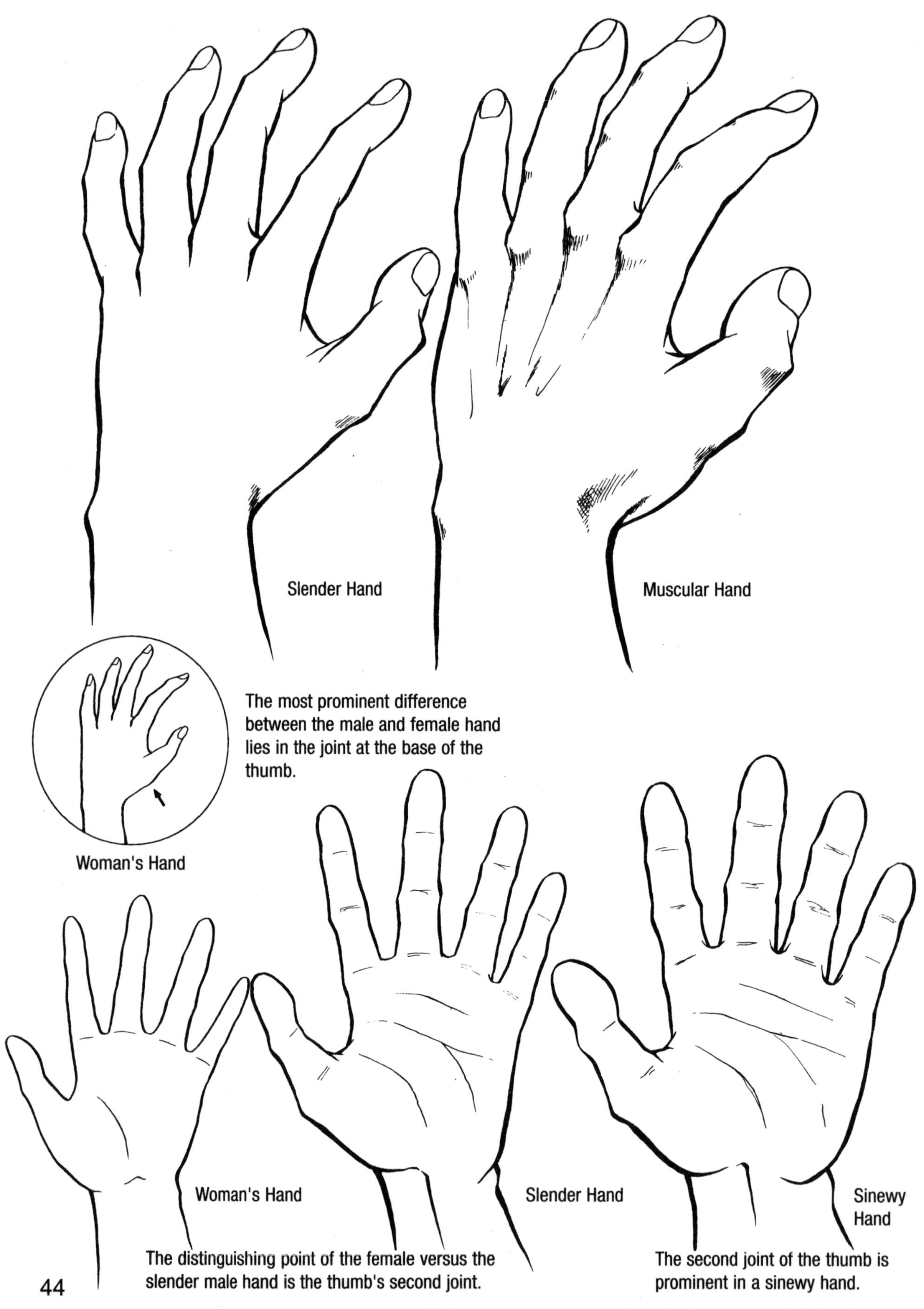

Distinguishing Male Hand Types

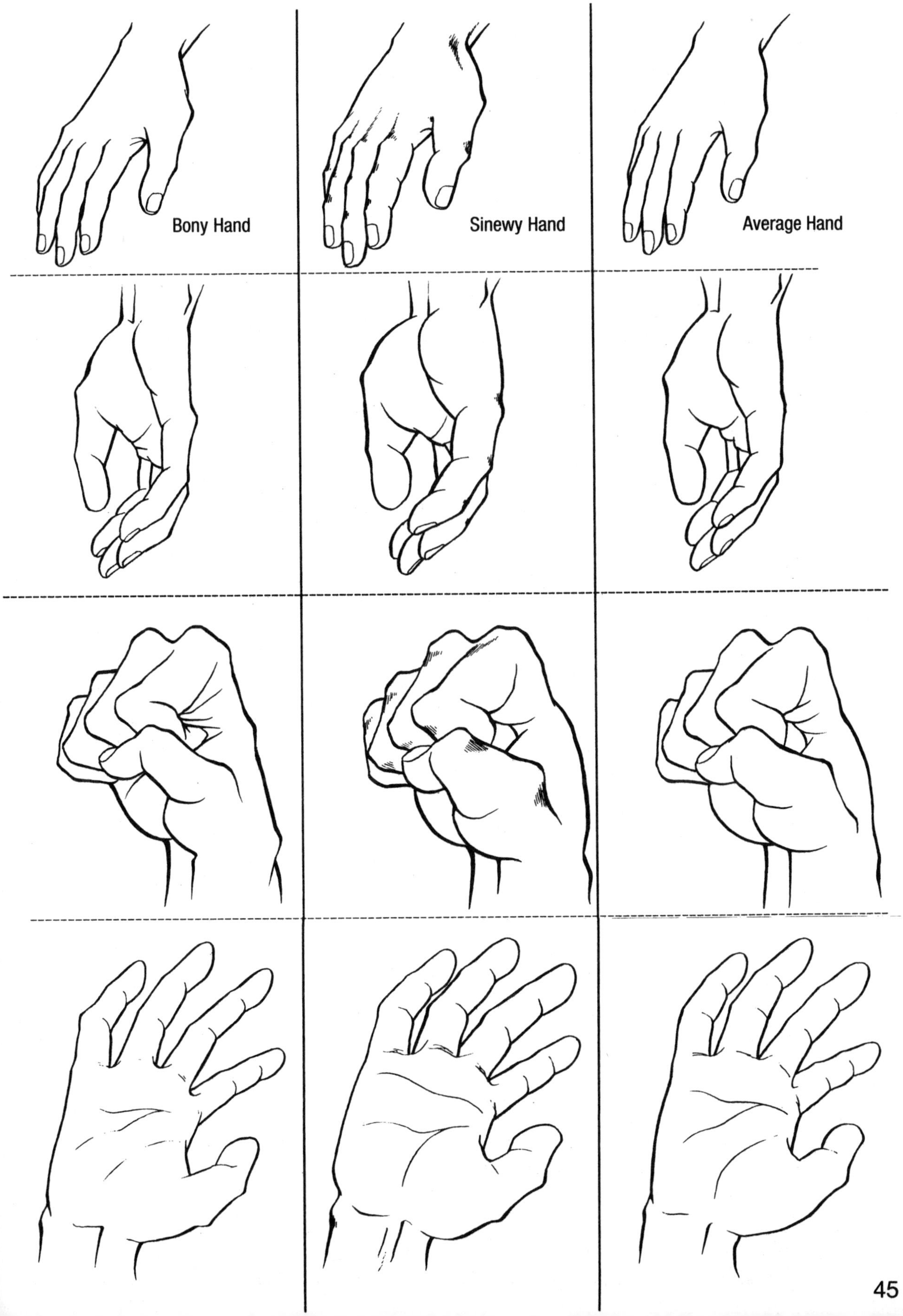

Bony Hand

Sinewy Hand

Average Hand

Adding the Body after Drawing the Face

1. The Upper Body

When adding the boy after having drawn the face, first consider the type of pose desired for the character.

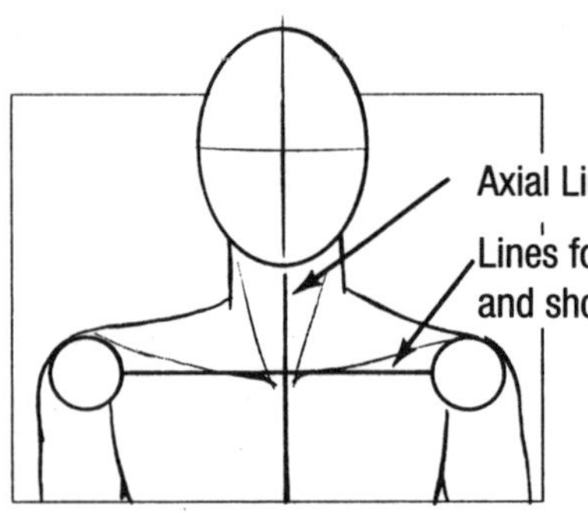

Basic Form: Clavicle and Shoulder Lines and Axial Line (Spine)

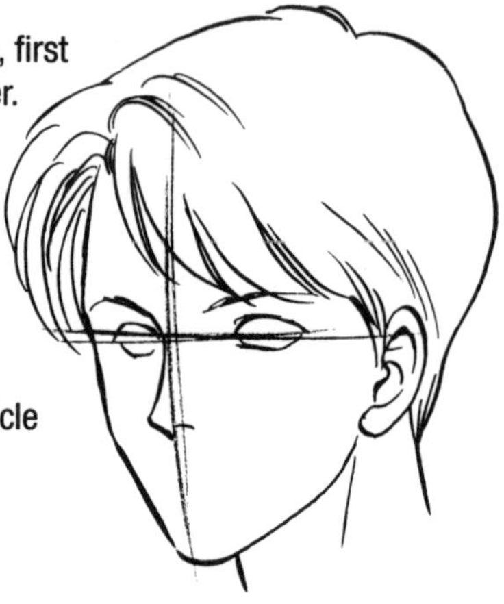

The face is drawn.
1. In which direction should the body face?
2. At which angle should the body be drawn?

Possible Directions for the Body with Respect to the Face (With the Face at a Common Angle)

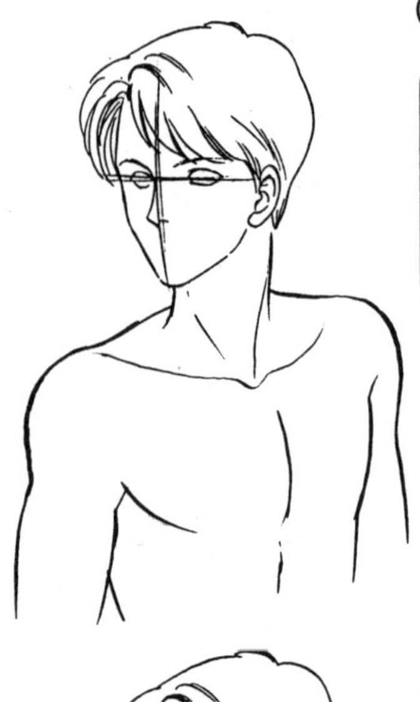

Face and Body in Opposing Directions
Note the direction of the neck. When drawing the trunk (mass between the back and chest), pay attention to its thickness.

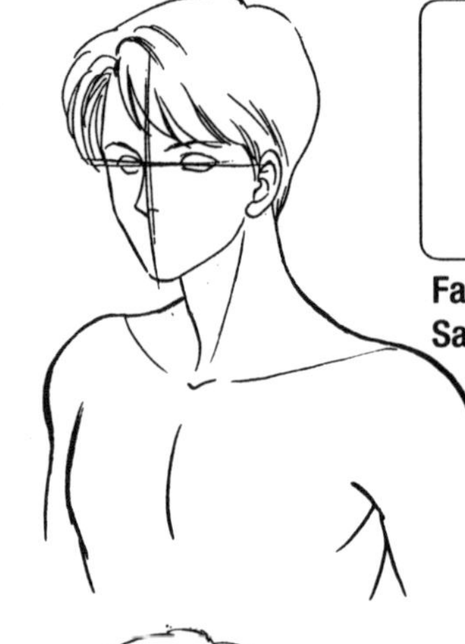

Face and Body in the Same Direction
Determine the direction of the body based on the abbreviated clavicle lines.

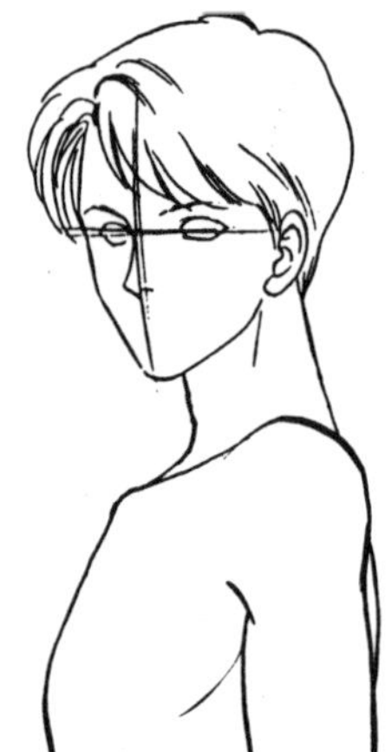

Body Turned 90° from the Picture Plane
Do not forget when drawing the body that the spine is attached from the back of the head.

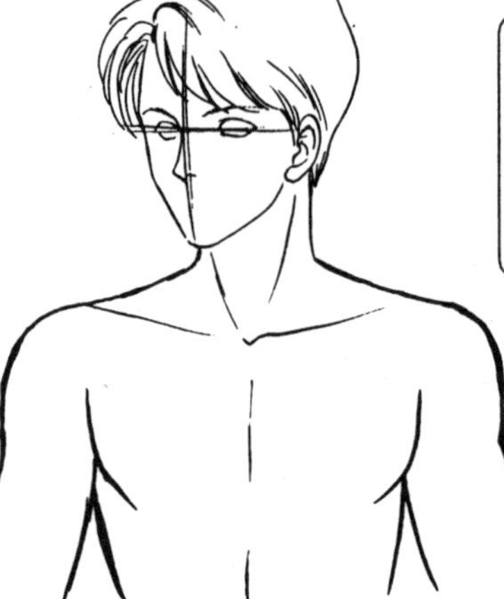

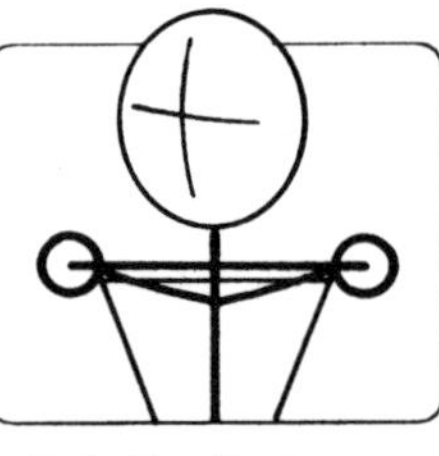

Only the Body Directed toward the Picture Plane

Body Facing the Picture Plane

The diameter of the circle determines the arm's thickness: a small circle means a slender arm; a big circle means a thick arm.

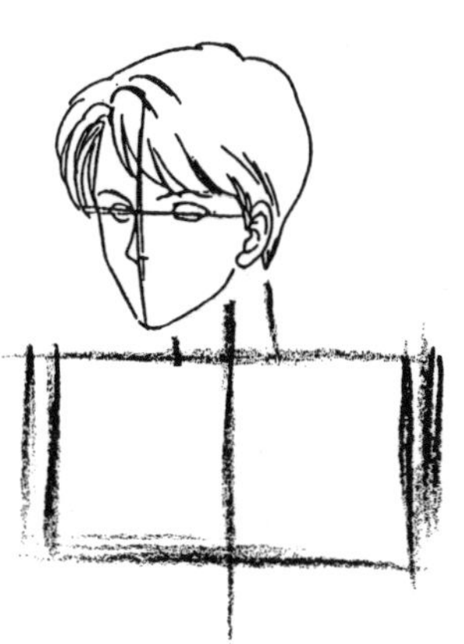

① Draw a box for the chest.

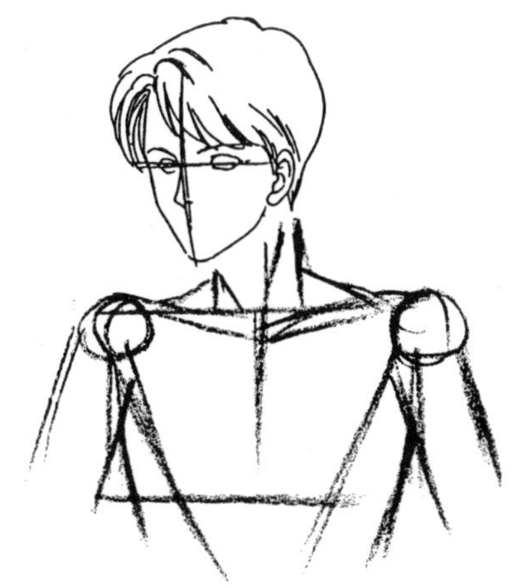

② Draw the clavicle and determine the positions and thickness of the arms.

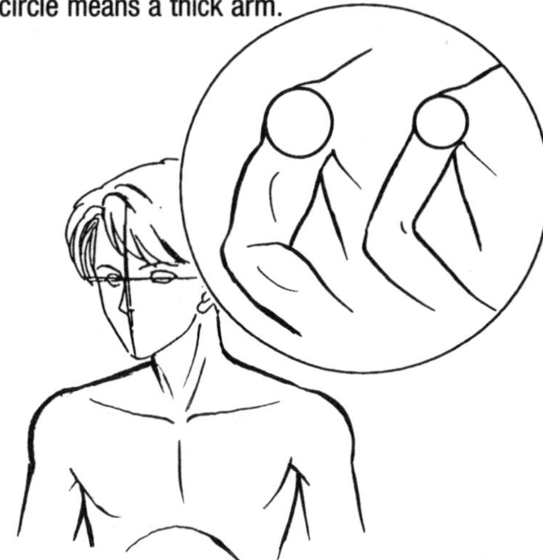

③ Clean up the figure's form
Draw the muscles and other features as desired.

Face and Body in the Same Direction

There is a risk of the arms being drawn inordinately thick from this angle, so use a shallow box for the chest when determining the girth of the arms.

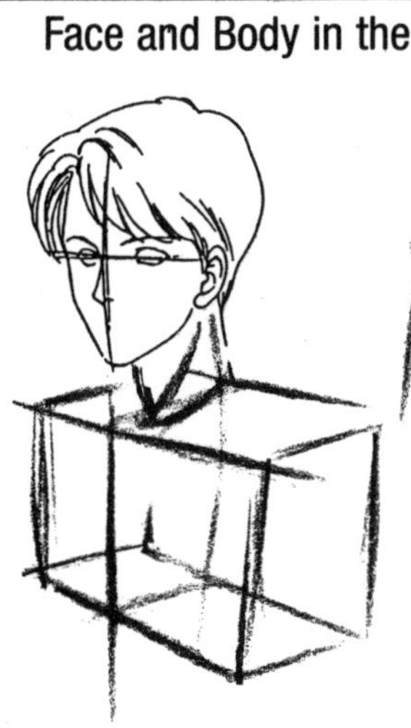

① Draw a box for the chest.

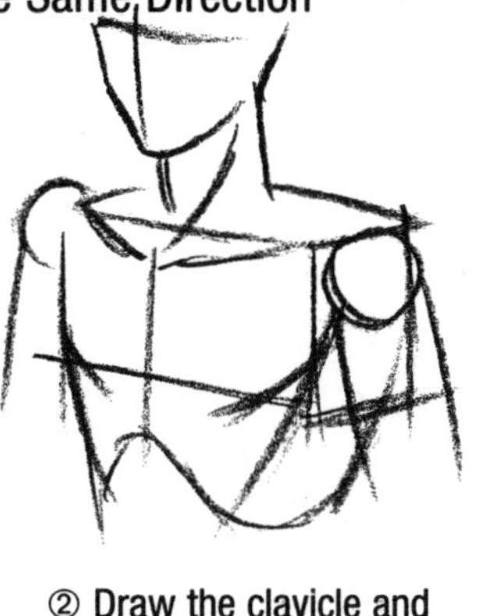

② Draw the clavicle and determine the positions and thickness of the arms.

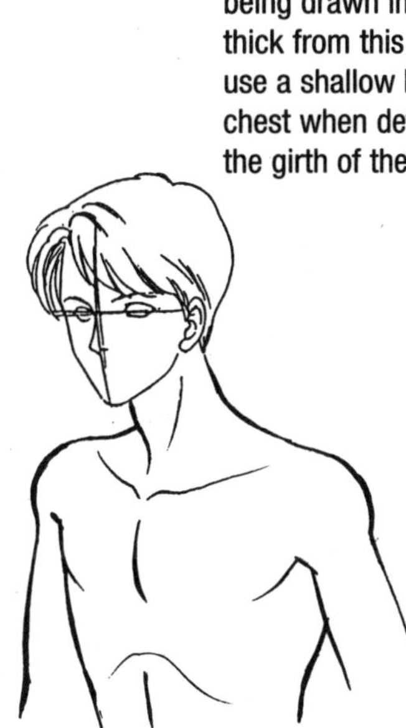

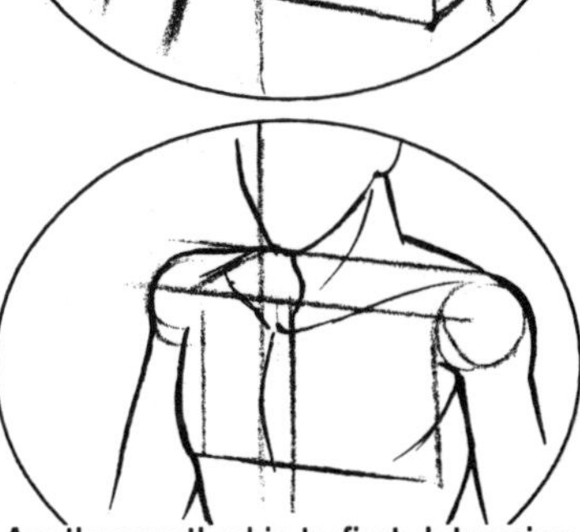

Another method is to first determine the girth of the arms and then make the chest box thicker as desired.

The Body Turned to the Side

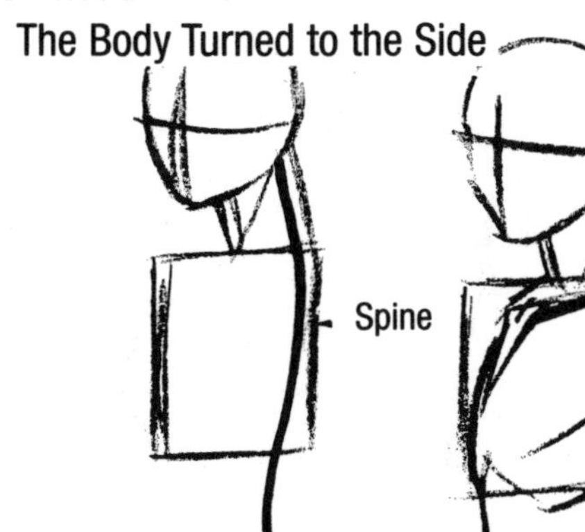

① Draw a box for the chest.
Pay close attention to the way the neck attaches to the body when drawing a side view.

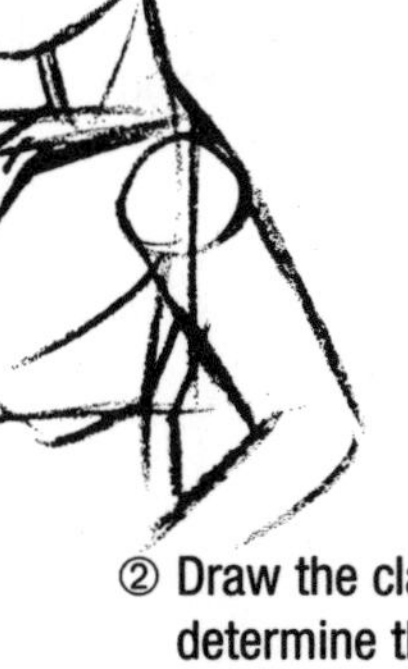

② Draw the clavicle and determine the positions and thickness of the arms.

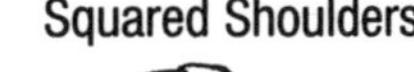

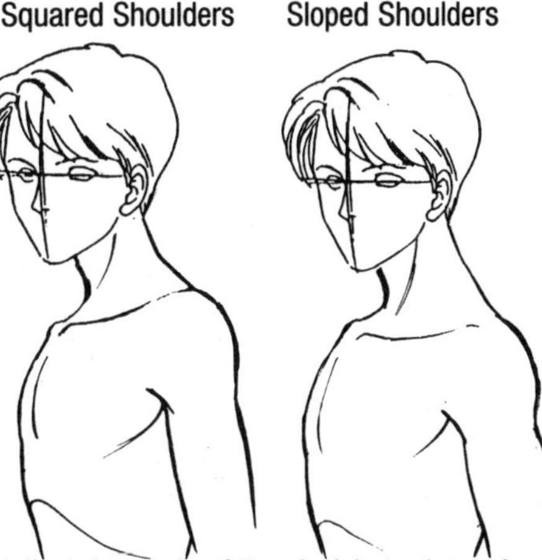

Adjust the angle of the clavicle to determine whether the character has sloped or squared shoulders.

When Drawing from a Moderate High Angle

Drawing the body as a box will allow you to study how to achieve 3-dimensionality in the chest region from an overhead perspective. Position the top of the shoulders and neck on the top of this box.

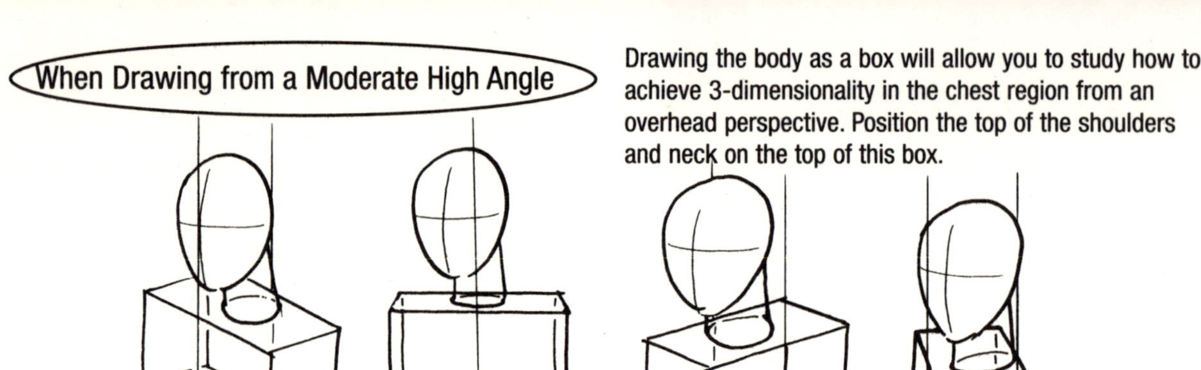

Face and Body in the Same Direction

Body Directed toward the Picture Plane

Face and Body in Opposing Directions

Body Turned 90° from the Picture Plane

Model 1: Face and Body in Opposing Directions

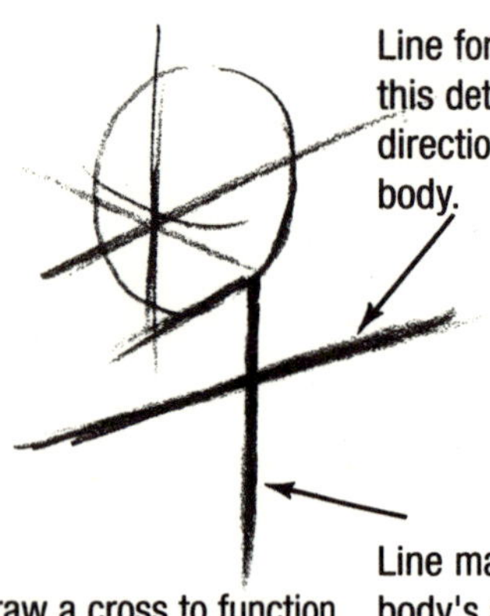

① Draw a cross to function as guides in determining the direction the body will face.

② Draw a box for the chest.

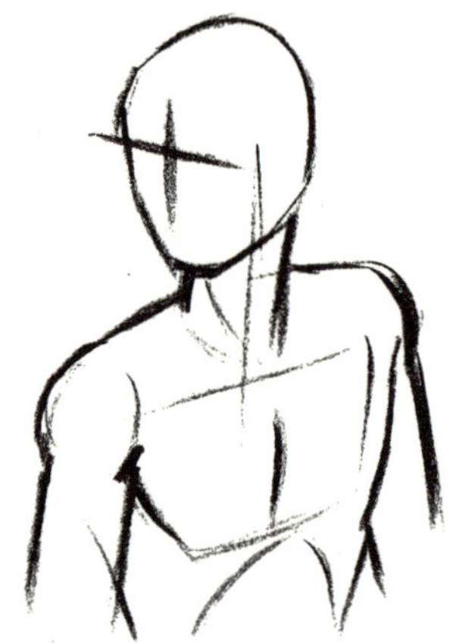

③ Clean up the figure's form.

Model 2: Face and Body in the Same Direction

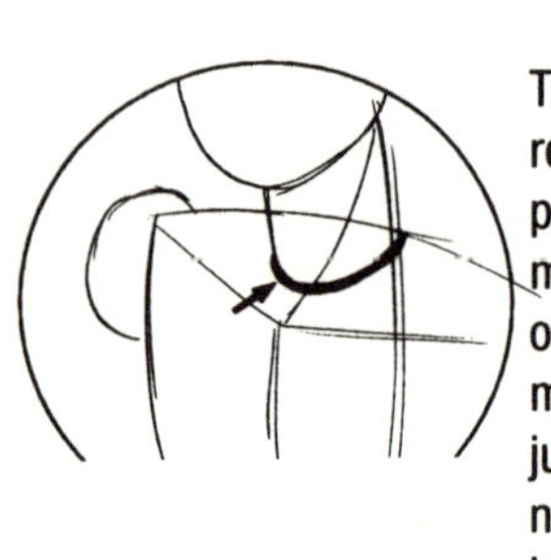

The overall relationship of parts will become more obvious once a curved line marking the juncture of the neck and body has been added.

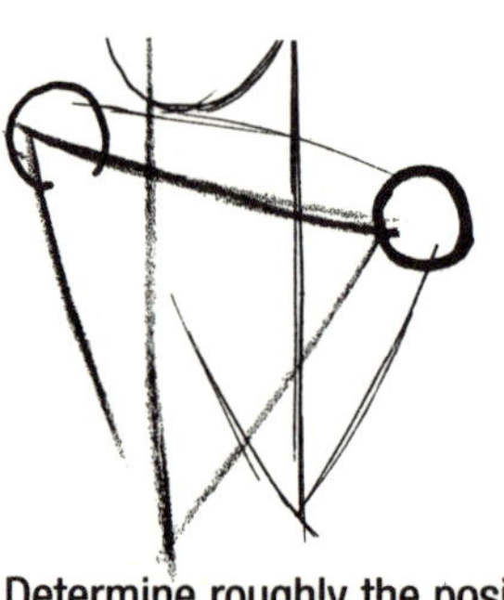

② Determine roughly the position of the shoulder joints and add a thumbnail sketch of the body.

④ Draw the chest.

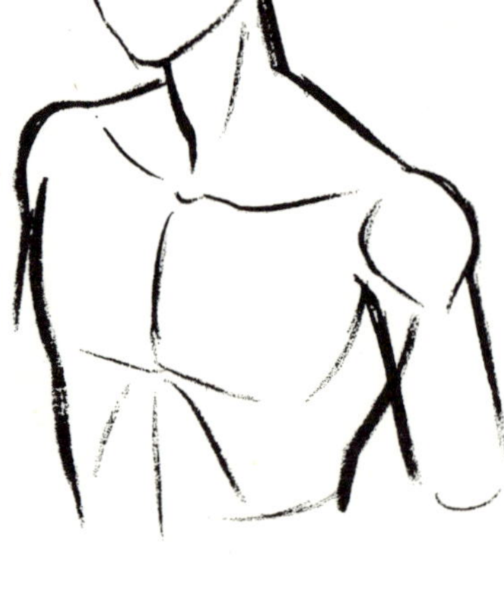

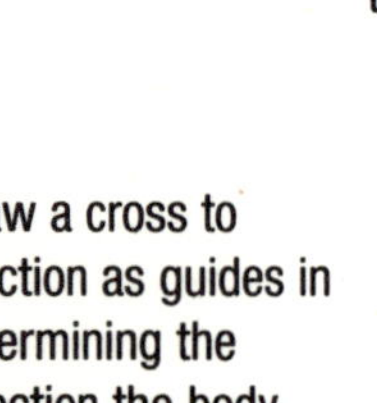

① Draw a cross to function as guides in determining the direction the body will face.

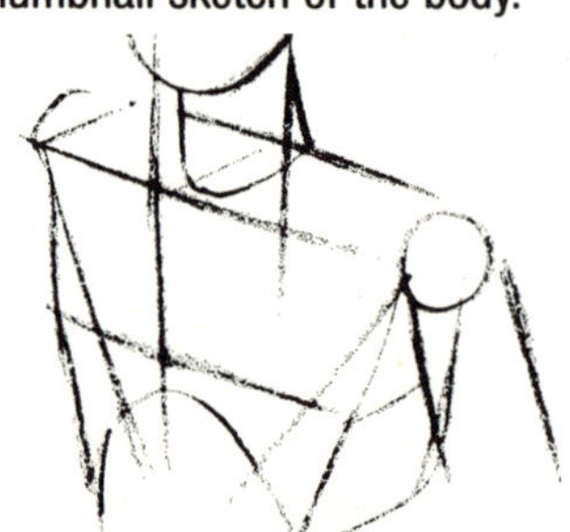

③ Draw boxes based on the thumbnail sketch of the body.

When Drawing from a Moderate Low Angle

Since the face is drawn in common bust format, it is unusual to draw the body from a low angle.

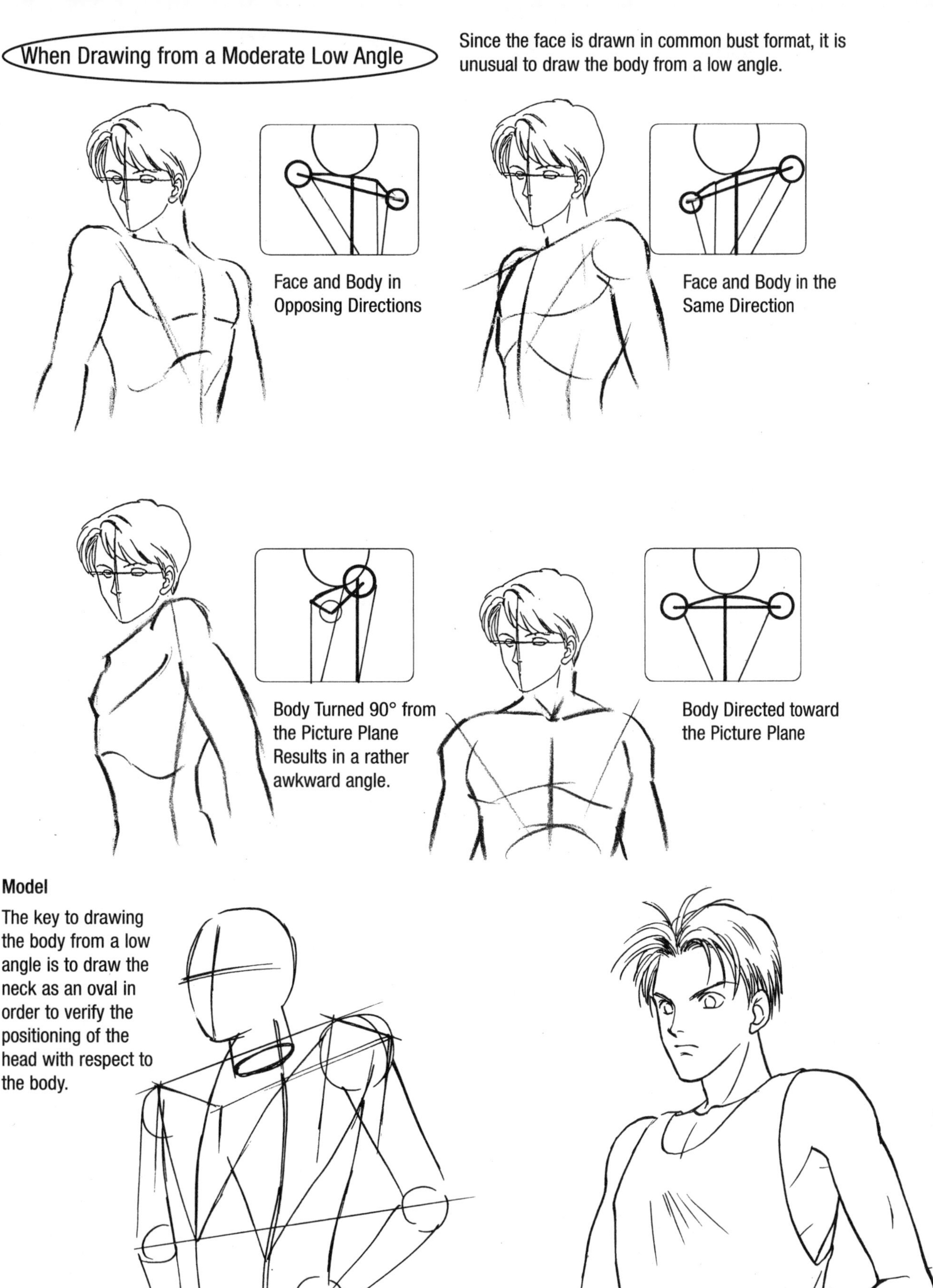

Face and Body in Opposing Directions

Face and Body in the Same Direction

Body Turned 90° from the Picture Plane Results in a rather awkward angle.

Body Directed toward the Picture Plane

Model

The key to drawing the body from a low angle is to draw the neck as an oval in order to verify the positioning of the head with respect to the body.

Composition Study: Rough Sketch

Drawing only the body from a low angle gives the character the appearance of looking down.

2. The Full Figure

When adding the full body after drawing the face, you must first have a clear idea of what sort of pose is desired.

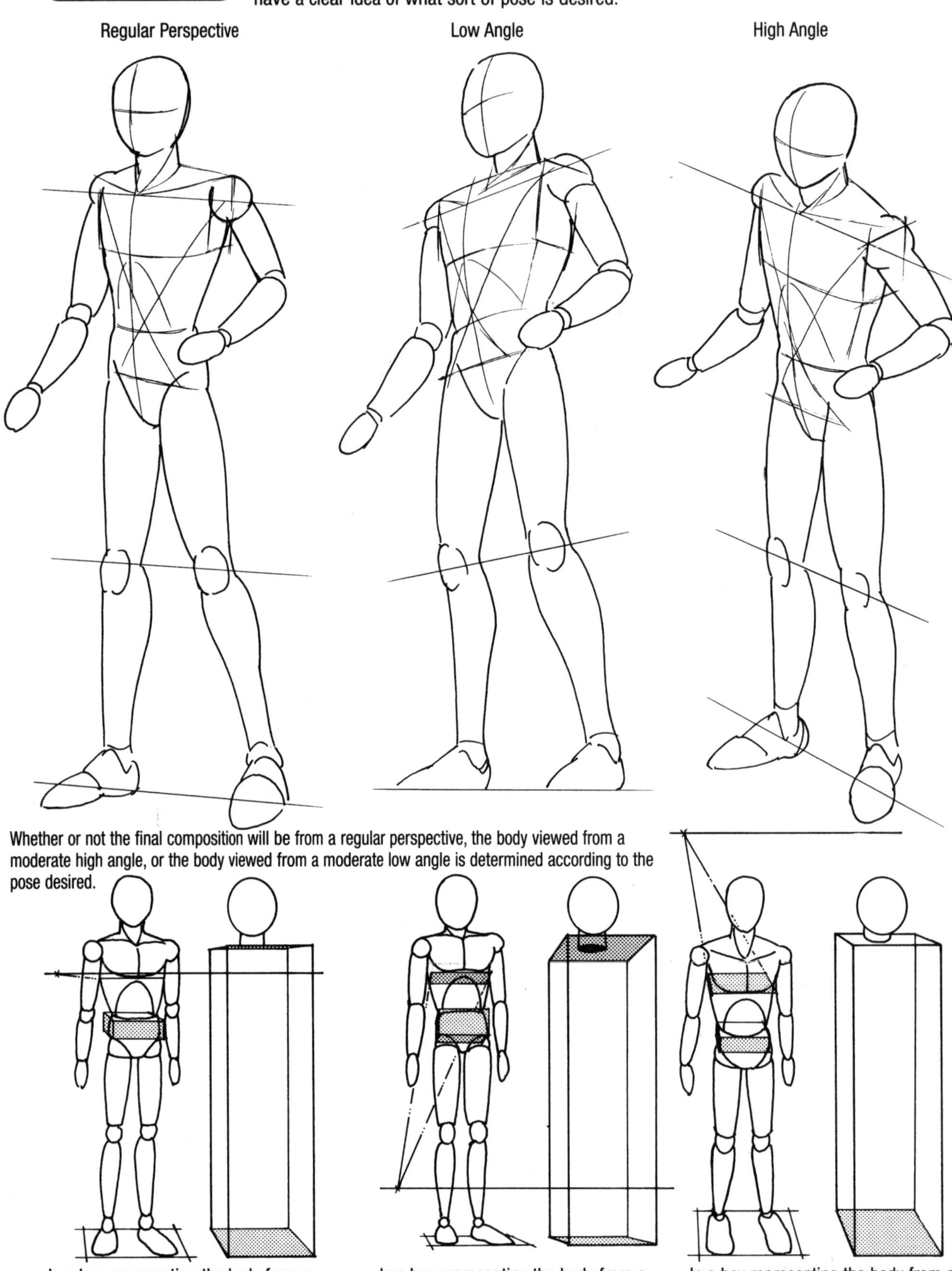

Whether or not the final composition will be from a regular perspective, the body viewed from a moderate high angle, or the body viewed from a moderate low angle is determined according to the pose desired.

In a box representing the body from a regular perspective, either the side or the front of the body is in view.

In a box representing the body from a low angle, the point of connection between the neck and the body is not visible.

In a box representing the body from a high angle, the top surface of the body and the neck is visible.

Regular Perspective

When drawing the body from a regular perspective, after having drawn the face, visualize the body as boxes with the horizon line about the level of the chest.

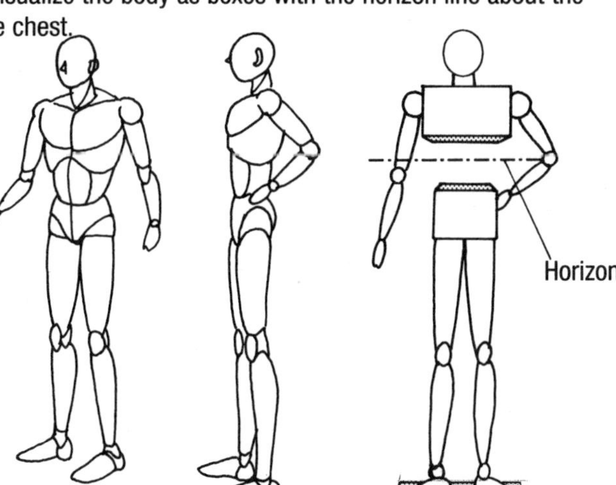

The appearance of the feet changes dramatically according to whether the view selected is from a regular perspective, a low angle, or a high angle.

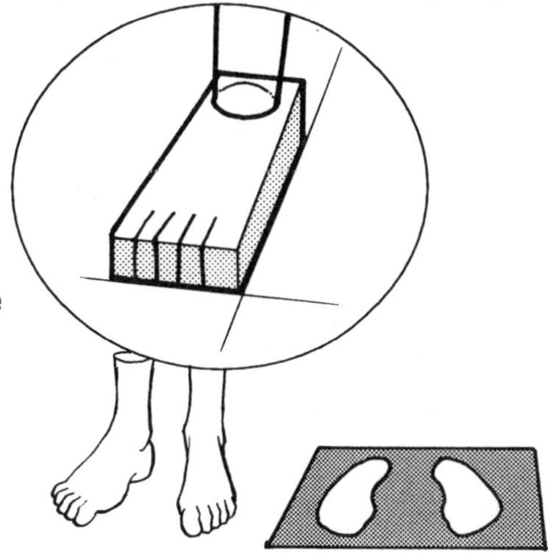

Low Angle

When drawing the body from a low angle, picture the horizon line somewhere between the hips and the knees. Boxes seen from a moderately low angle will then represent the body.

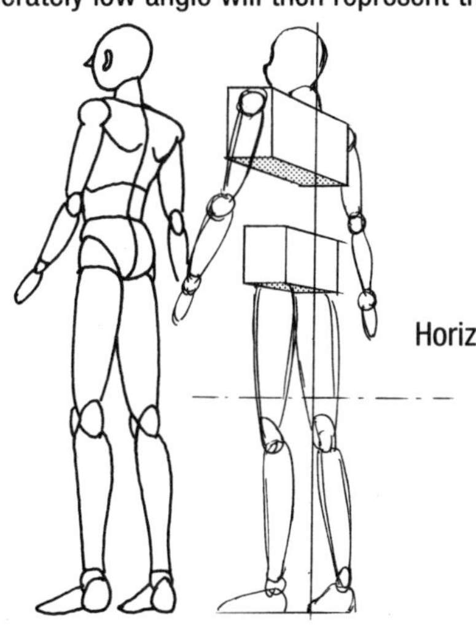

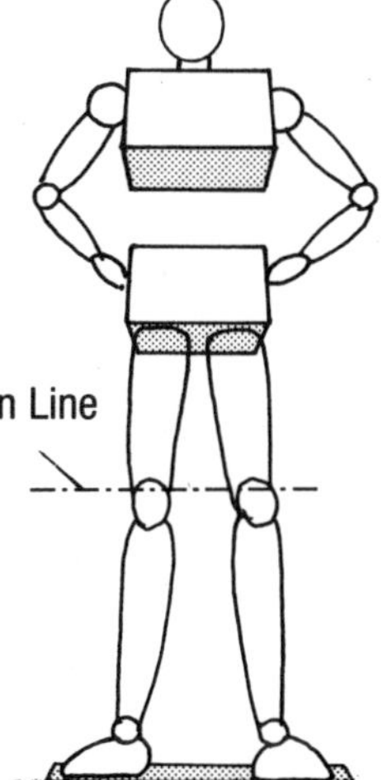

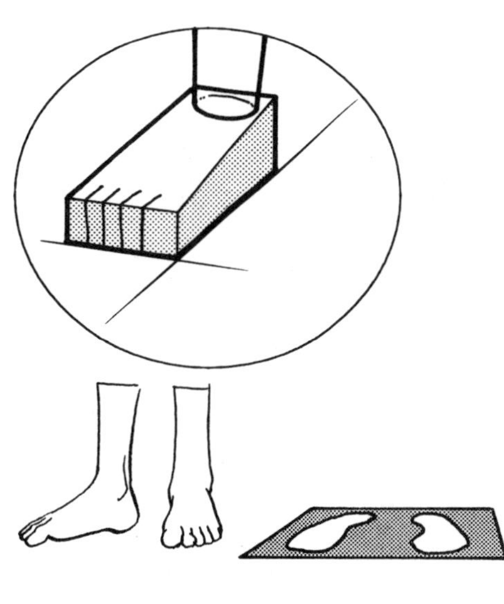

Low Angle: The neck becomes shortened and the body takes on a bold stance.

High Angle

Because the face has already been completed, the horizon line cannot go above the head. Picture the body as boxes with the top surface visible.

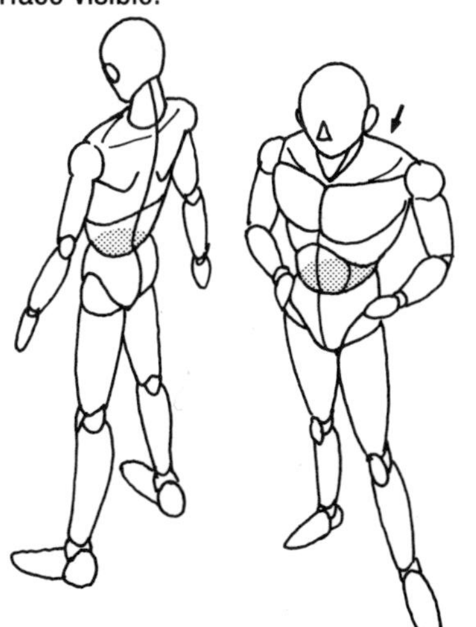

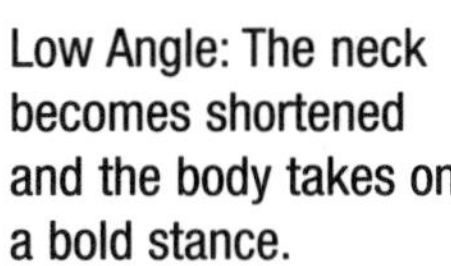

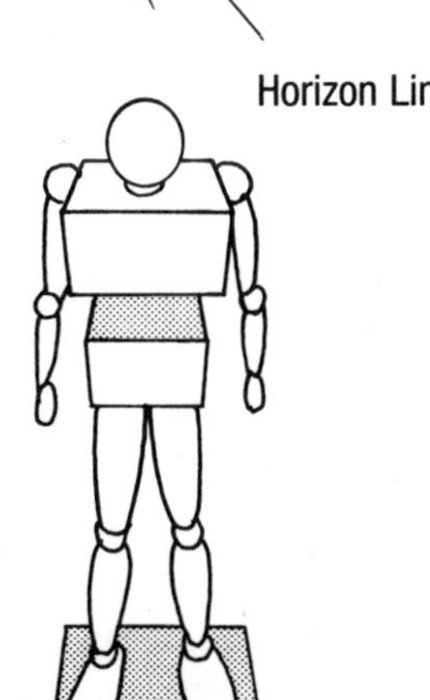

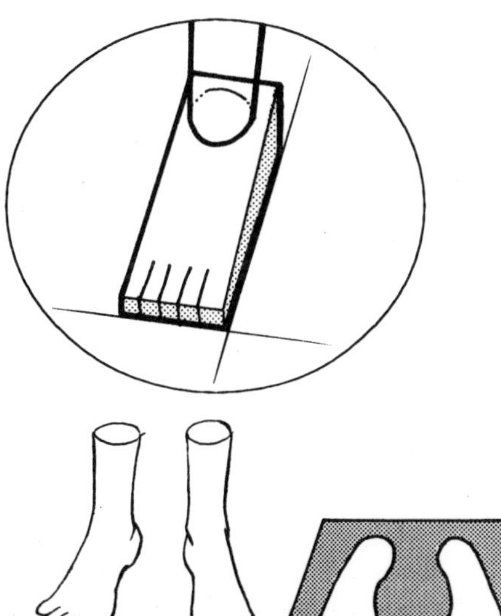

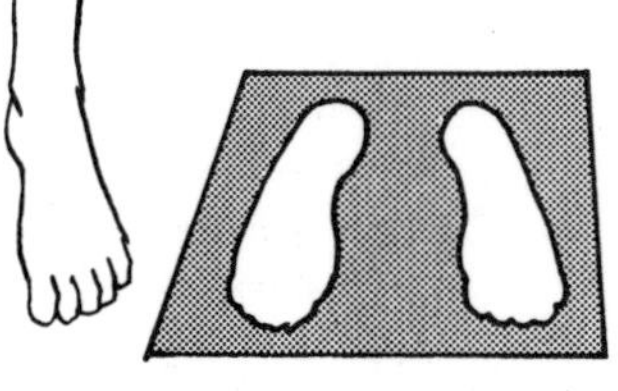

High Angle

The upper surface of the shoulders is visible.

Conceiving the Figure as a Whole

The male body is composed of blocks. Visualizing the character as combinations of blocks allow you to create a solid, powerful, masculine-looking figure with volume.

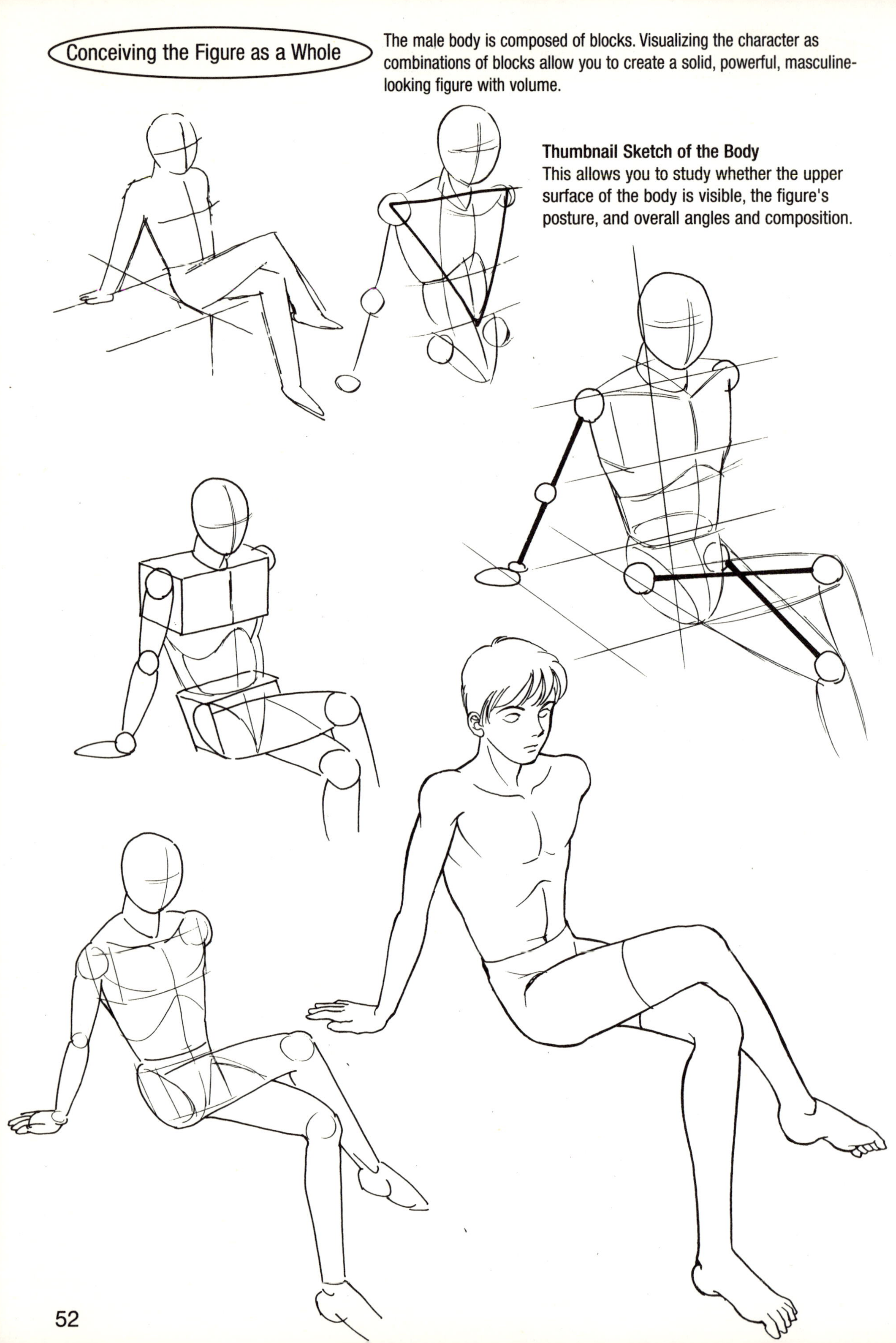

Thumbnail Sketch of the Body

This allows you to study whether the upper surface of the body is visible, the figure's posture, and overall angles and composition.

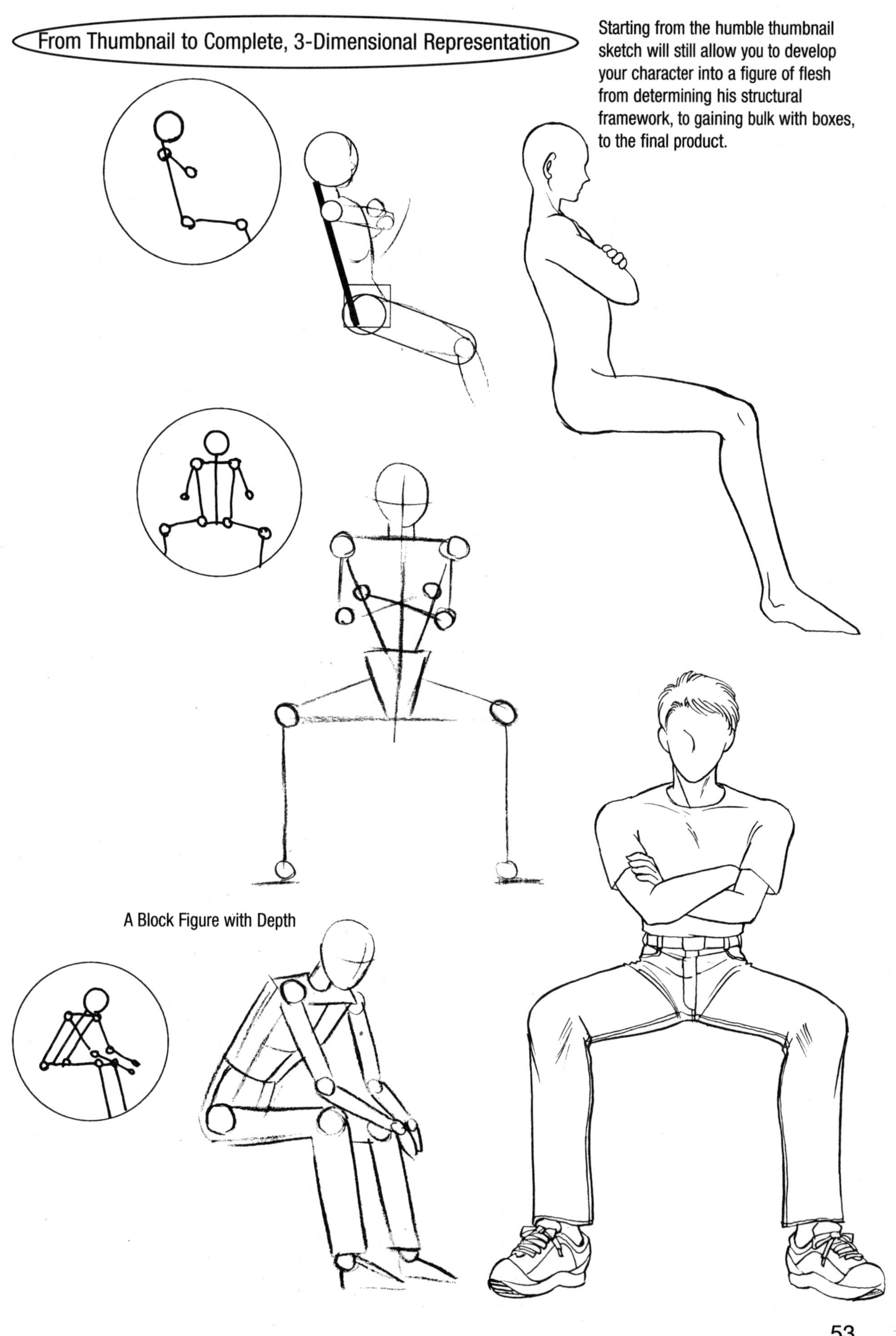
From Thumbnail to Complete, 3-Dimensional Representation
Starting from the humble thumbnail sketch will still allow you to develop your character into a figure of flesh from determining his structural framework, to gaining bulk with boxes, to the final product.
A Block Figure with Depth

Planning the Figures Height

1. Drawing Small, Lean Male Figures

Lean Build, Average Stature

a) Have the legs, arms, and body remain slender, and enlarge the head.
b) Raise the waist for a shorter trunk.

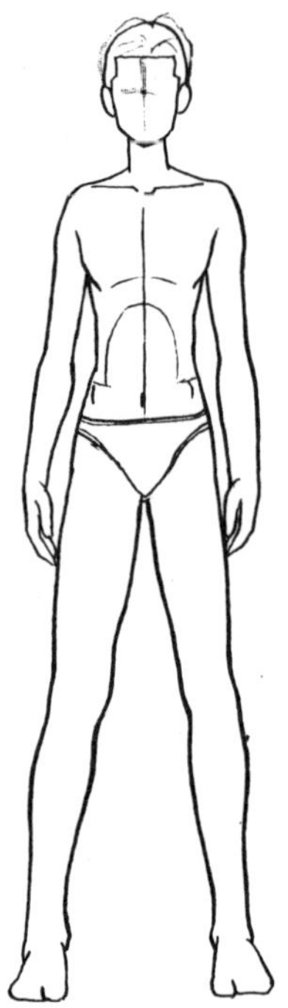

Distinguishing features of a lean build are narrow shoulders and a long neck, trunk, arms, and legs.

Lean Figure of Short Stature

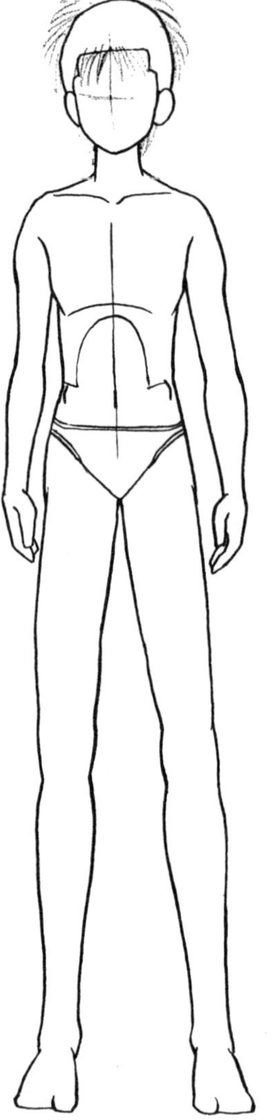

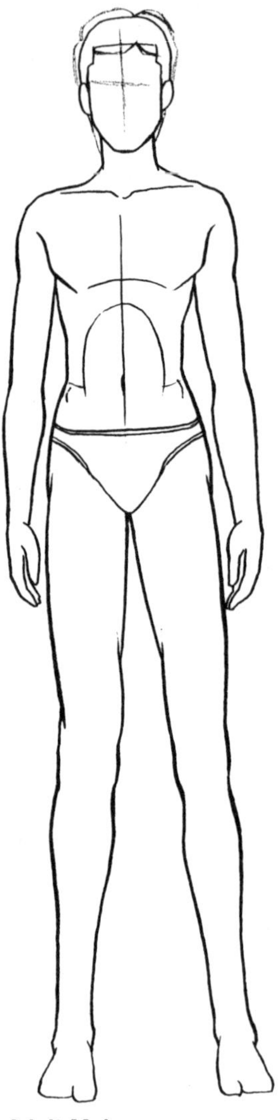

Adolescent Boy
The pelvis is long and narrow, but somewhat wider. (Use a smaller shoulder to hips ratio.)

Adult Male
Lengthen the height of the pelvis for the adult male.

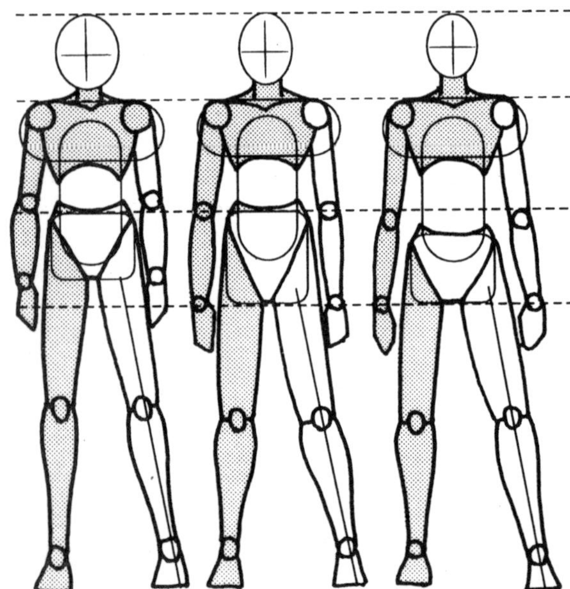

Adolescent Boy　Adult Male　Lean Build, Average Stature

2. Drawing Well-Proportioned Male Figures

1. Draw the head smaller.
2. Give the trunk an elongated appearance (i.e. lower the position of the waist).
3. Lengthen the arms and legs. (Make no change to the amount of curves and crevices in the muscles.)

Well-Proportioned Build, Average Stature

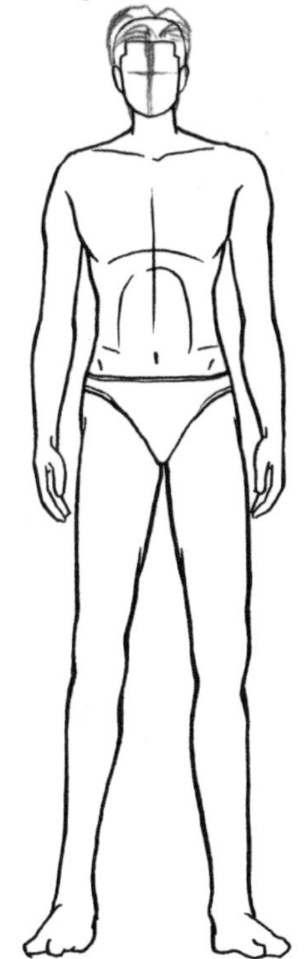

Distinguishing features of the well-proportioned build are wide shoulders, a deep chest cavity, a slender waist (taught abdomen), and robust appearance.

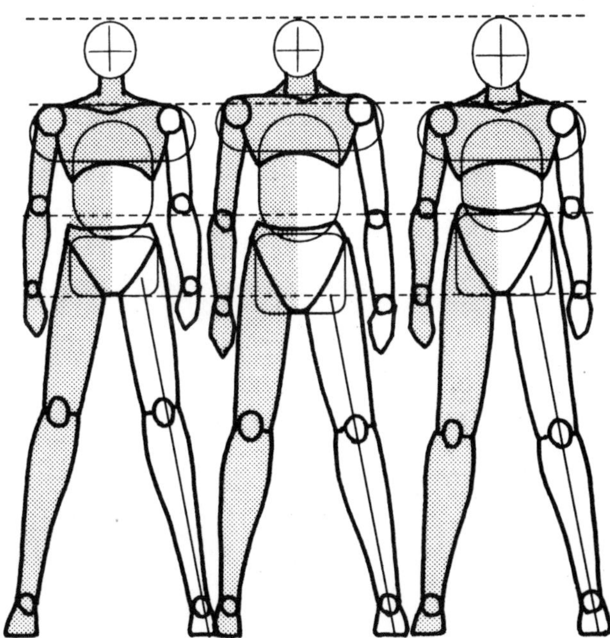

Adolescent Boy　　Adult Male　　Lean Build, Average Stature

Well-Proportioned Build, Tall Stature

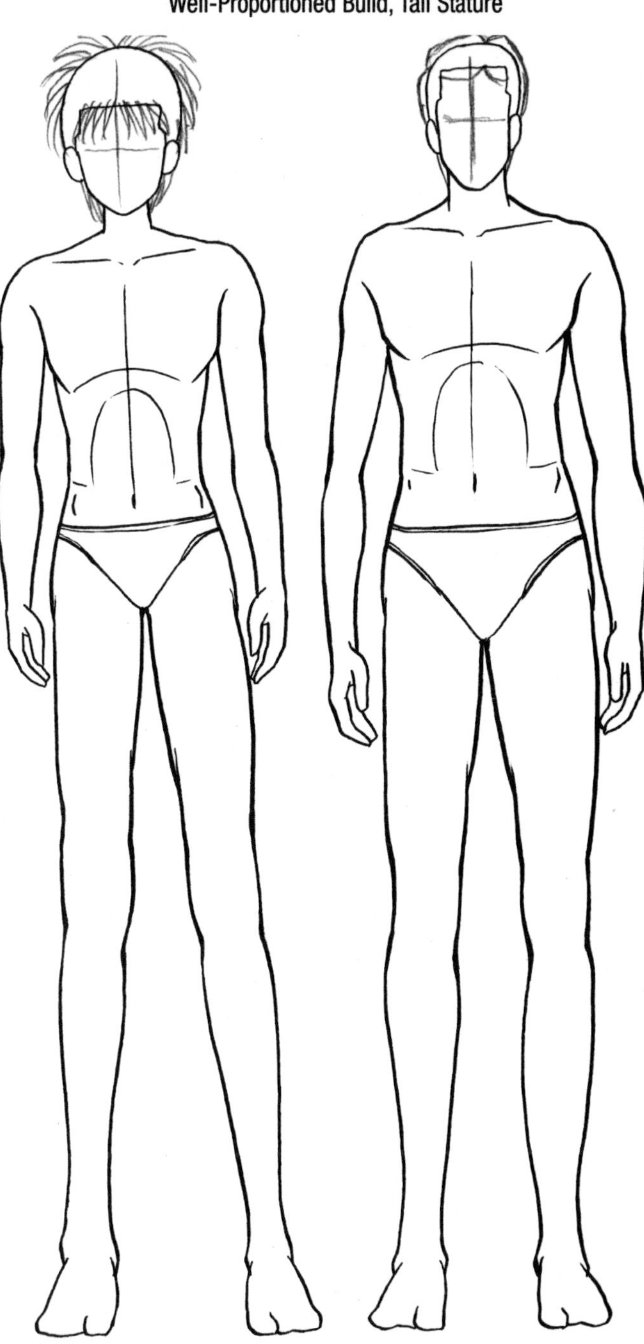

Adolescent Boy
Give the pelvis a less sturdy appearance by shortening hips in height and width.

Adult Male
Give the pelvis a stable appearance by elongating the hips.
Give the figure a thick, muscular neck.

Drawing Middle-Aged and Older Male Figures

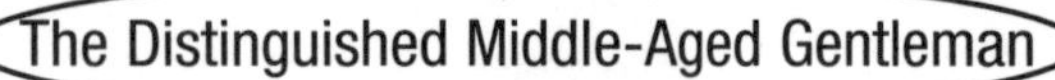

The Distinguished Middle-Aged Gentleman

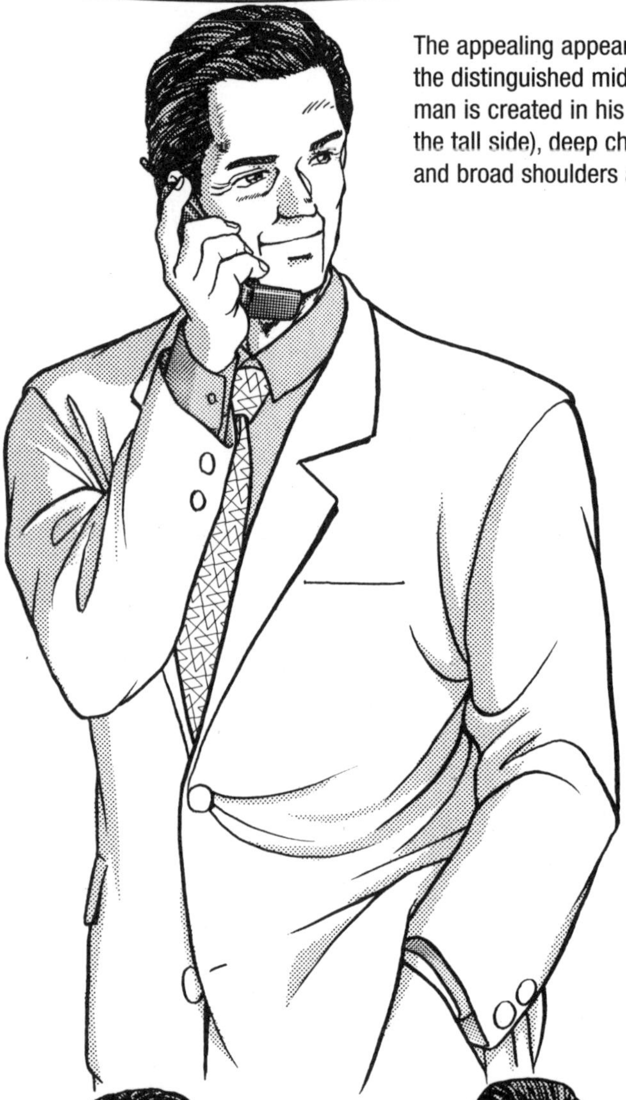

The appealing appearance of the distinguished middle-aged man is created in his height (on the tall side), deep chest cavity, and broad shoulders and back.

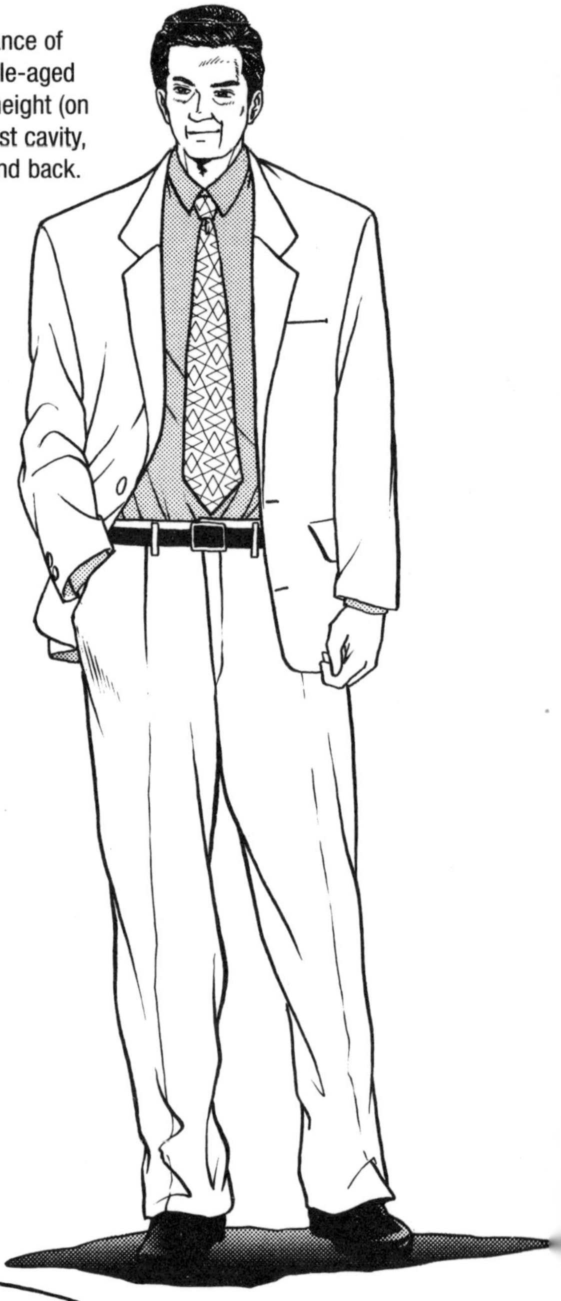

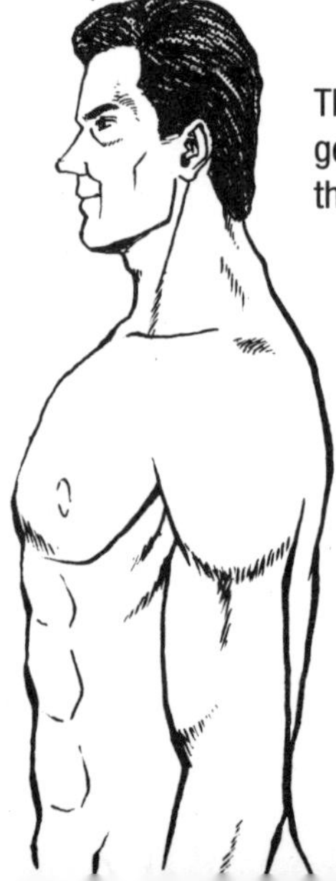

The middle-aged gentleman's neck is thick and robust.

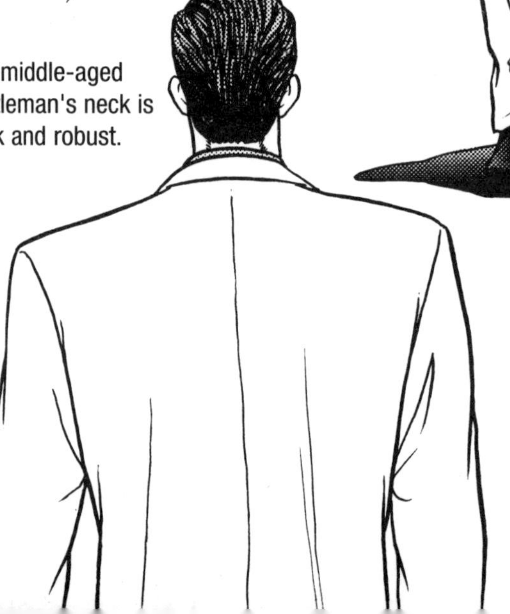

Use the back of a middle-aged character, a man in his prime, to give him a distinguished air.

Hunched Over Male Figures (Sloped Shoulders)

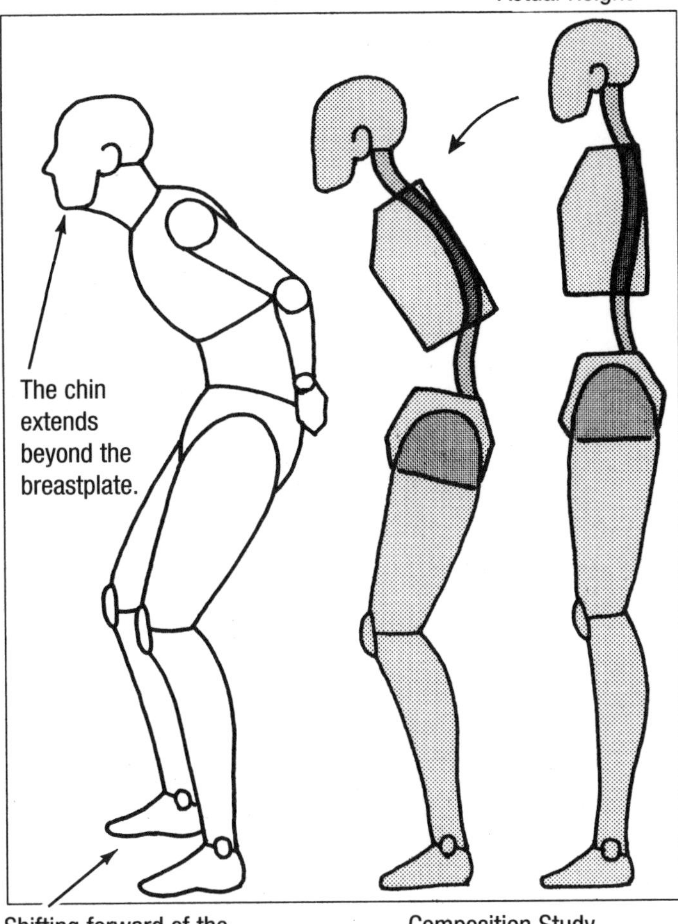

Shifting forward of the body's center of gravity causes the character to adopt a pronounced bowlegged gait.

Composition Study

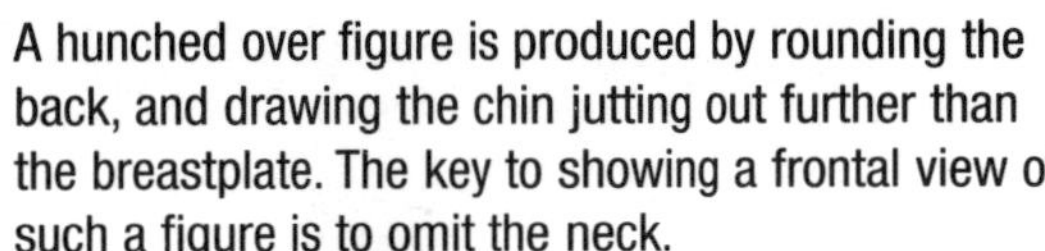

A hunched over figure is produced by rounding the back, and drawing the chin jutting out further than the breastplate. The key to showing a frontal view of such a figure is to omit the neck.

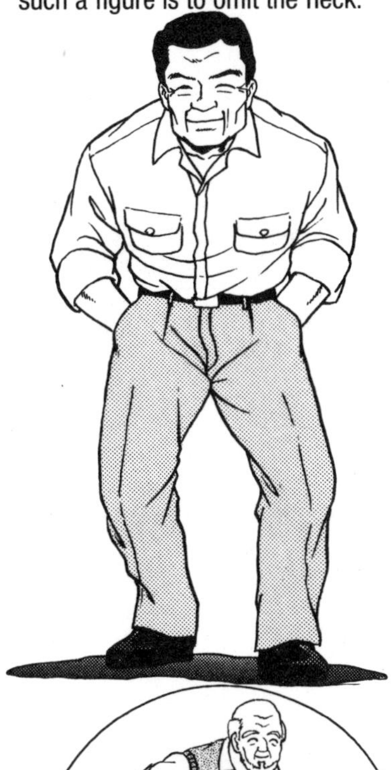

A hunched over figure can be applied to drawing an elderly male character.

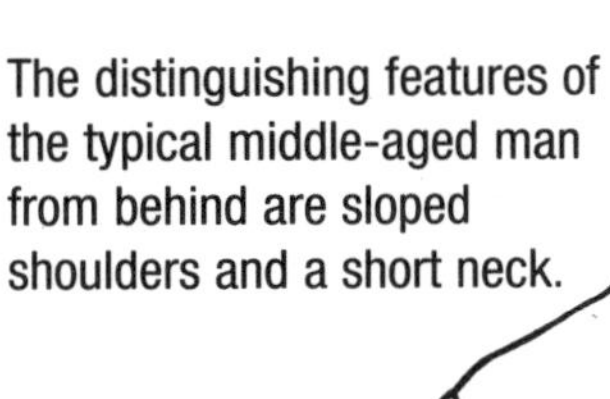

The distinguishing features of the typical middle-aged man from behind are sloped shoulders and a short neck.

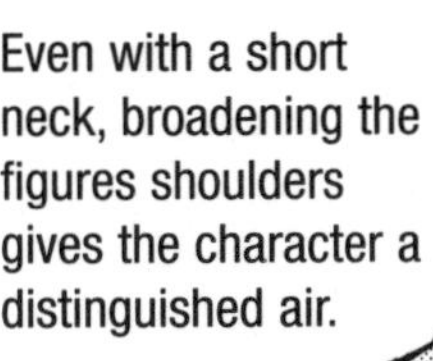

Even with a short neck, broadening the figures shoulders gives the character a distinguished air.

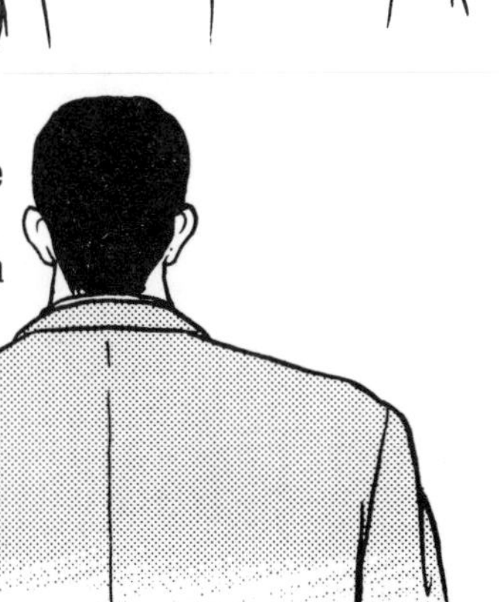

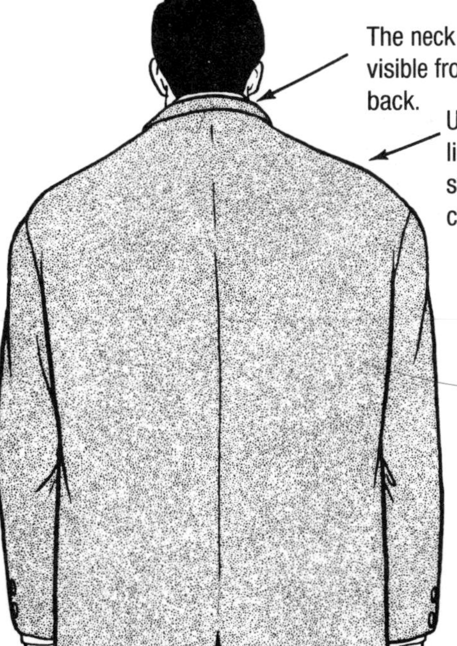

The neck is not visible from the back.

Use an arced line for the shoulder contour.

Drawing a Wizened (Wrinkled) Face

Wrinkles, which function to suggest age in elderly characters, tend to appear consistently in the same locations.

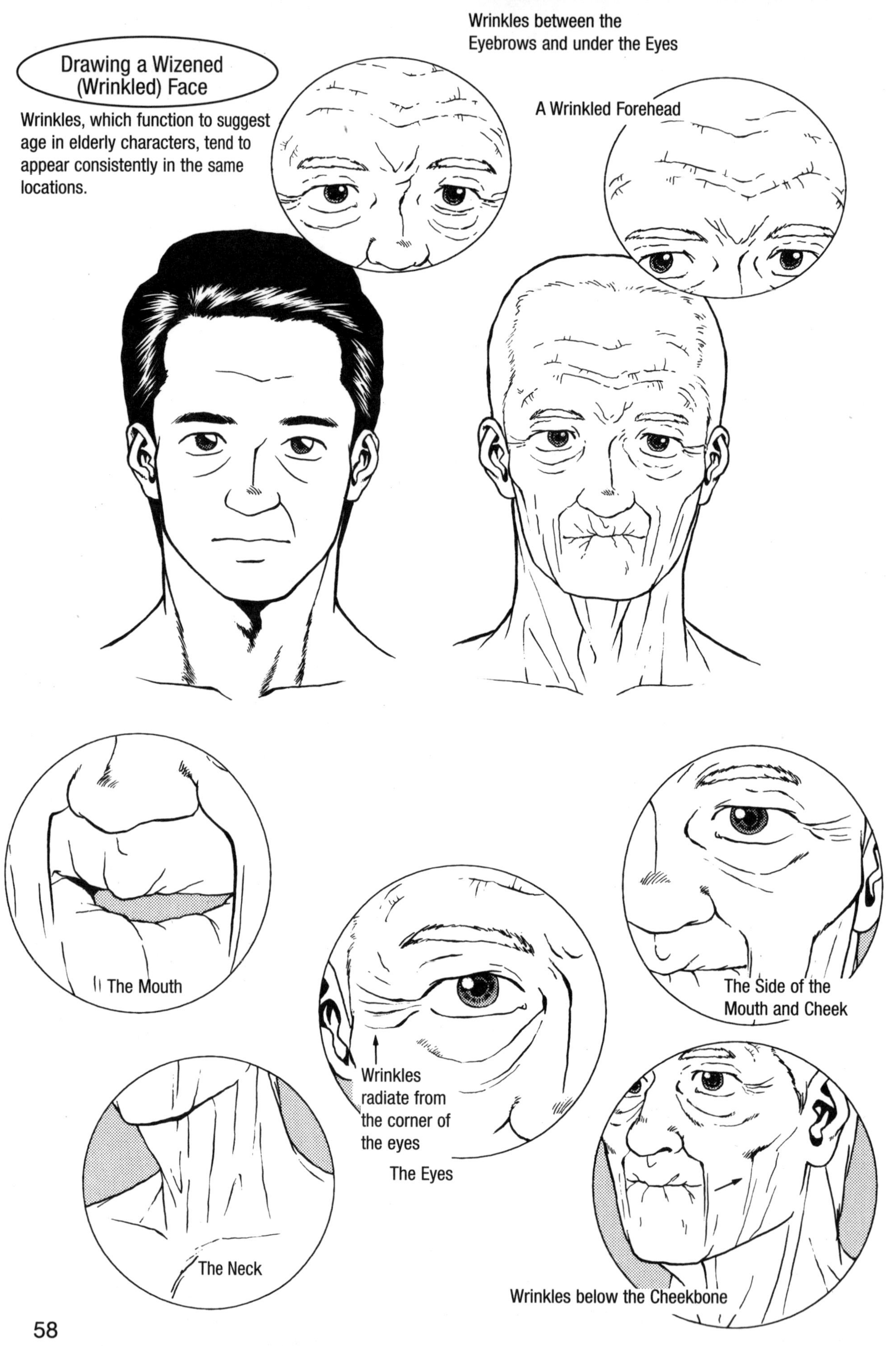

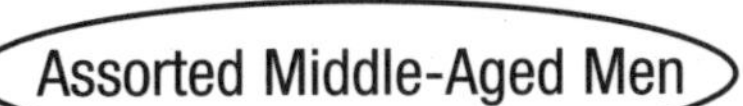

Assorted Middle-Aged Men

The shapes of the faces of middle-aged male characters tend to be round, triangular, rectangular, and pentagonal-the same, typical face shapes used in manga. The common distinguishing features of middle-aged males are wrinkles around the mouth and eyes and a strong jaw.

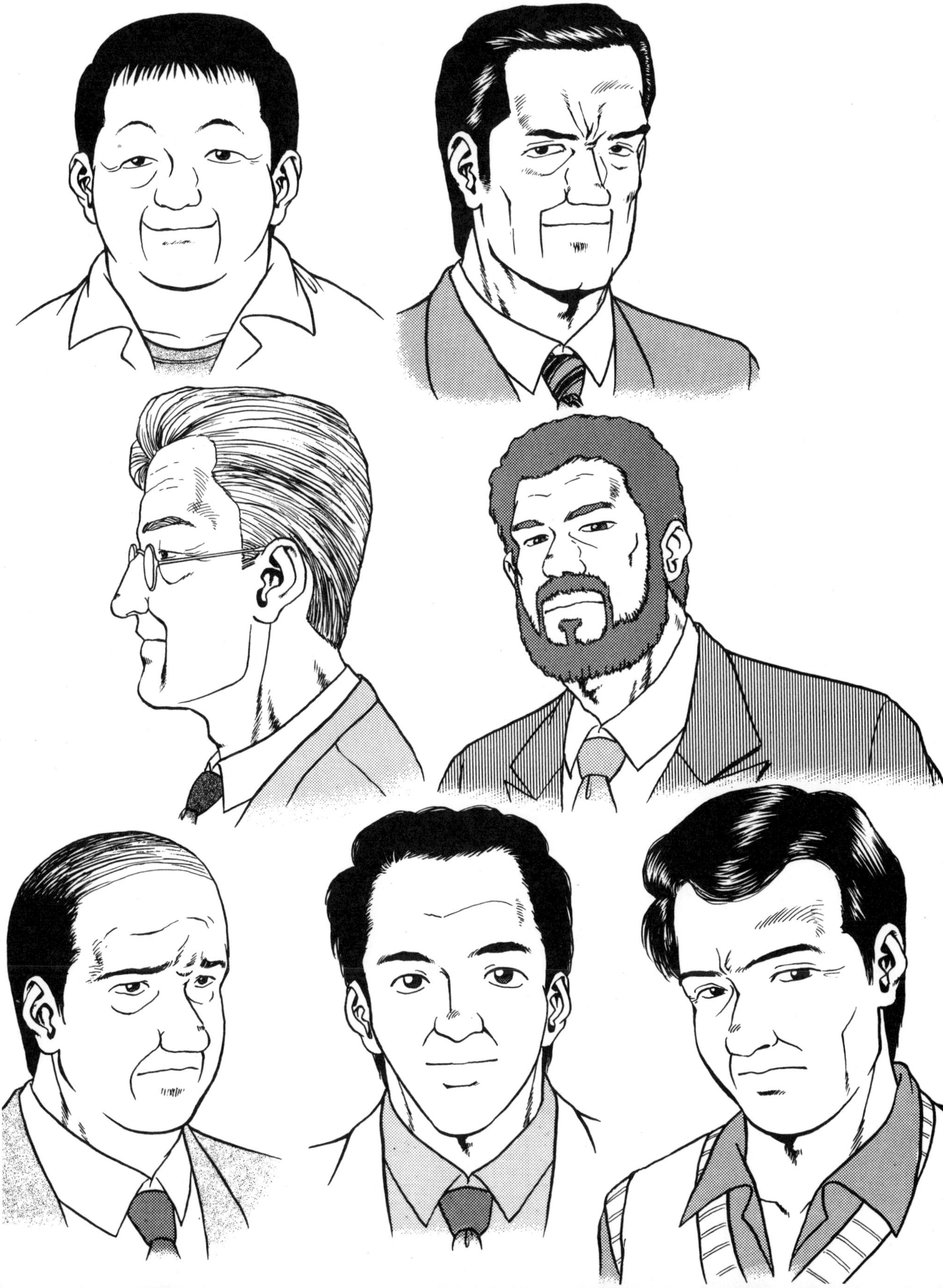

Hair

1. Wavy Hair

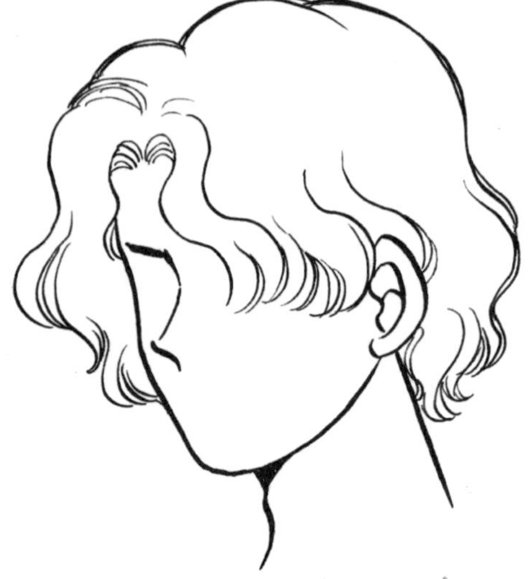

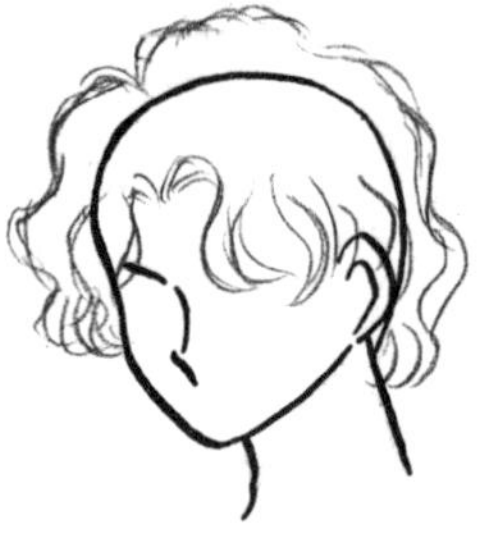

Draw the silhouette of the hair generally following the outline of the head.

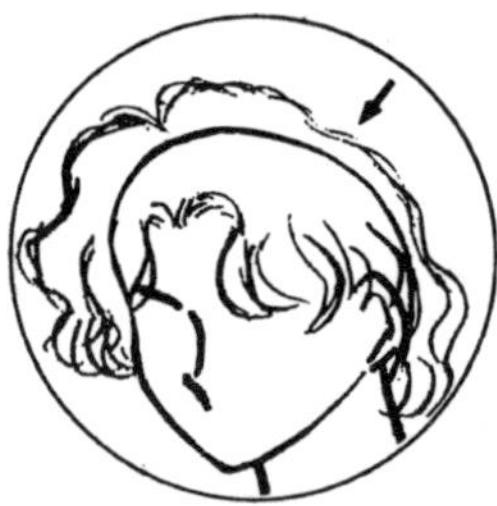

Drawing the silhouette of the hair with disregard for the shape of the head produces a bizarre appearance.

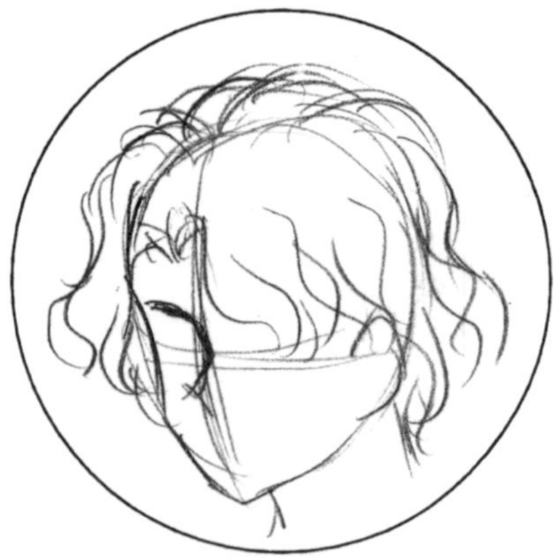

① Do a rough sketch in pencil of the hair. A penciled under drawing as precise as the finished work may also be used.

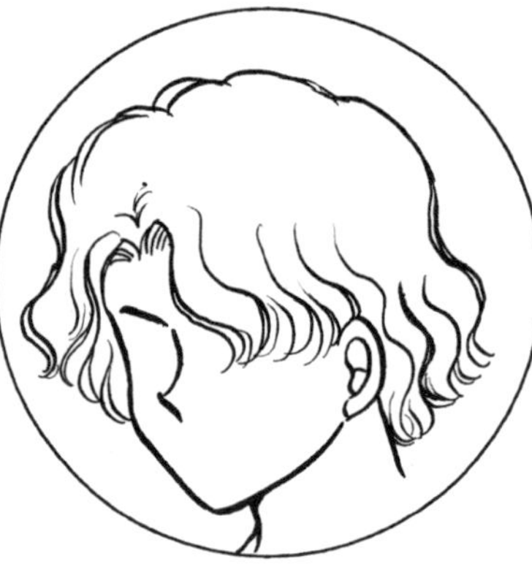

② Ink the sketch.

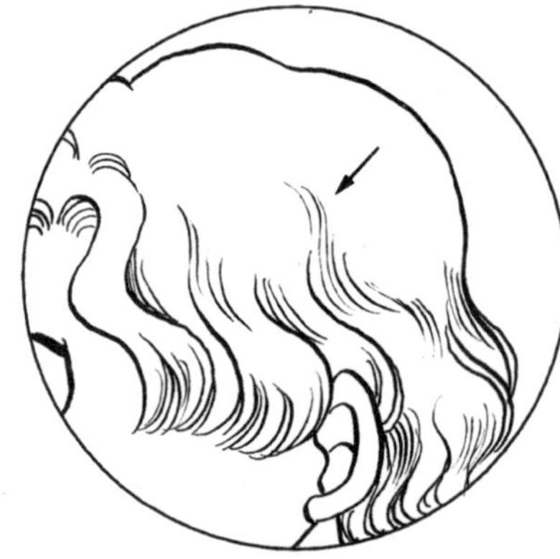

③ Add waves and movement to the hair by mixing in finer lines.

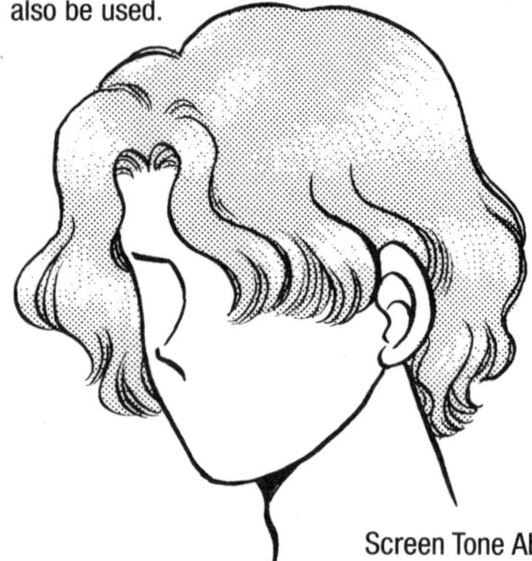

Screen Tone Abrading

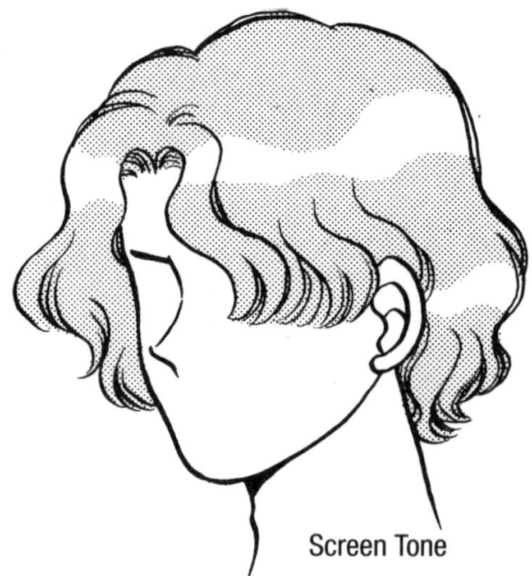

Screen Tone

2. Straight Hair

① Pencil Sketch (Under Drawing)
Draw the sketch while planning to leave white areas reflecting light (highlights) and while estimating which areas to leave white. The pencil should not touch areas of highlight.

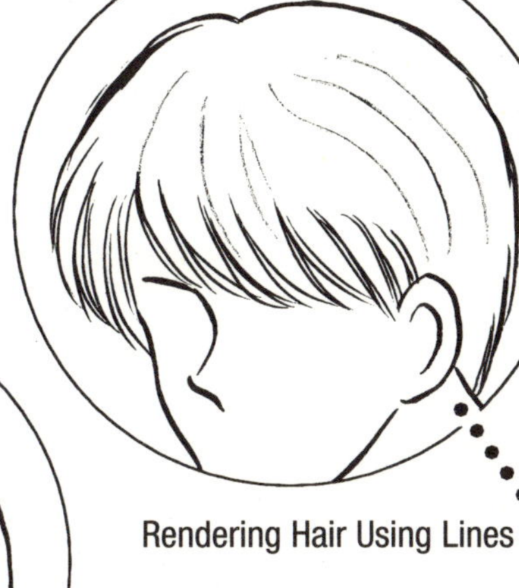

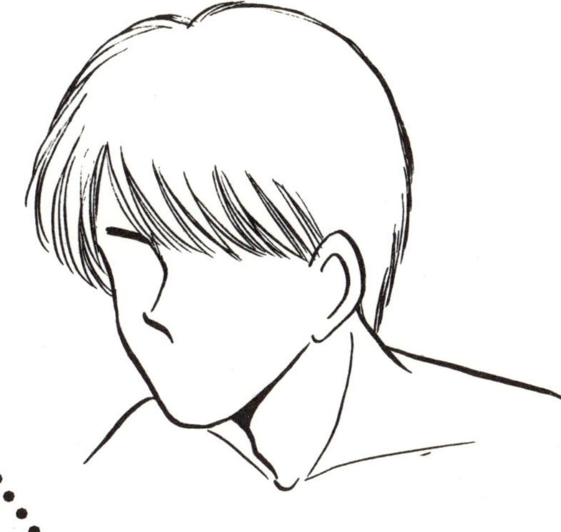

Rendering Hair Using Lines

The Solid Tone Approach

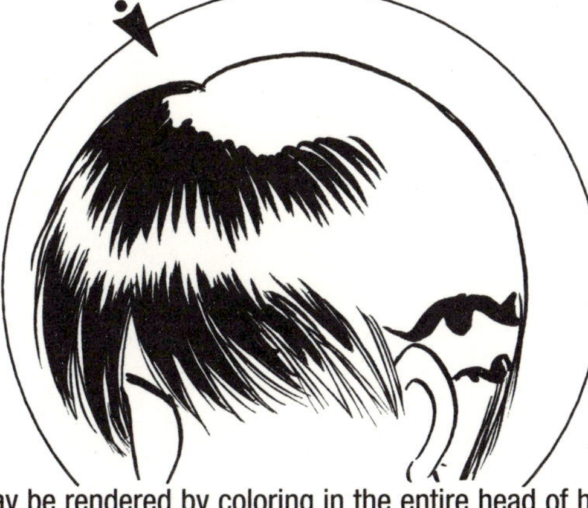

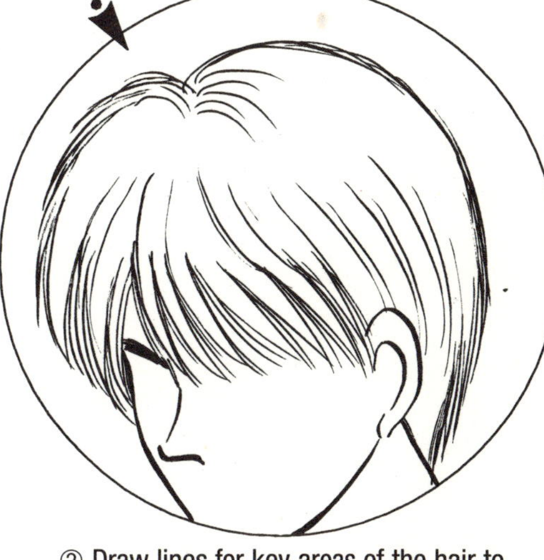

② Hair may be rendered by coloring in the entire head of hair (leaving out the white areas) with a calligraphy pen [fude felt pen] or using a calligraphy pen to mark off the areas to keep white and then filling in the rest with a felt marker.

② Draw lines for key areas of the hair to show its flow.

③ Assorted Finishes to the Solid Tone Approach

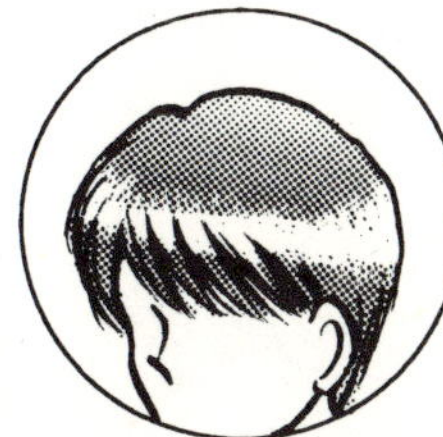

Use a gradation screen tone in lieu of a solid tone, abrading off highlights with a craft knife.

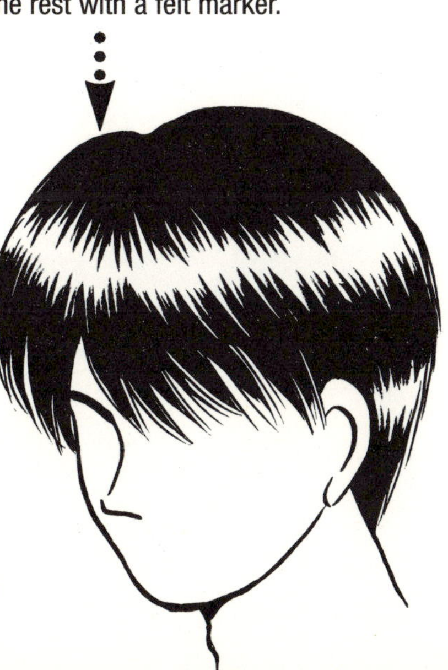

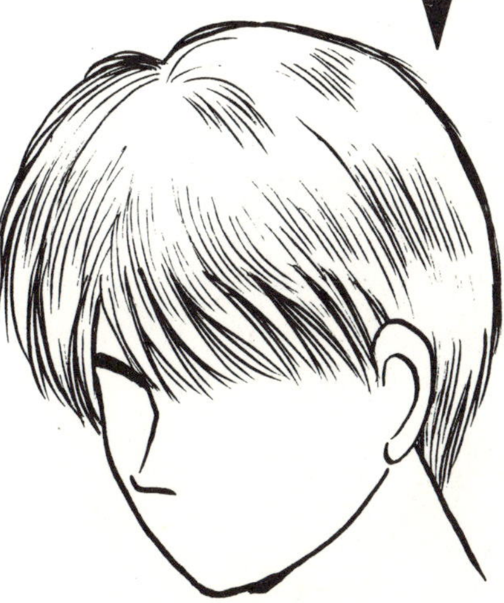

③ Add fine lines to create tousled hair or other looks as desired.

Rendering Hair Using Lines Only

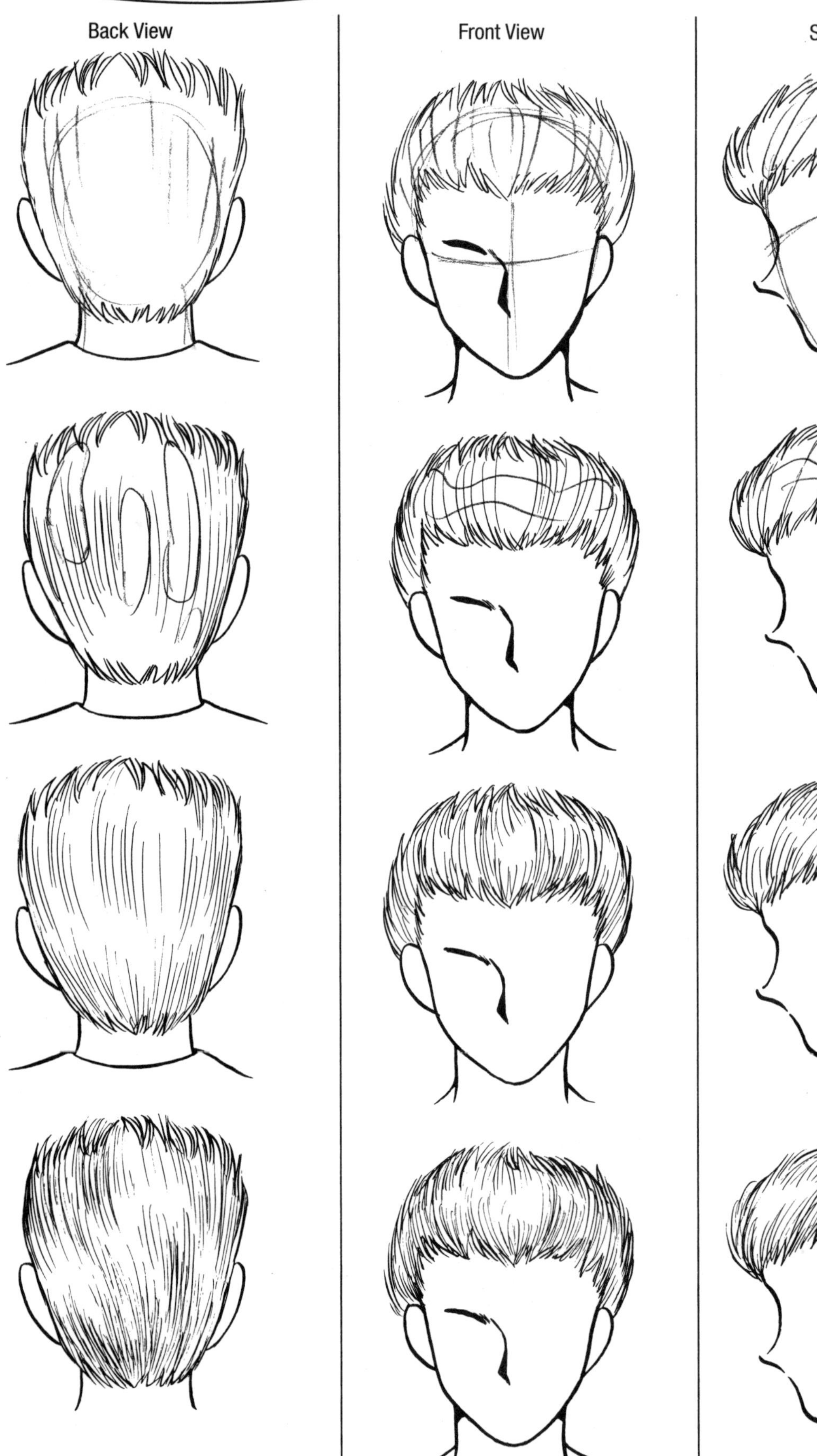

The Solid Tone Hair Approach

Back View	Front View	Side View
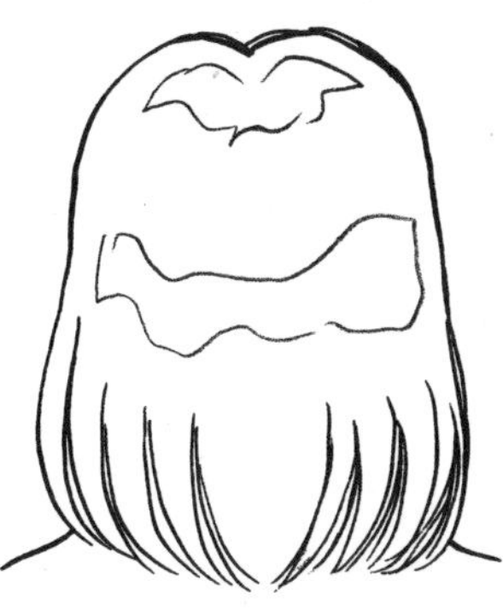	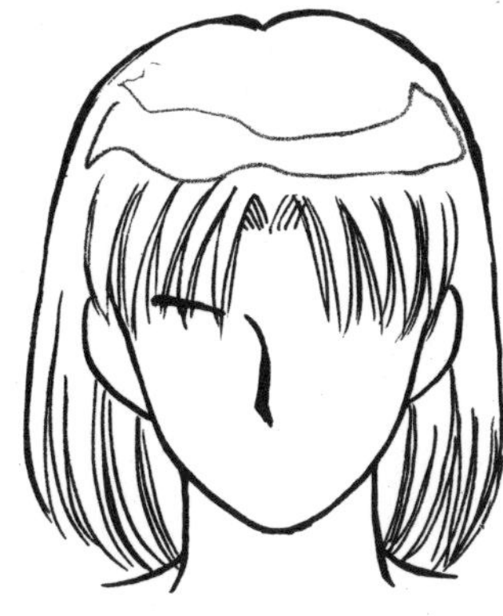	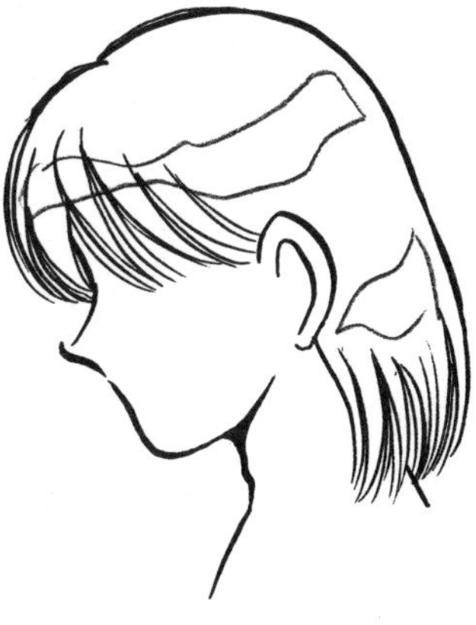
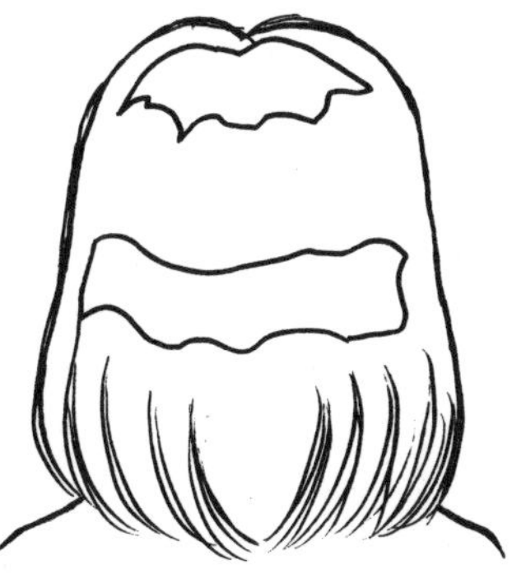	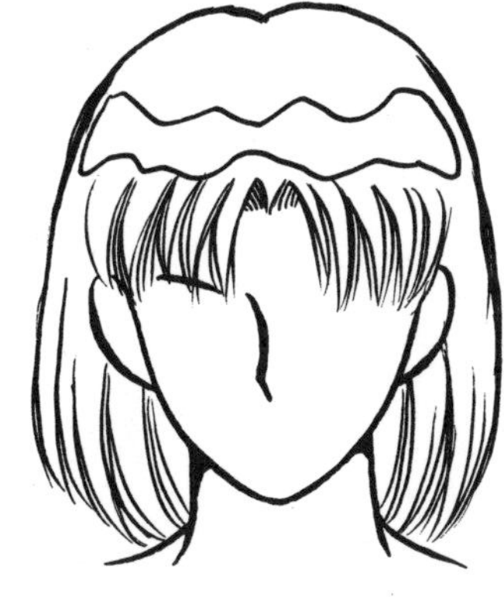	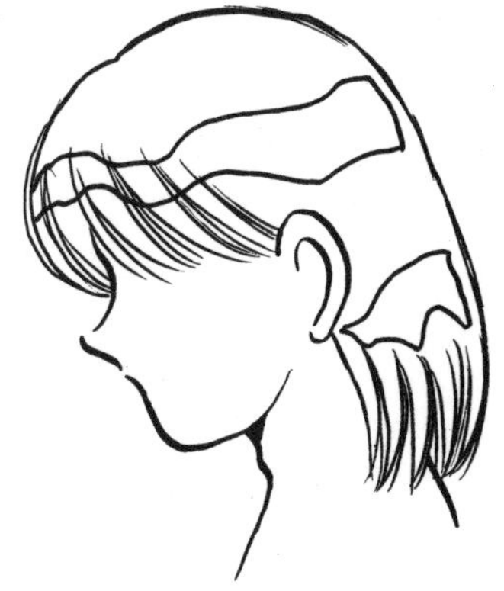
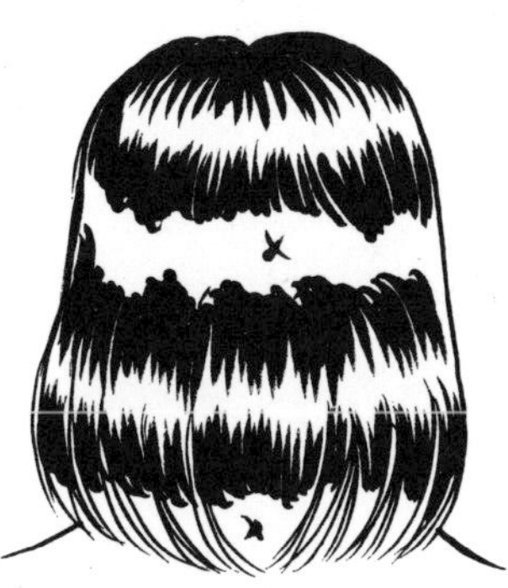	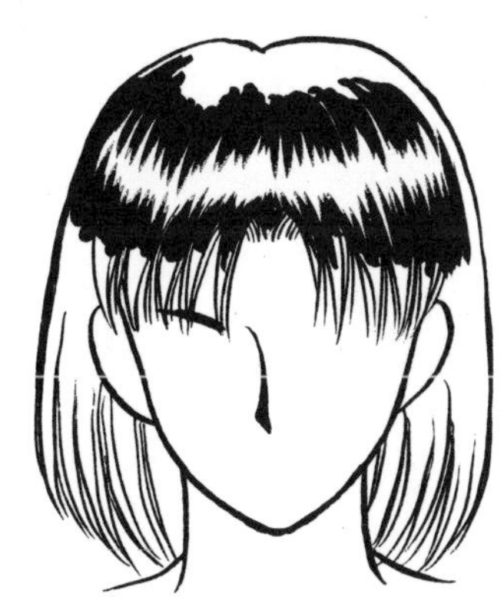	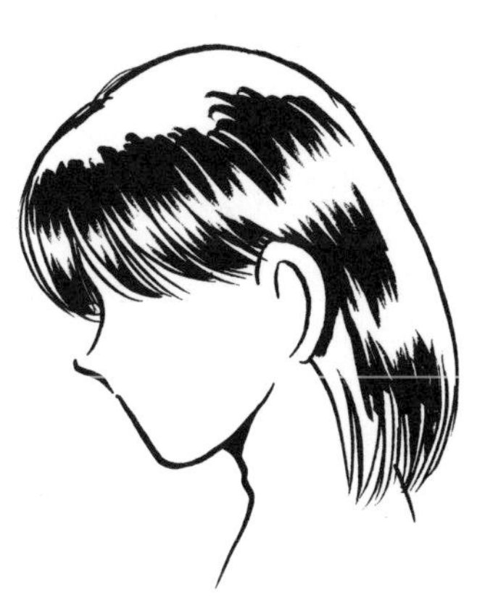
✗ ··Indicates where to add solid tone.		
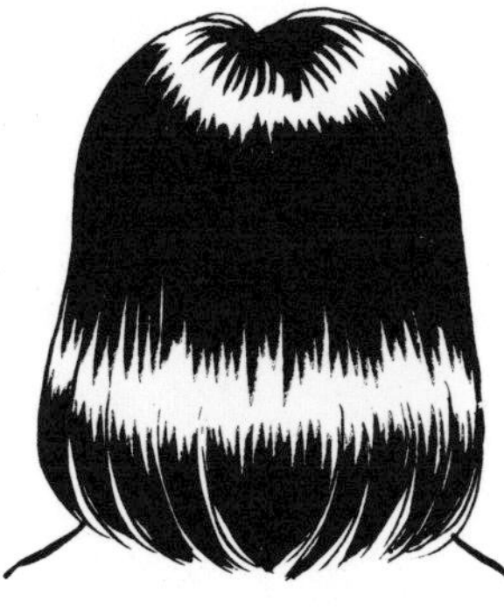	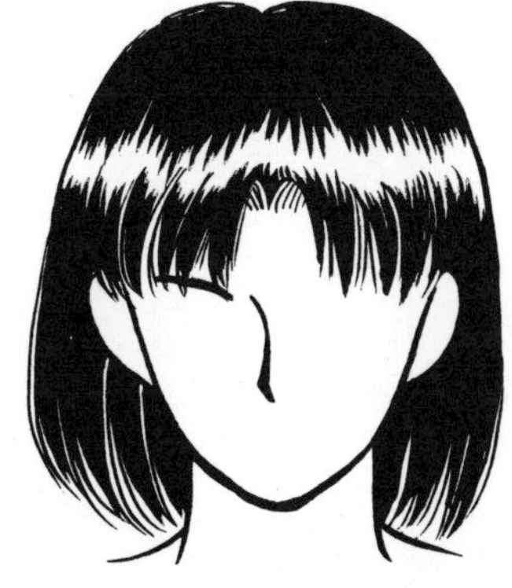	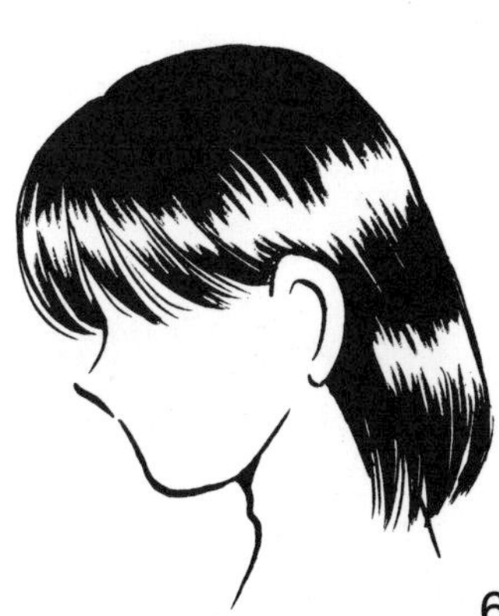

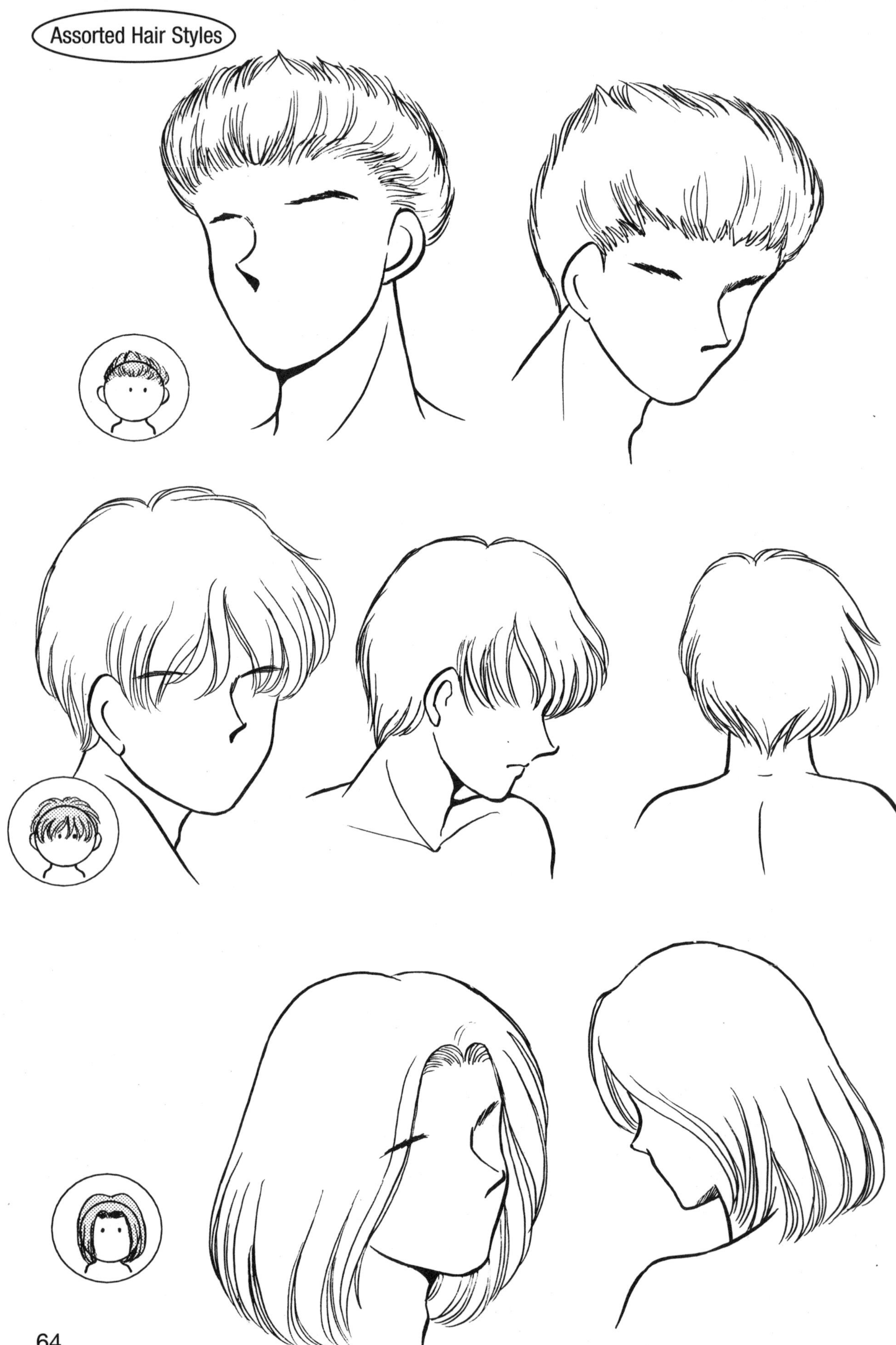

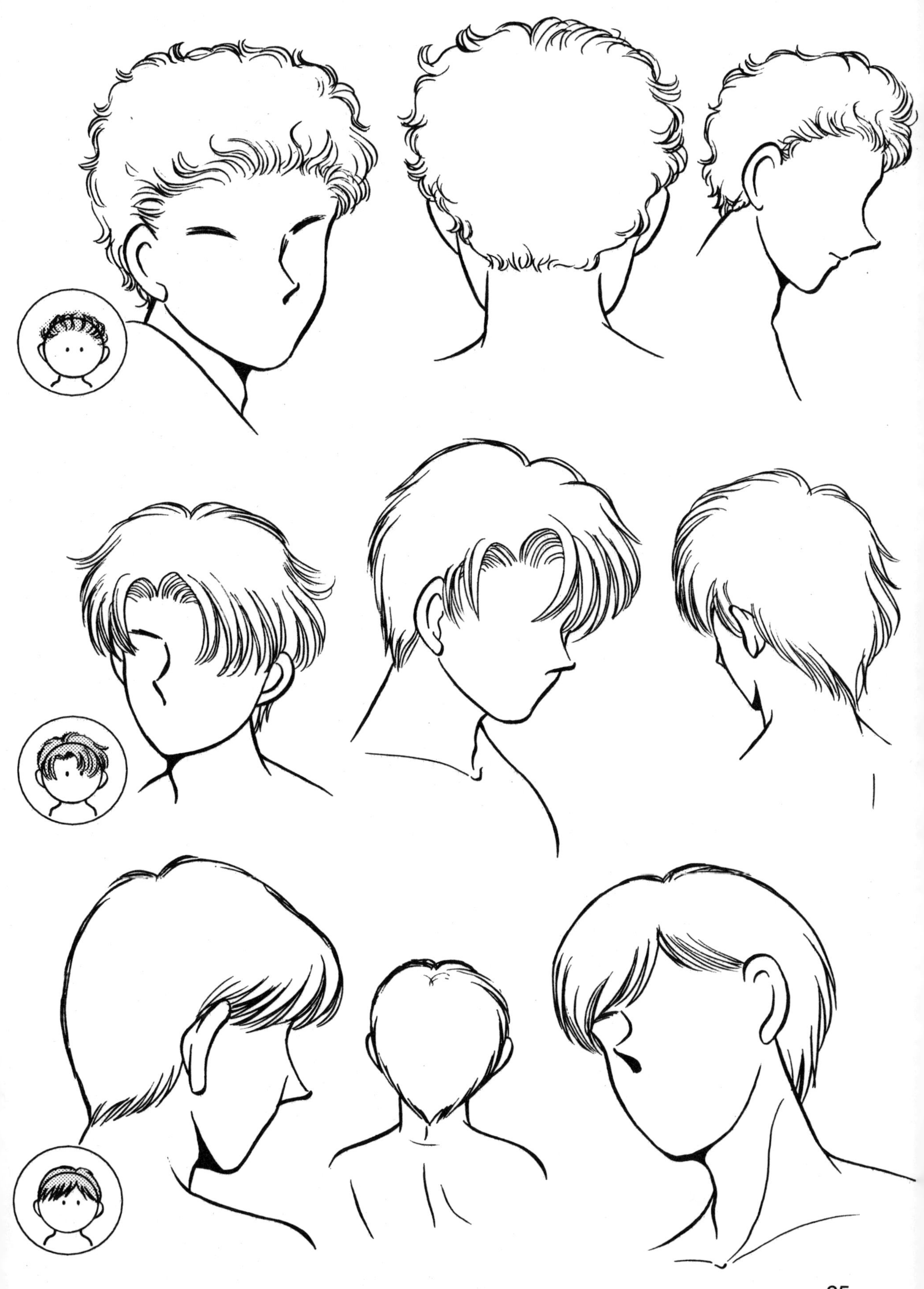

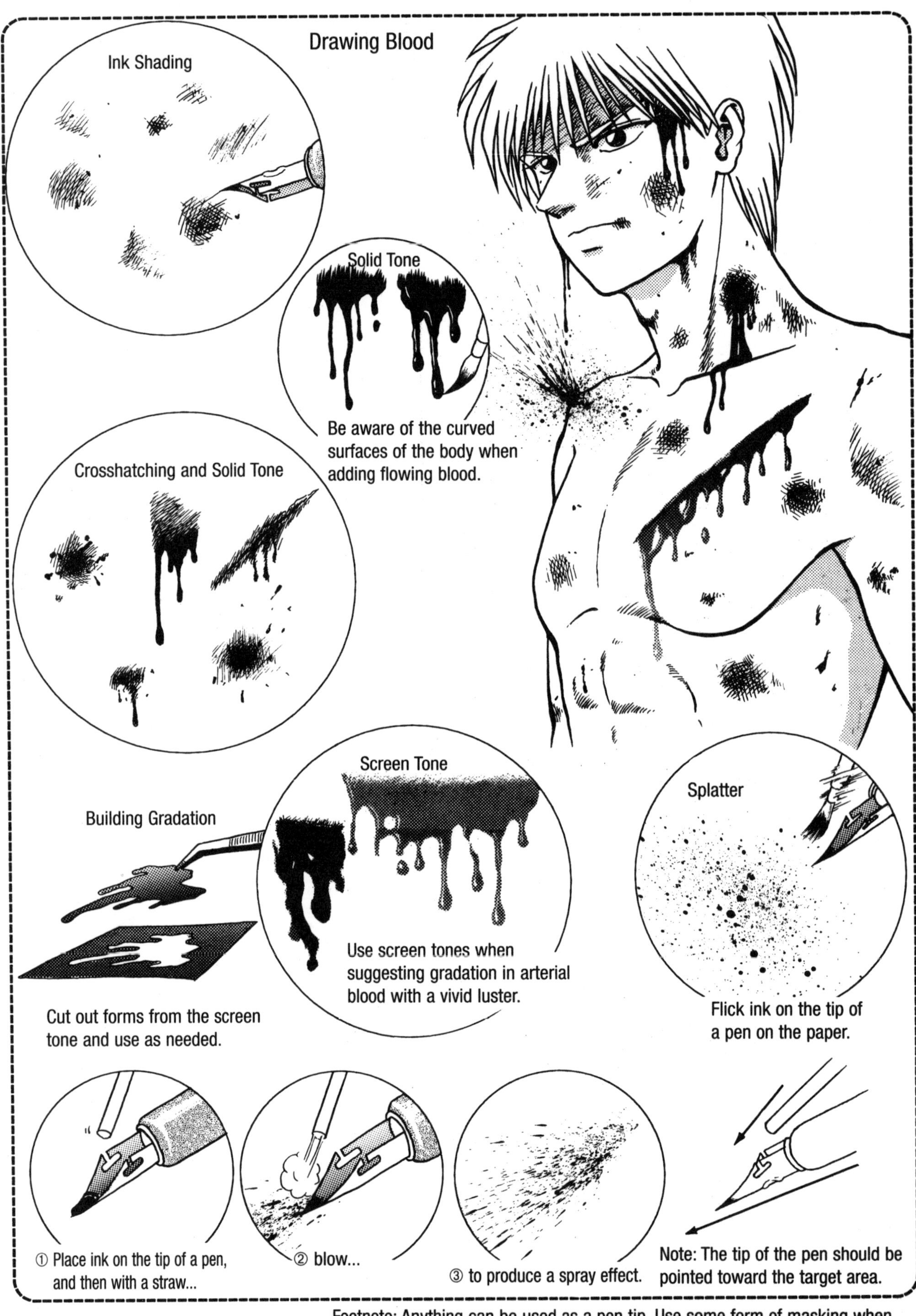

Footnote: Anything can be used as a pen tip. Use some form of masking when spraying or blowing ink so that no unwanted ink ends up in another panel.

Chapter 3
Basic Poses
The Figure Clothed and Unclothed

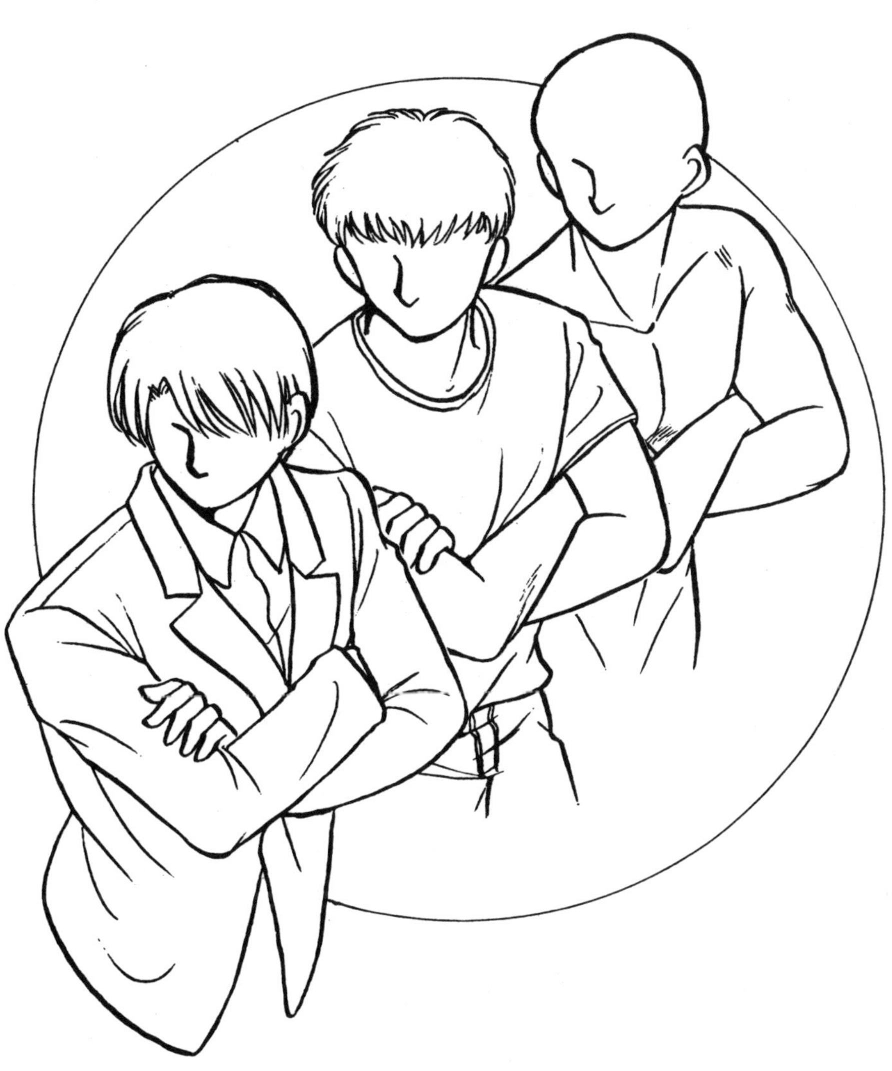

1. Standing

The shoulder rises slightly when the hand is placed on the hip. Creases formed from the shoulder of the jacket to the elbow are common and will be those most commonly drawn.

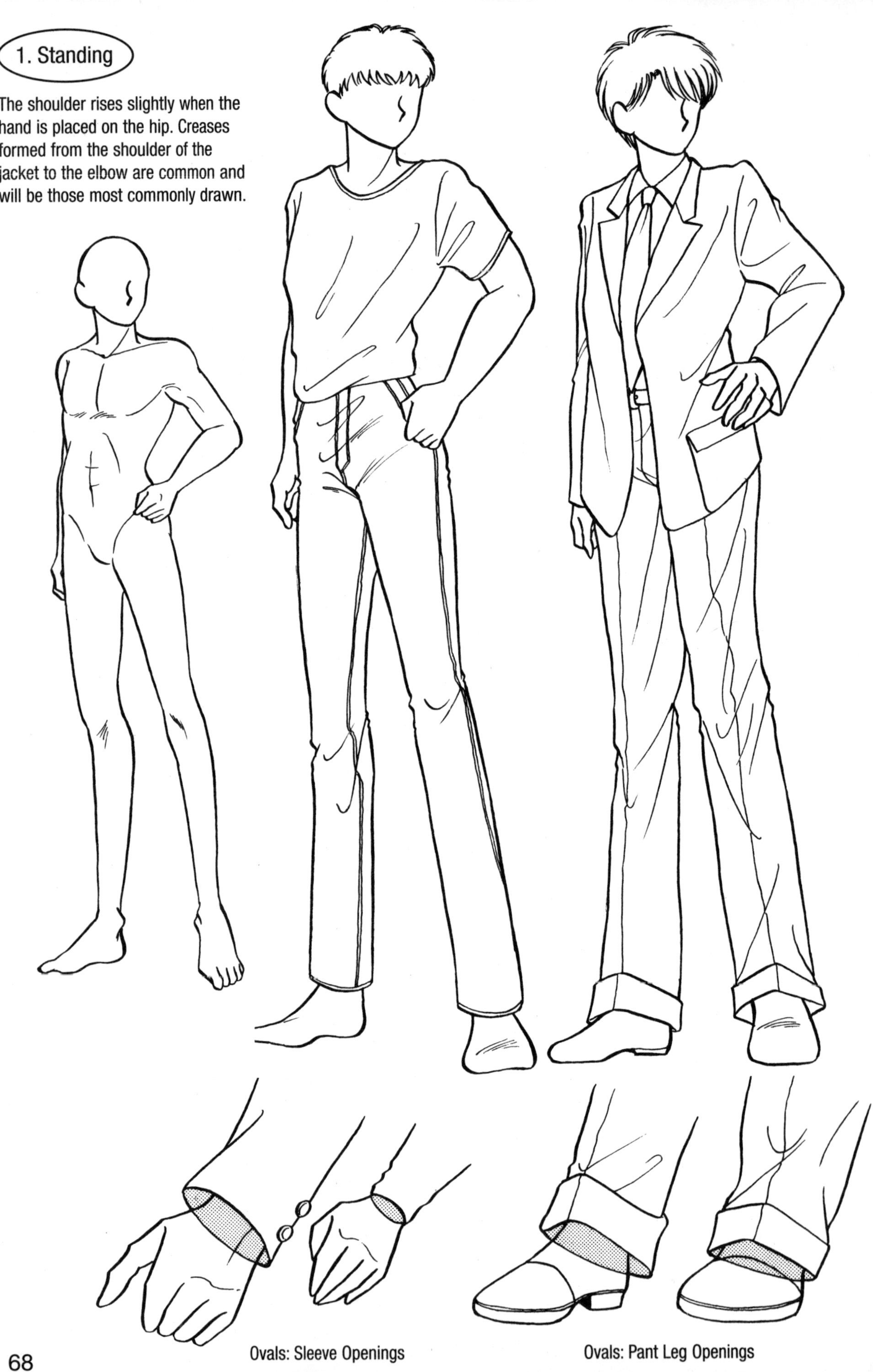

Ovals: Sleeve Openings

Ovals: Pant Leg Openings

2. Walking-Back View

The flow from the shoulders to the lower back generates creases in clothing scene in the back of a walking figure.

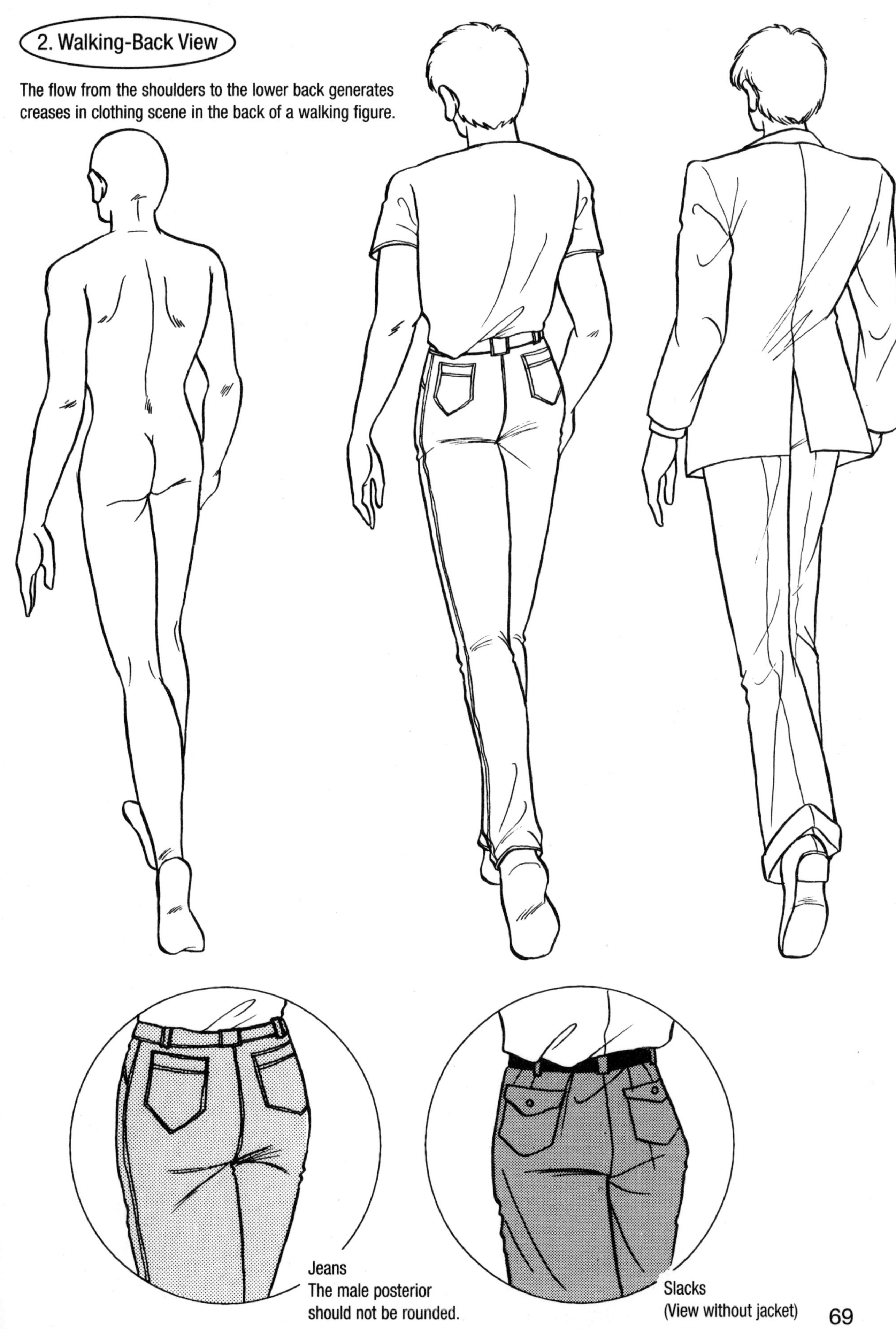

Jeans
The male posterior should not be rounded.

Slacks
(View without jacket)

3. Standing-Moderate Low Angle

Horizontal lines (clothing cuffs and hems) take on an upward arc when drawn from a low angle.

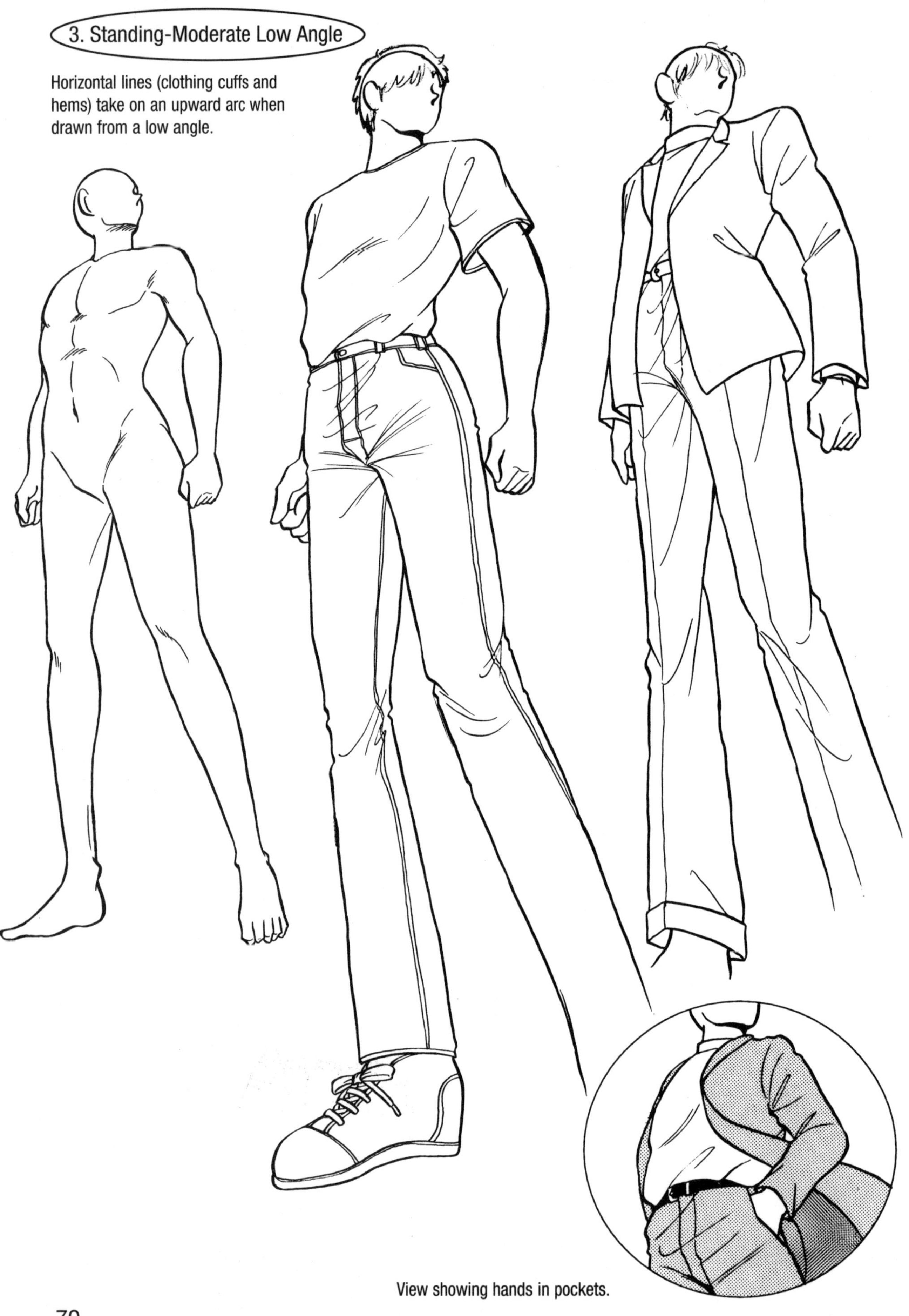

View showing hands in pockets.

4. Walking-Side View

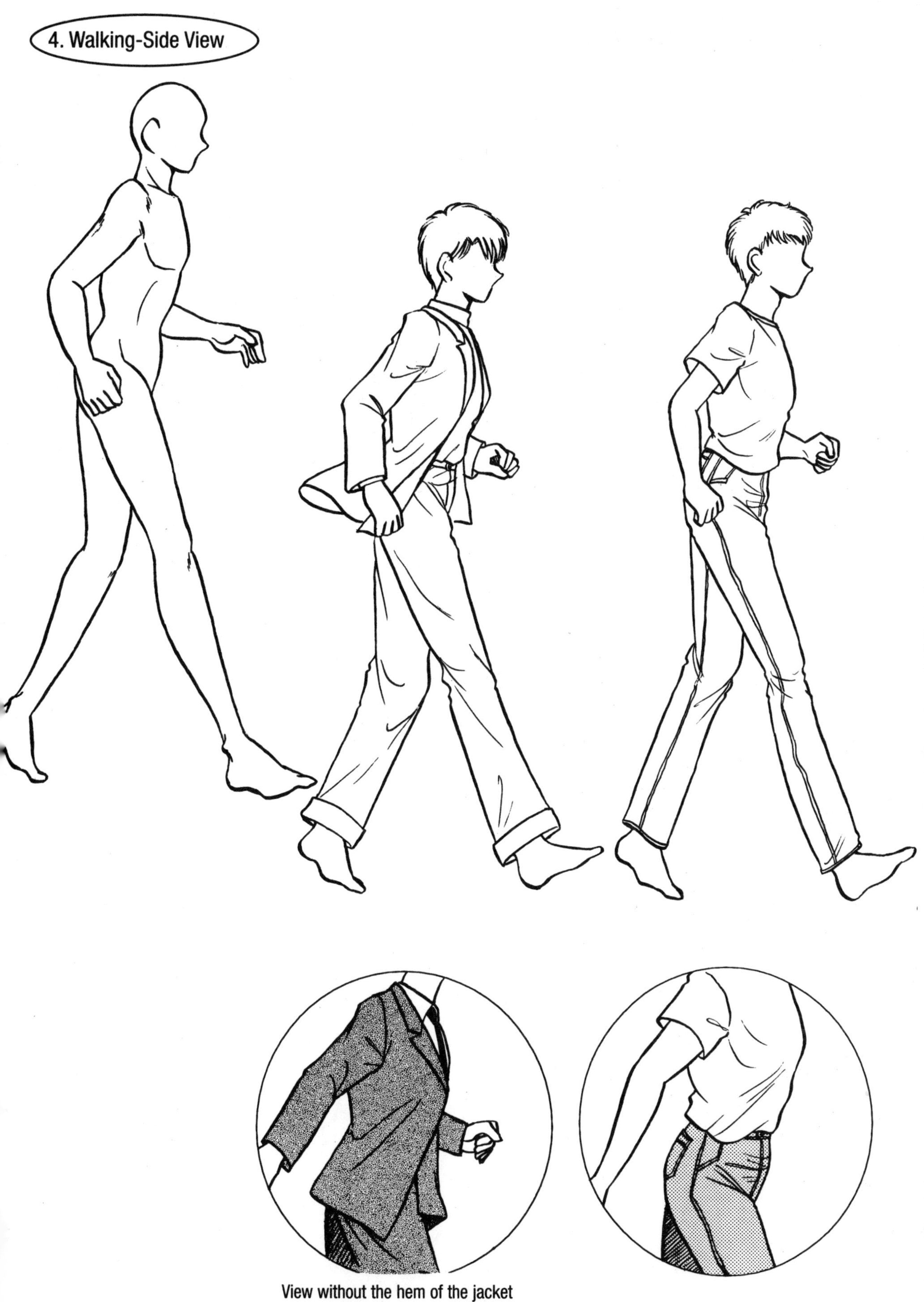

View without the hem of the jacket flipping up.

5. Standing & Walking-High Angle

6. Stretching

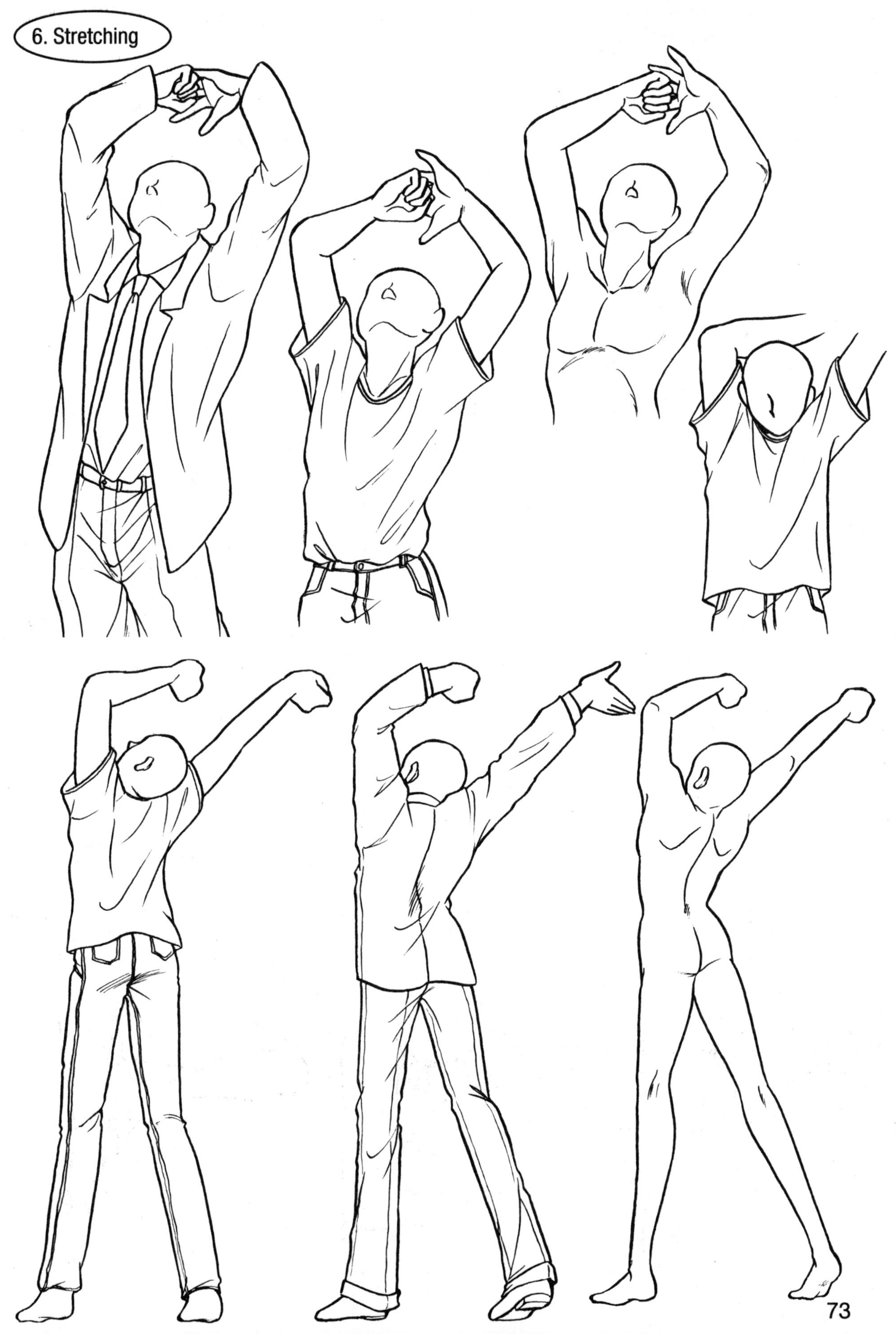

7. Sitting on the Floor/Ground

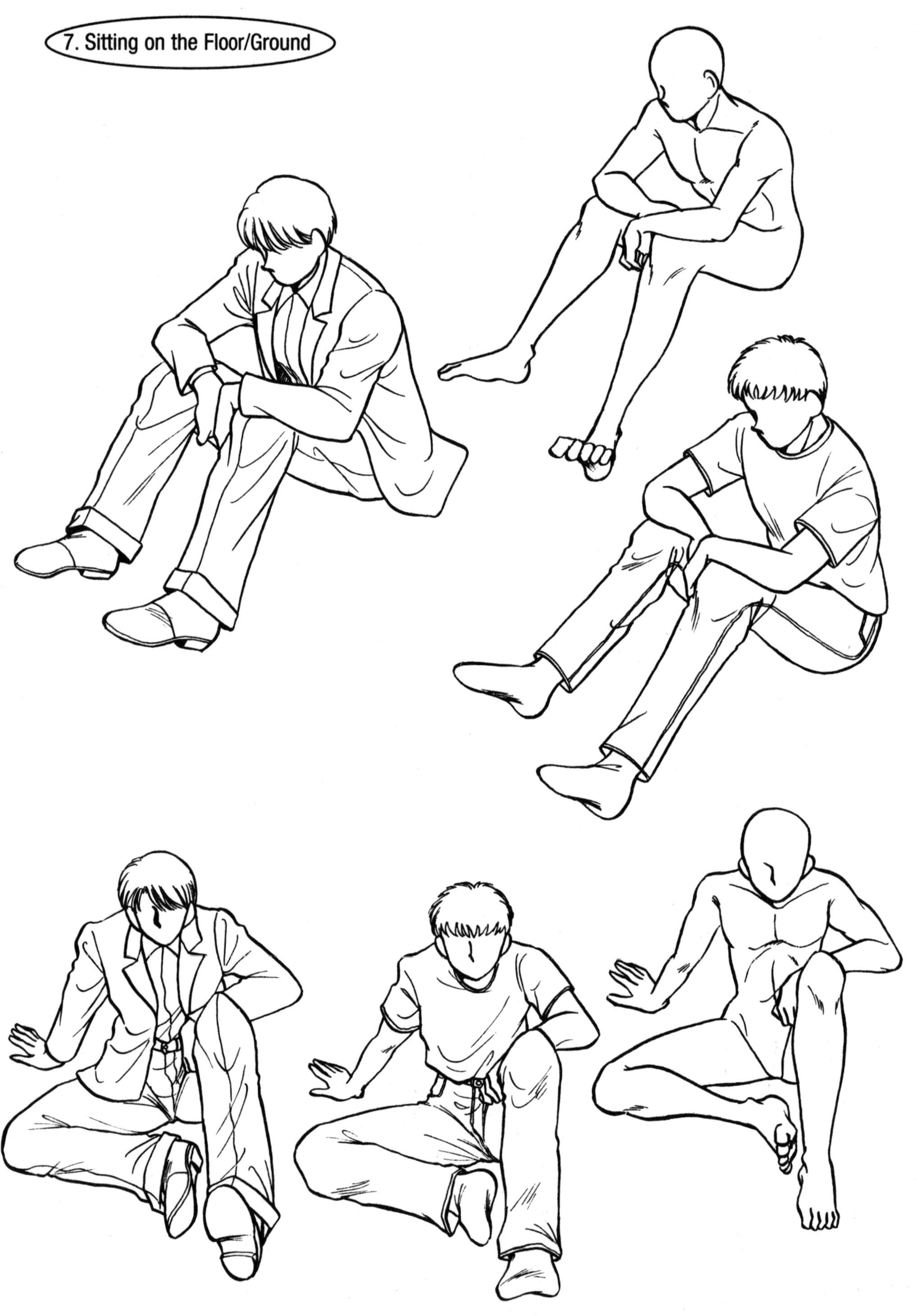

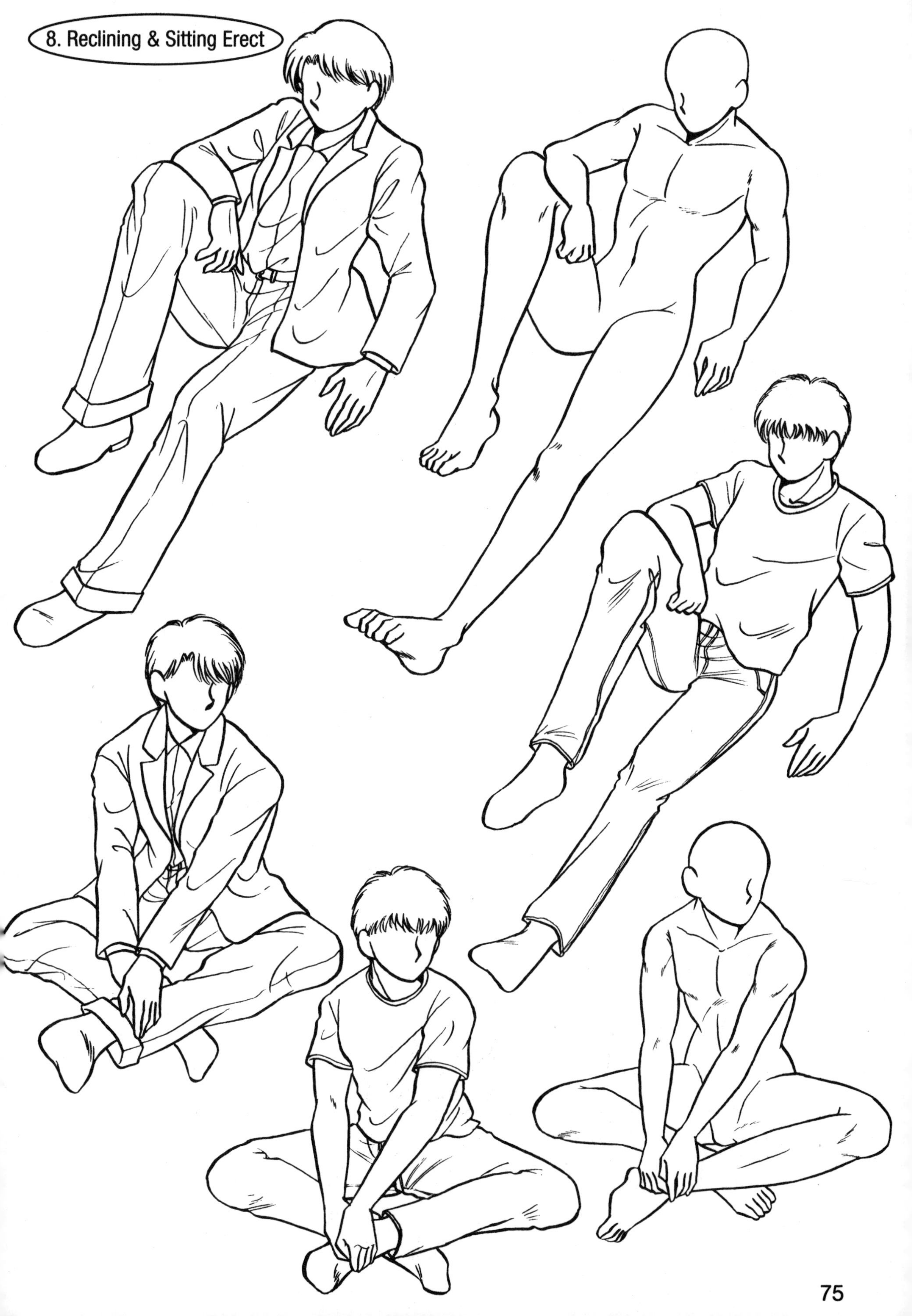
8. Reclining & Sitting Erect

9. Sitting in a Chair

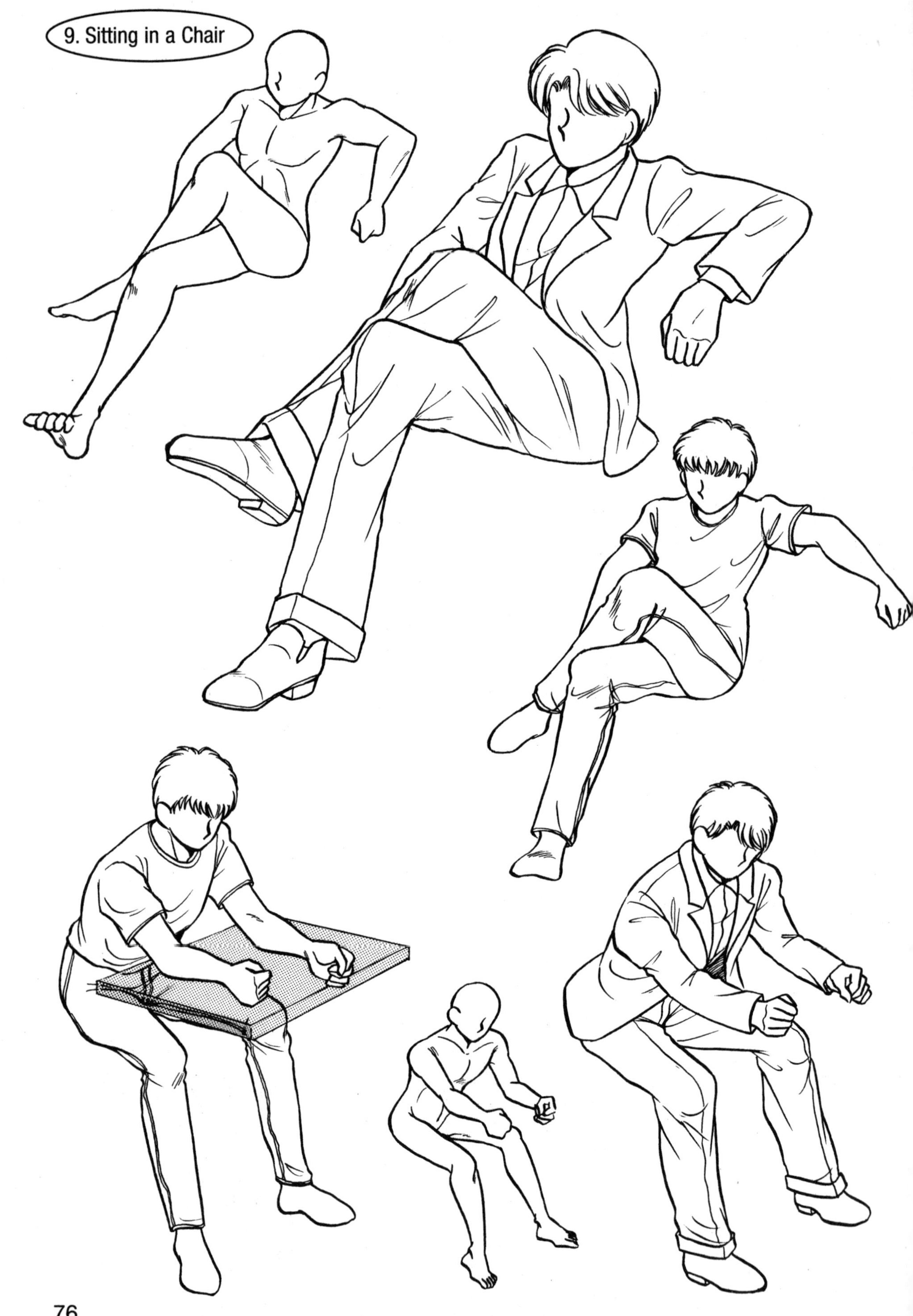

10. Squatting & Sitting on the Ground with the Trunk Erect

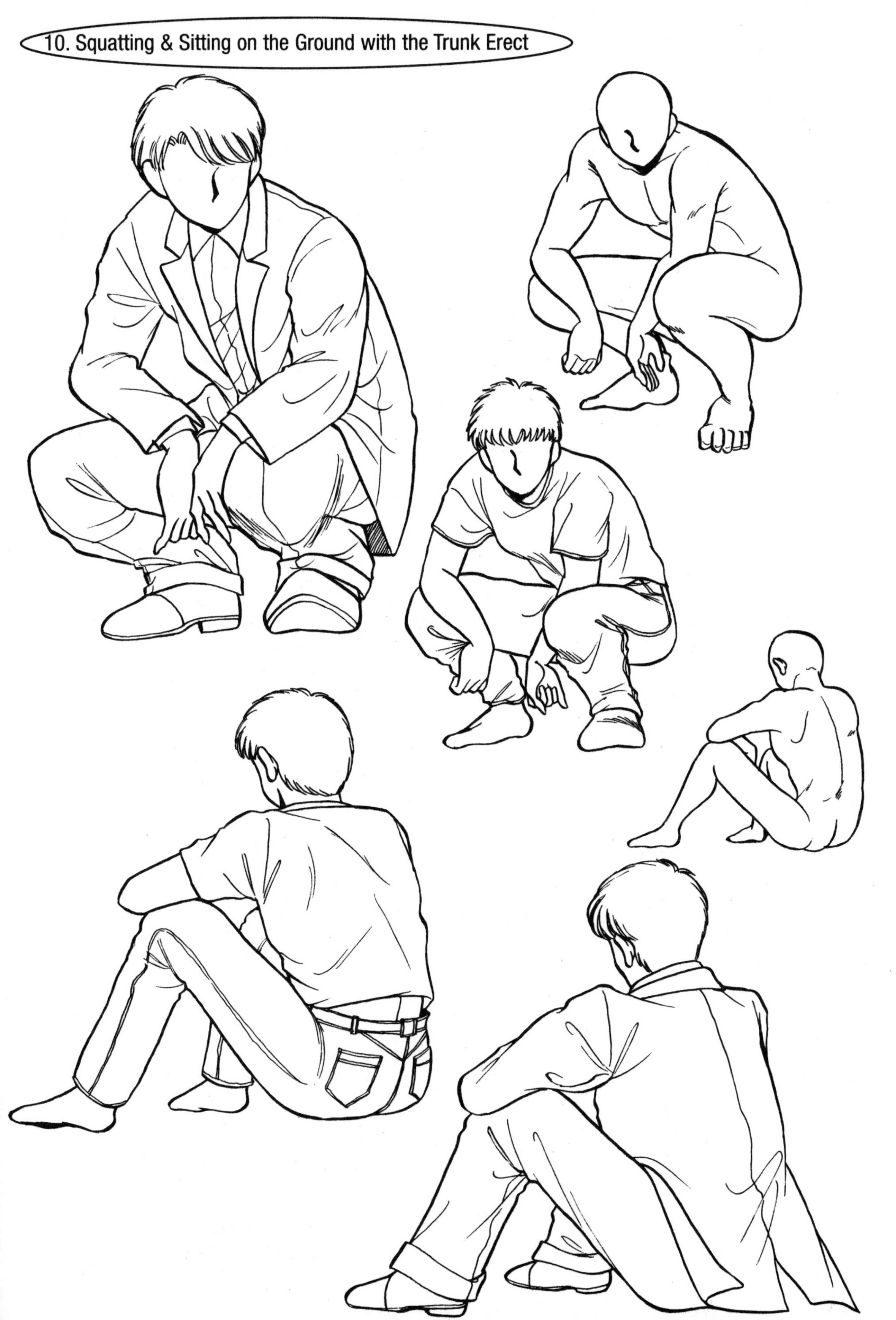

11. Crouching on One Knee

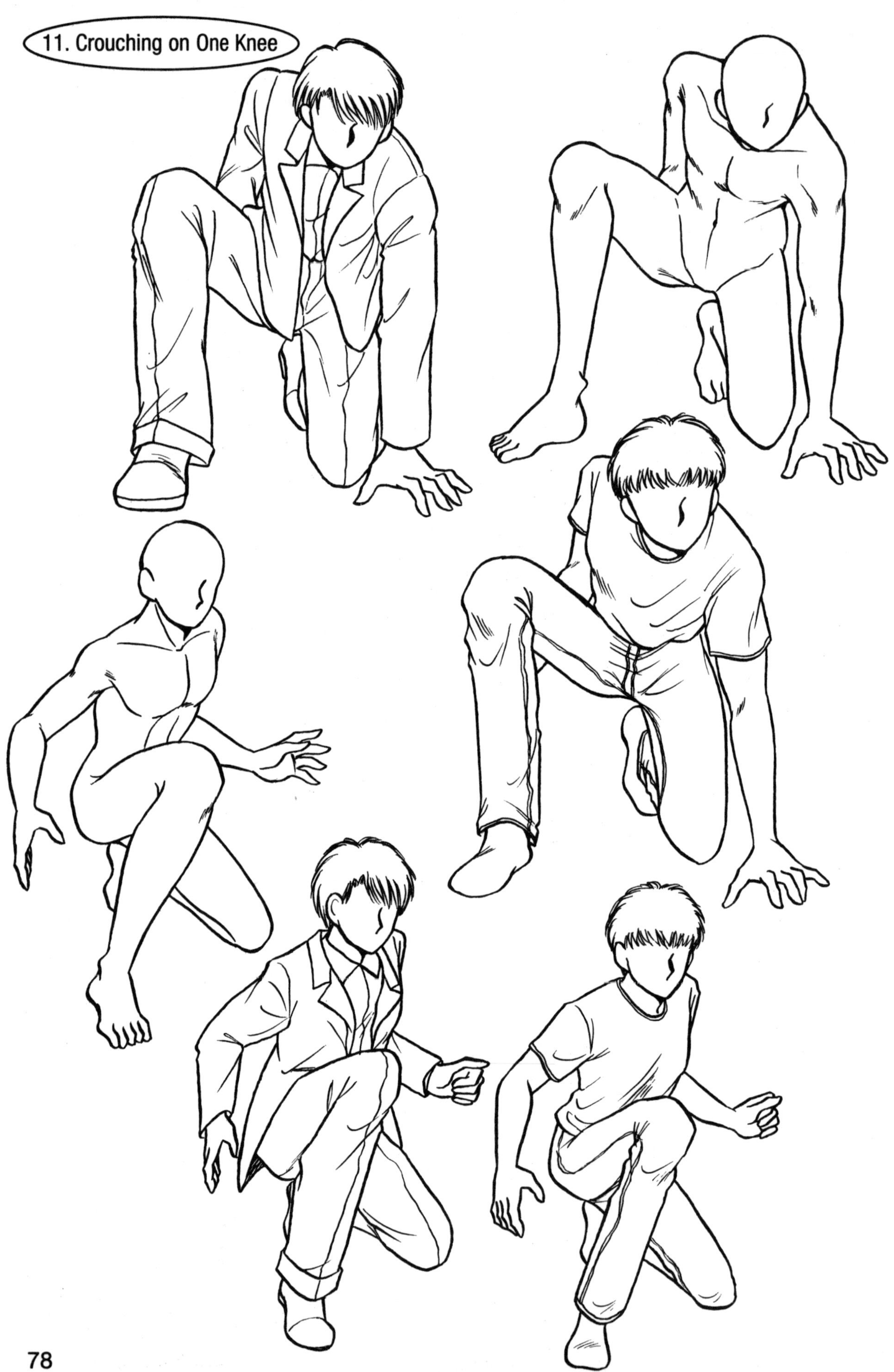

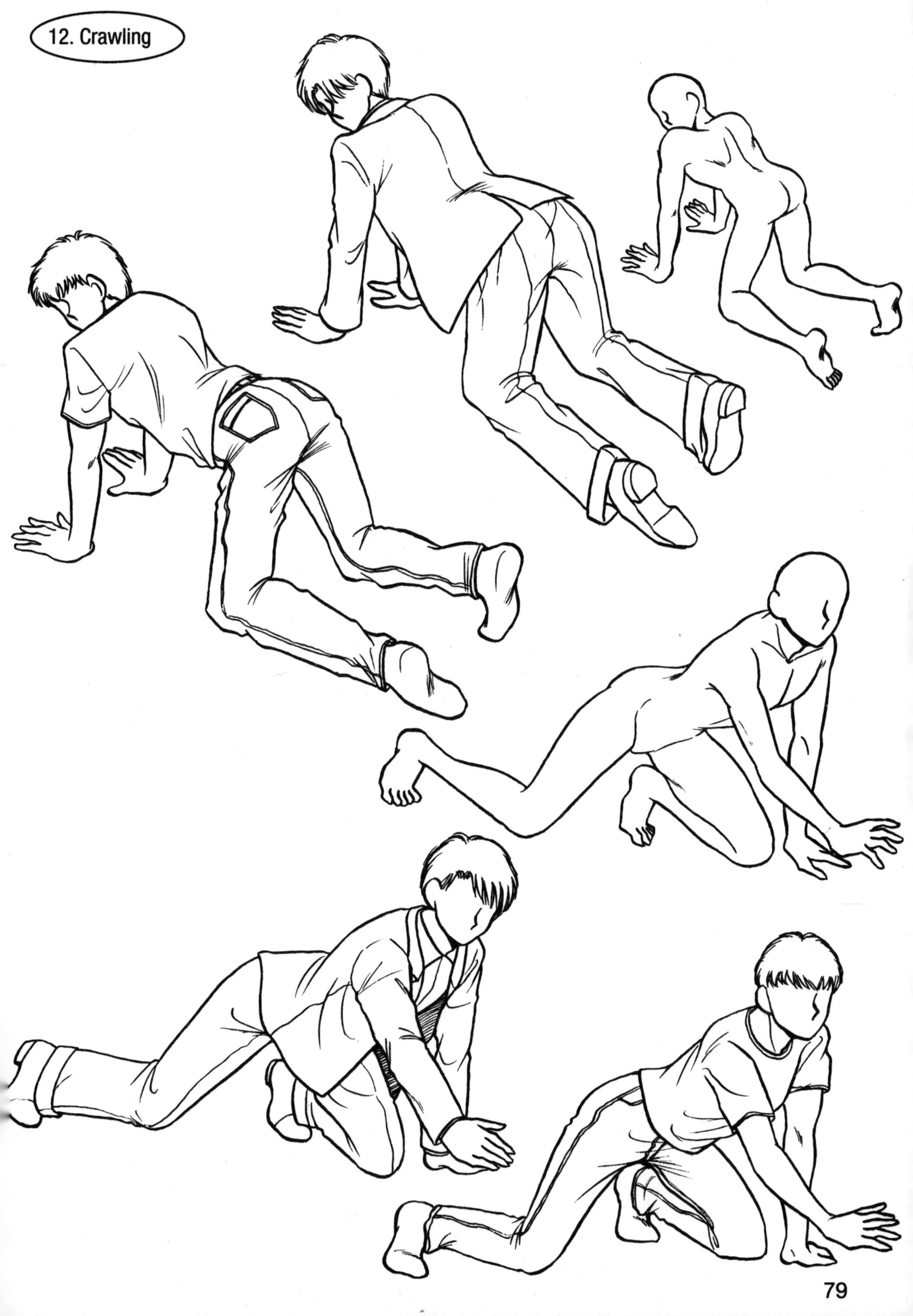
12. Crawling

13. Reclining-1

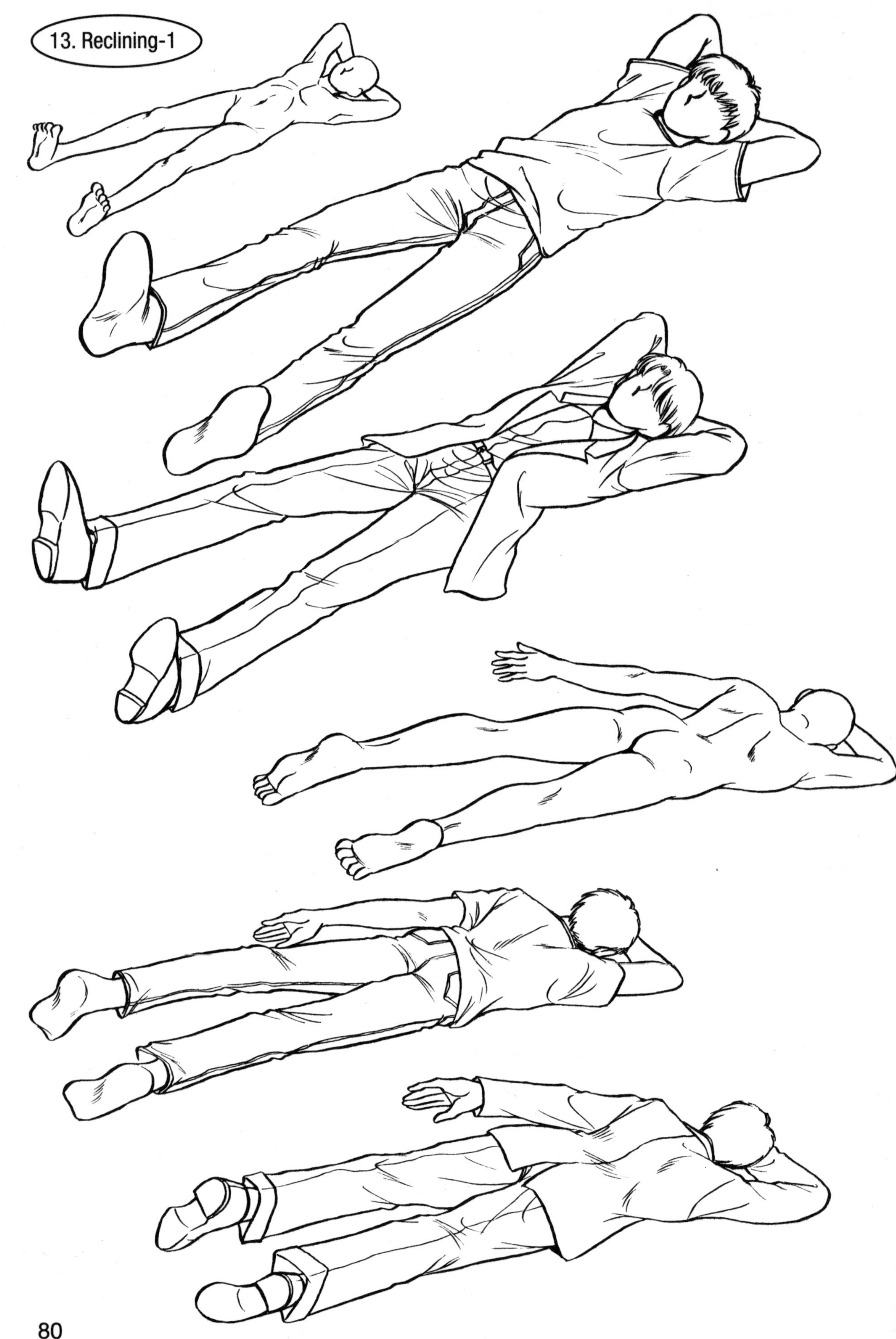

14. Reclining-2

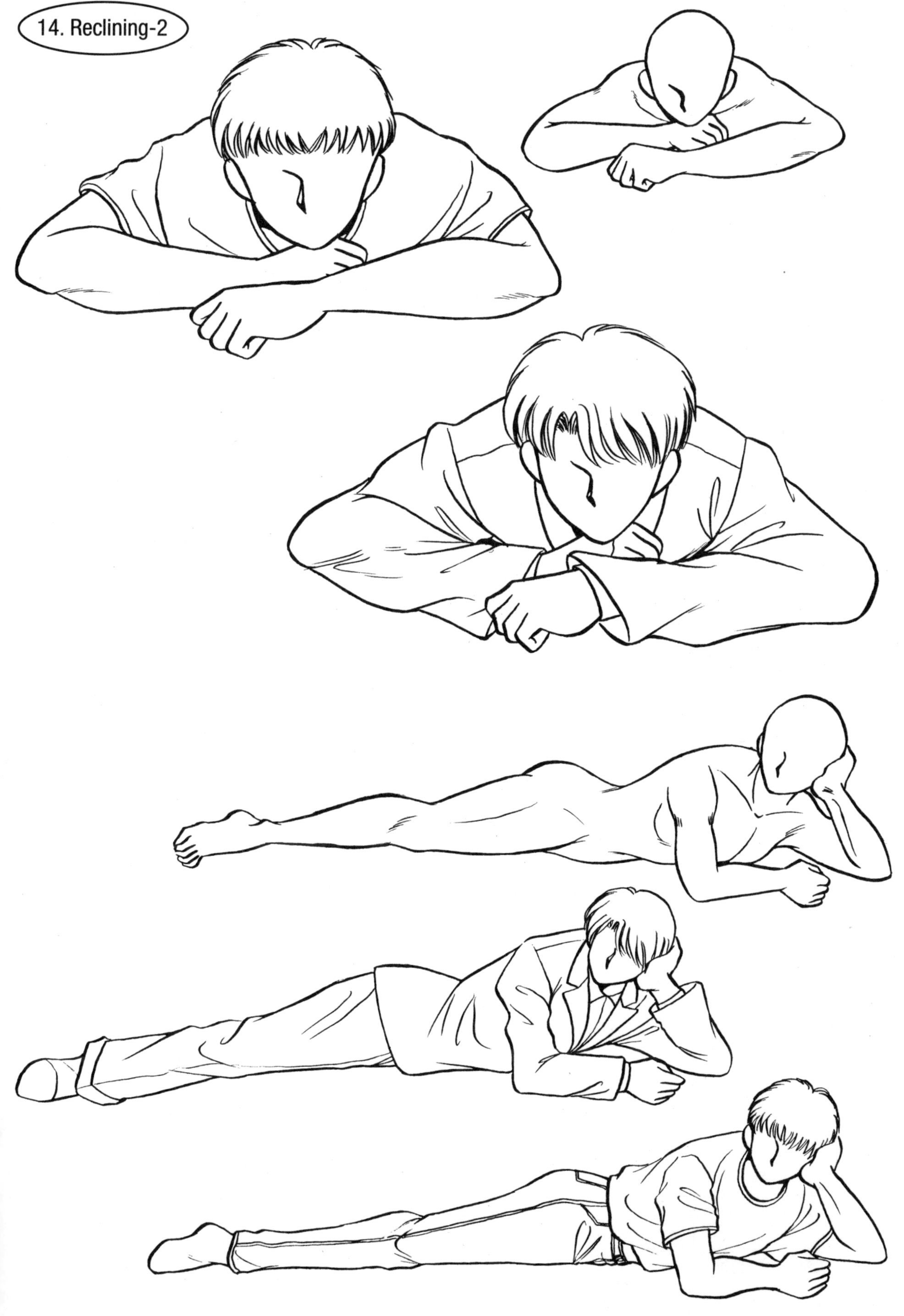

15. Crossed Arms

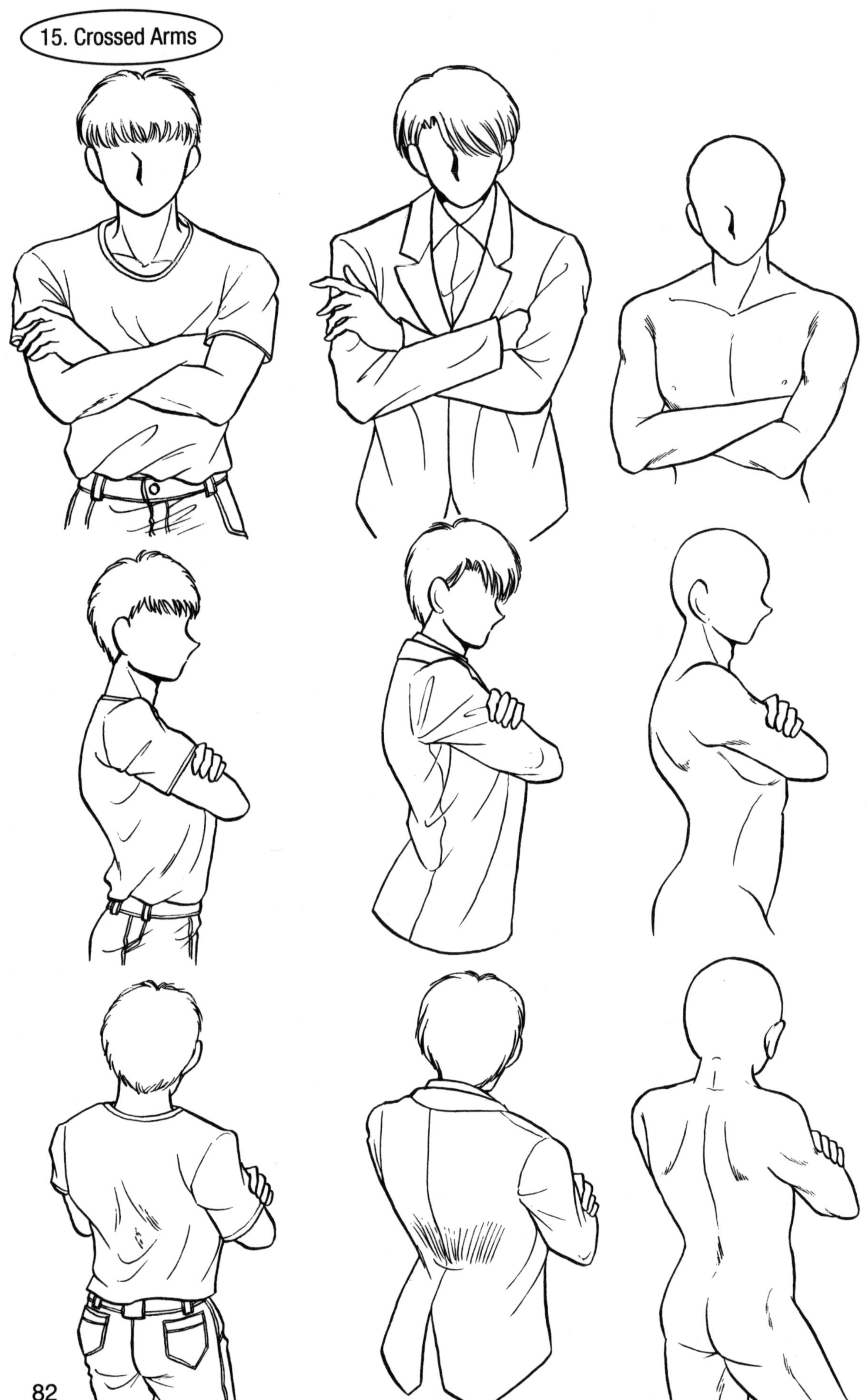

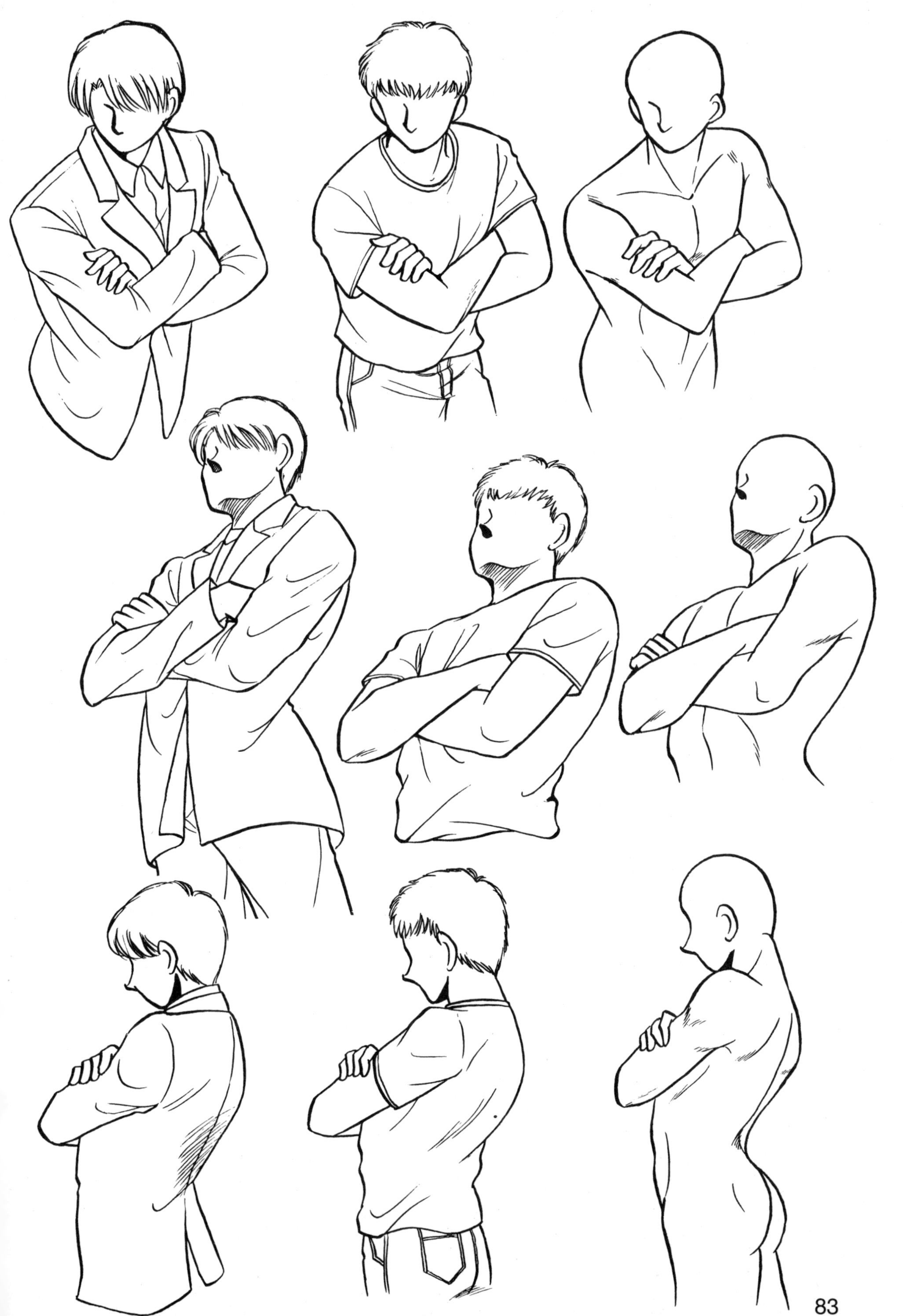

Athletic Wear and Undergarments

Tank Top

Use the flow of creases formed to suggest limpness in the tank top.

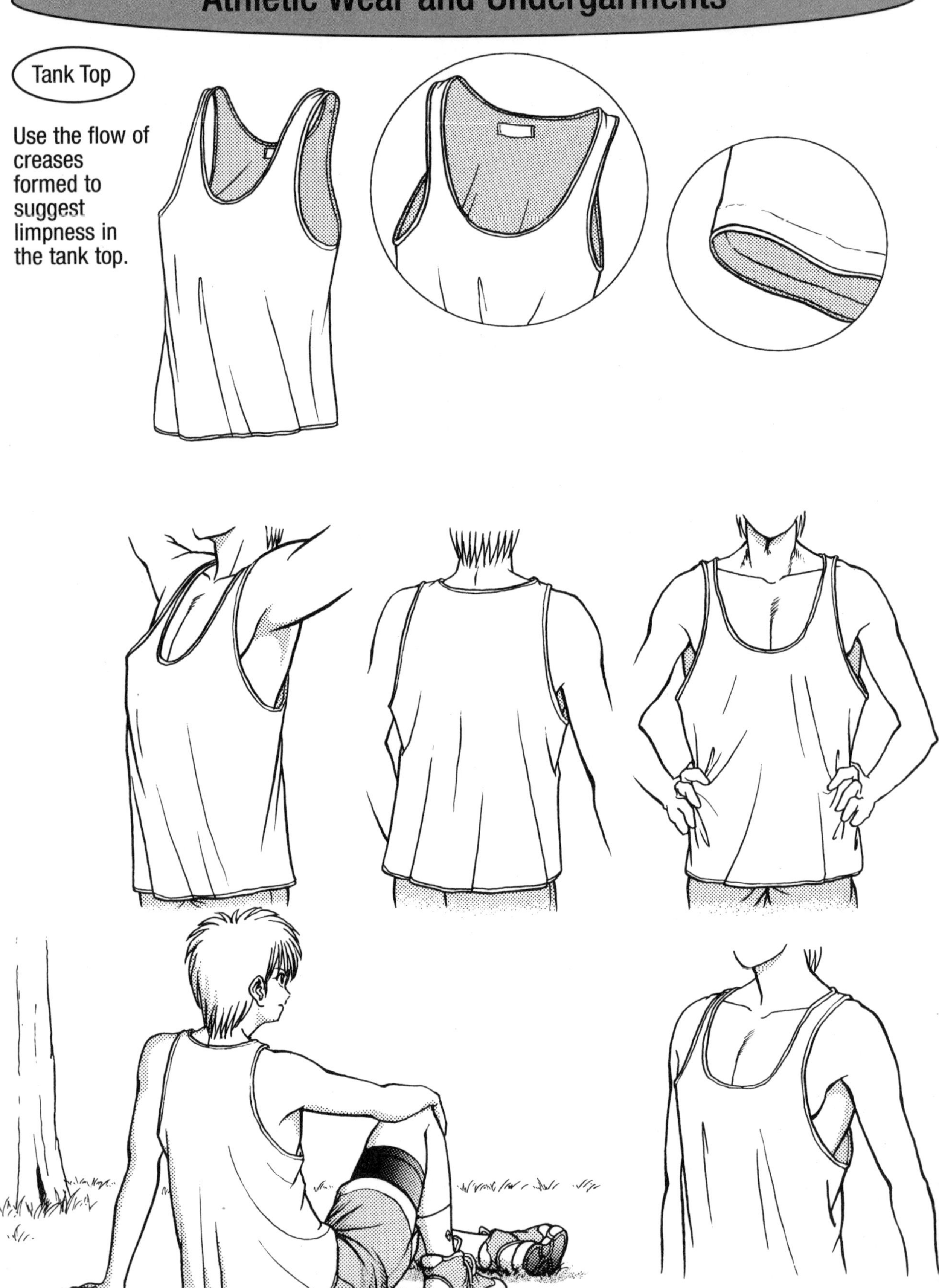

Briefs and Boxers

There are three common types of men's underwear: bikini briefs, regular briefs, and boxers

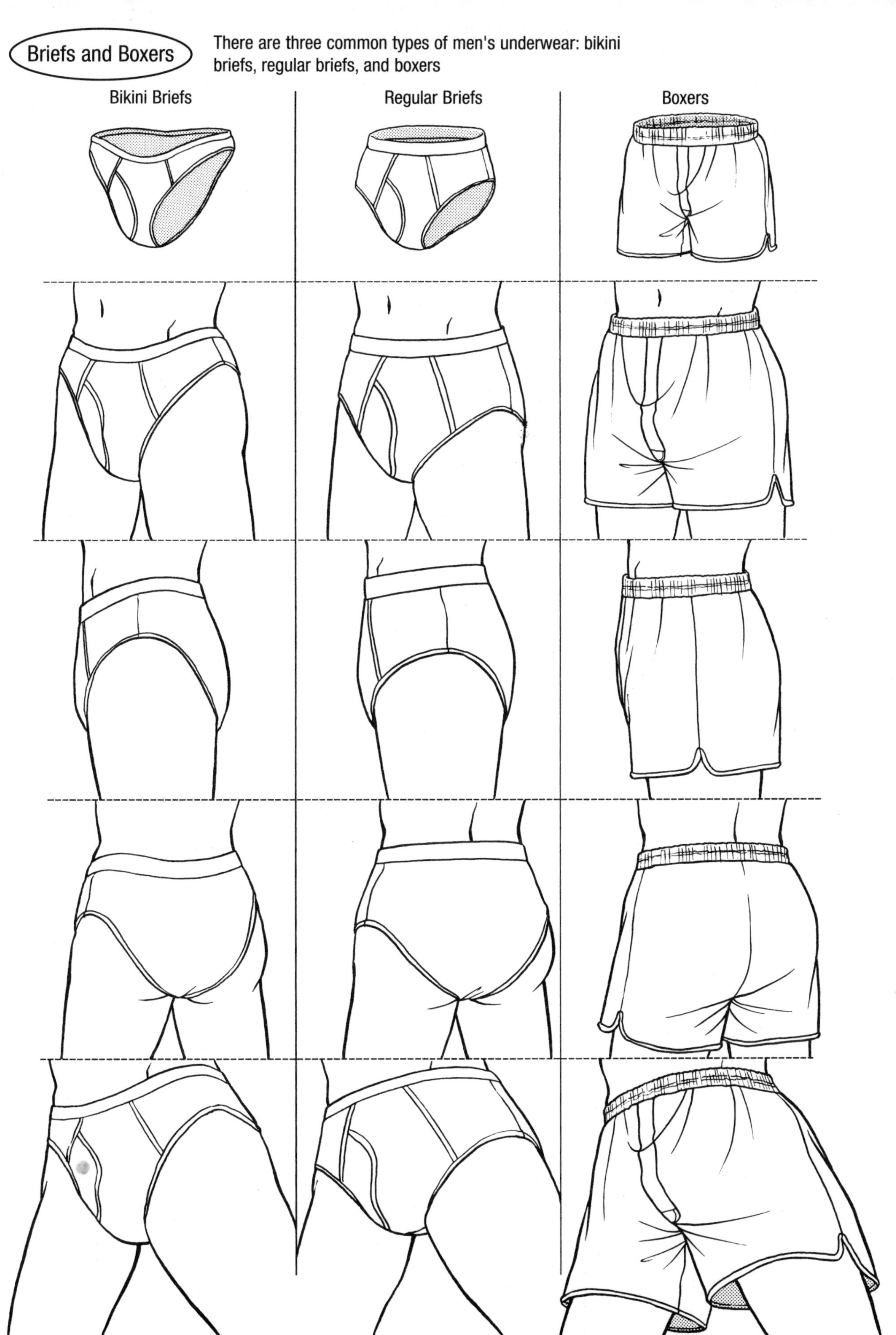

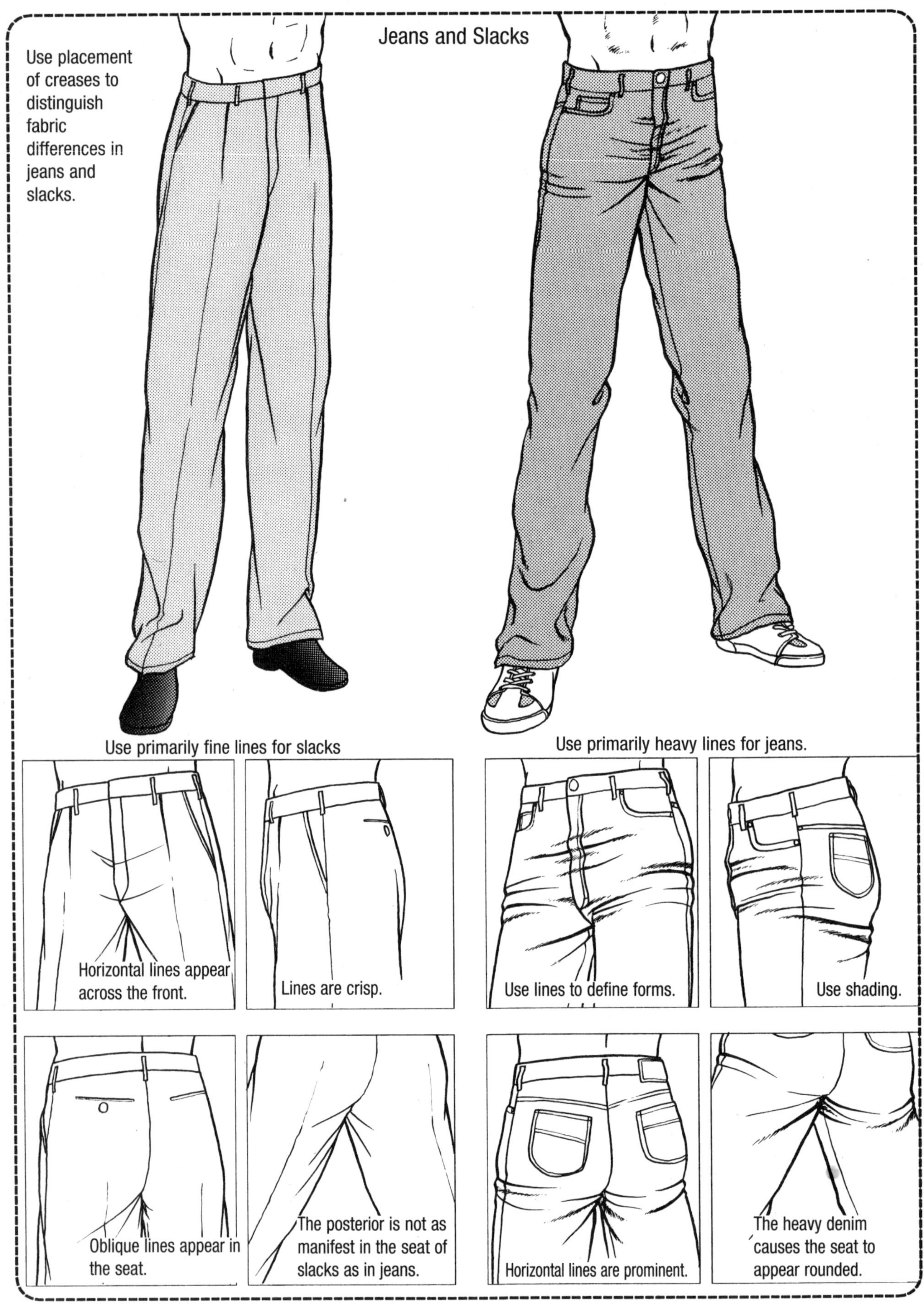
Jeans and Slacks
Use placement of creases to distinguish fabric differences in jeans and slacks.
Use primarily fine lines for slacks
Use primarily heavy lines for jeans.
Horizontal lines appear across the front.
Lines are crisp.
Use lines to define forms.
Use shading.
Oblique lines appear in the seat.
The posterior is not as manifest in the seat of slacks as in jeans.
Horizontal lines are prominent.
The heavy denim causes the seat to appear rounded.

Chapter 4
Male Clothing and Accessories

Uniforms, Japanese Dress, Representing the Hand, Eyeglasses & Shoes

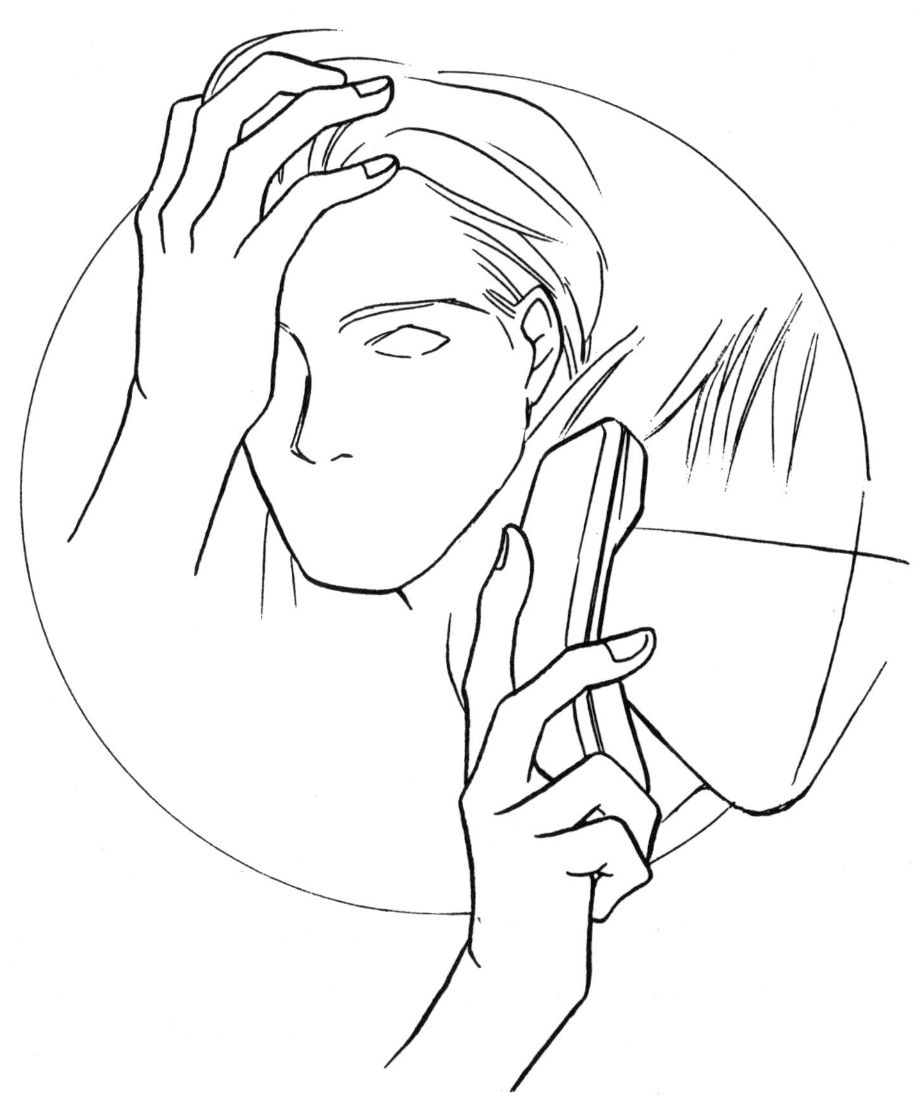

Assorted Uniforms

In manga, a uniform is a popular means of making a male character appealing.

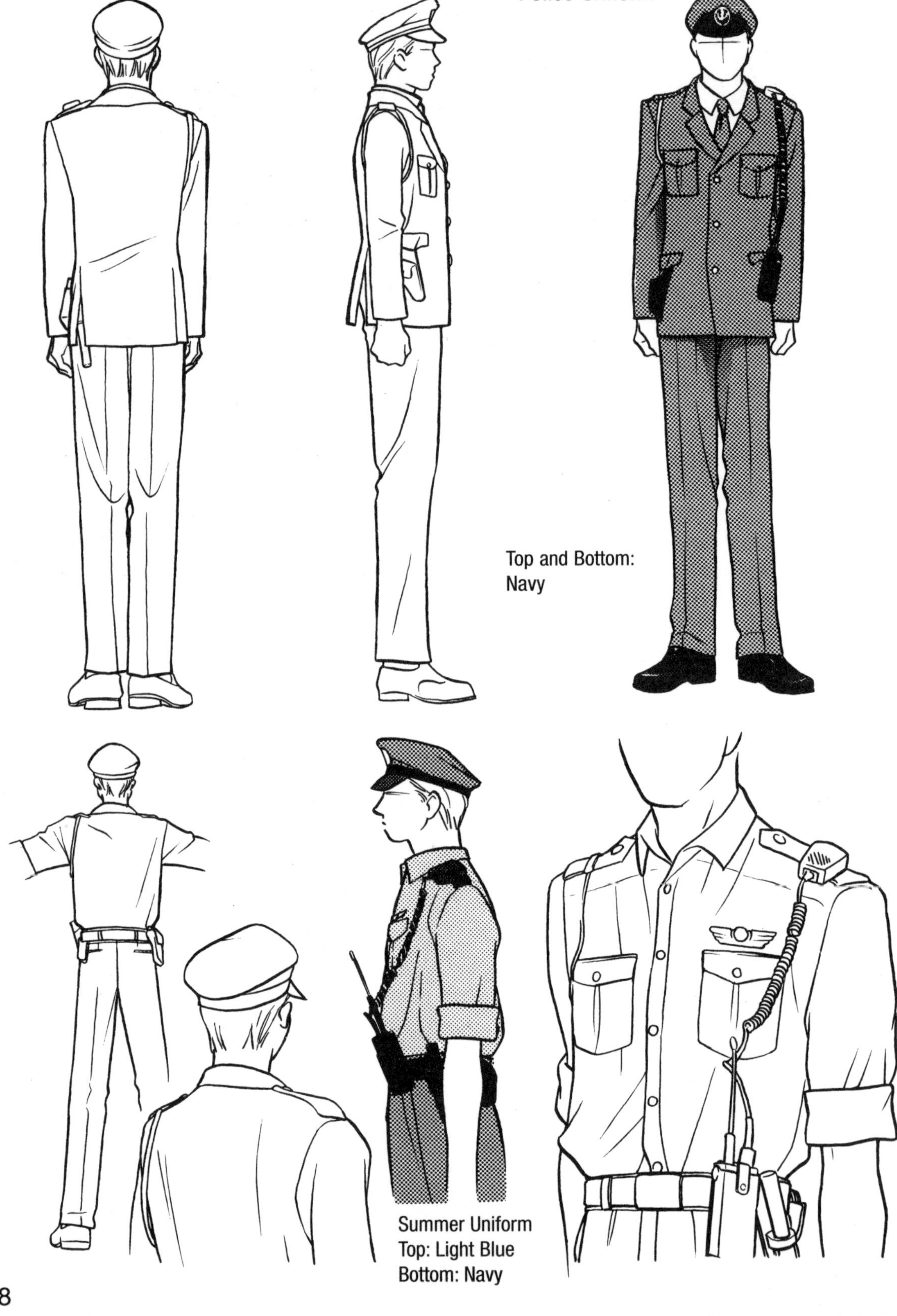

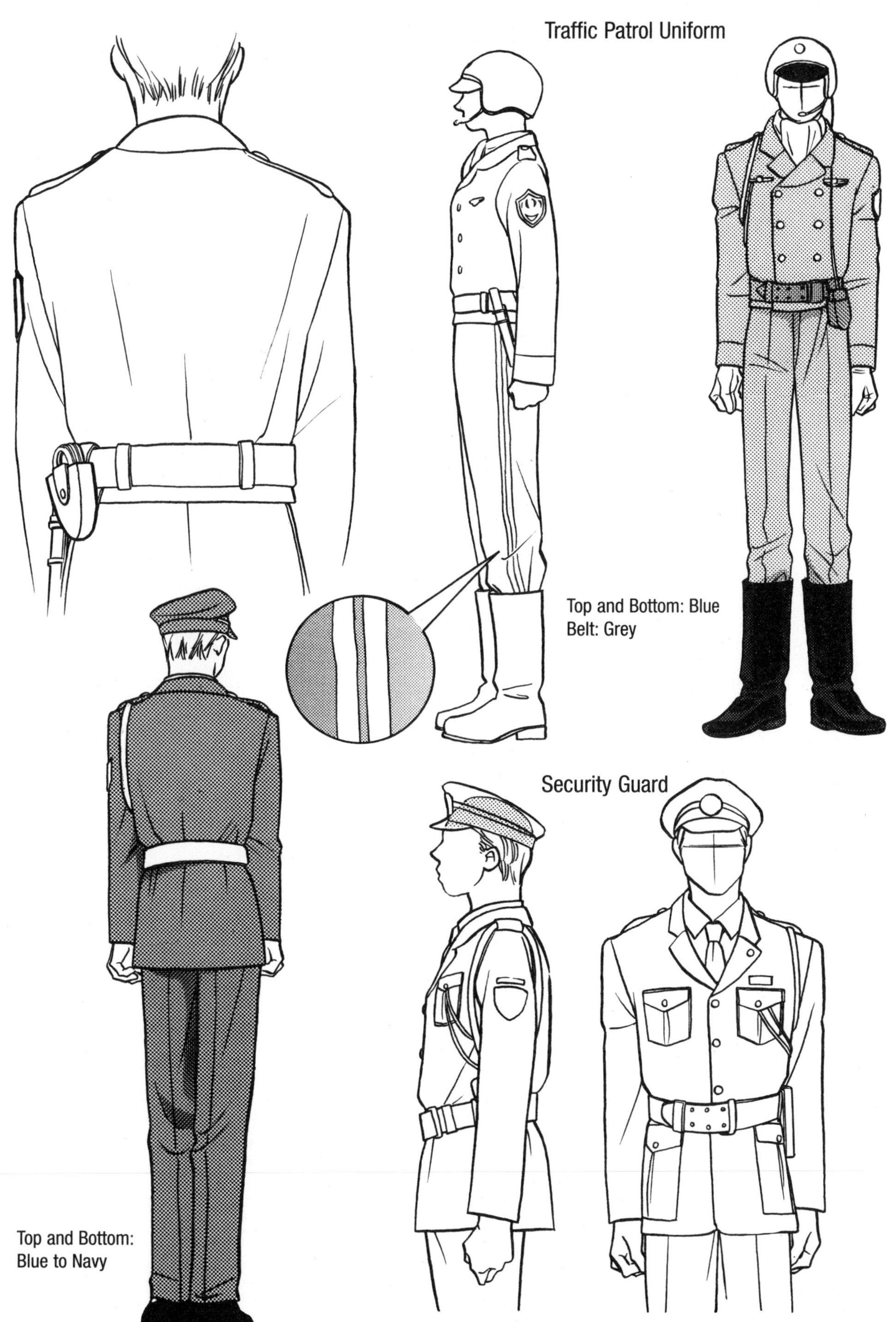
Traffic Patrol Uniform
Top and Bottom: Blue
Belt: Grey
Security Guard
Top and Bottom:
Blue to Navy

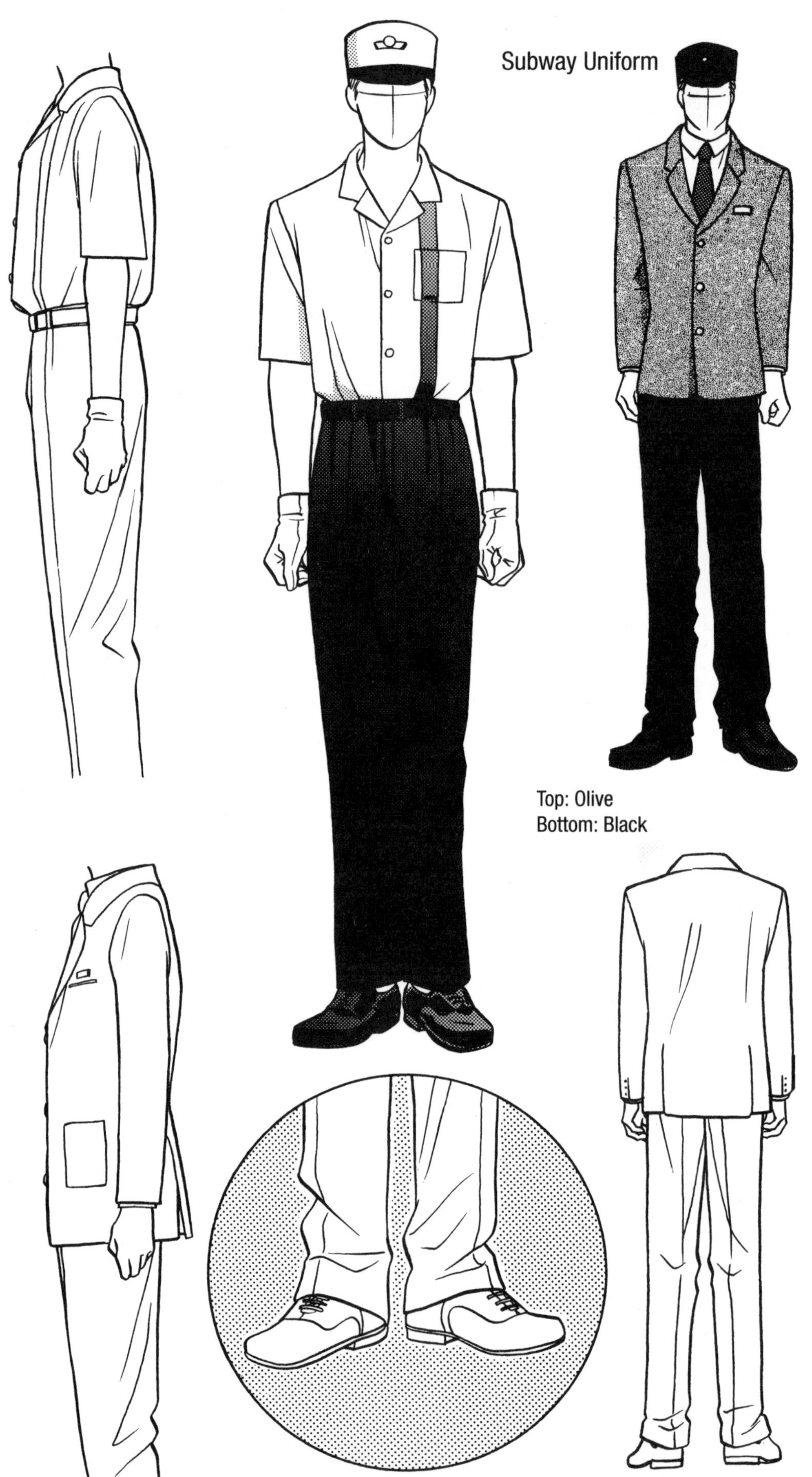
Subway Uniform
Top: Olive
Bottom: Black

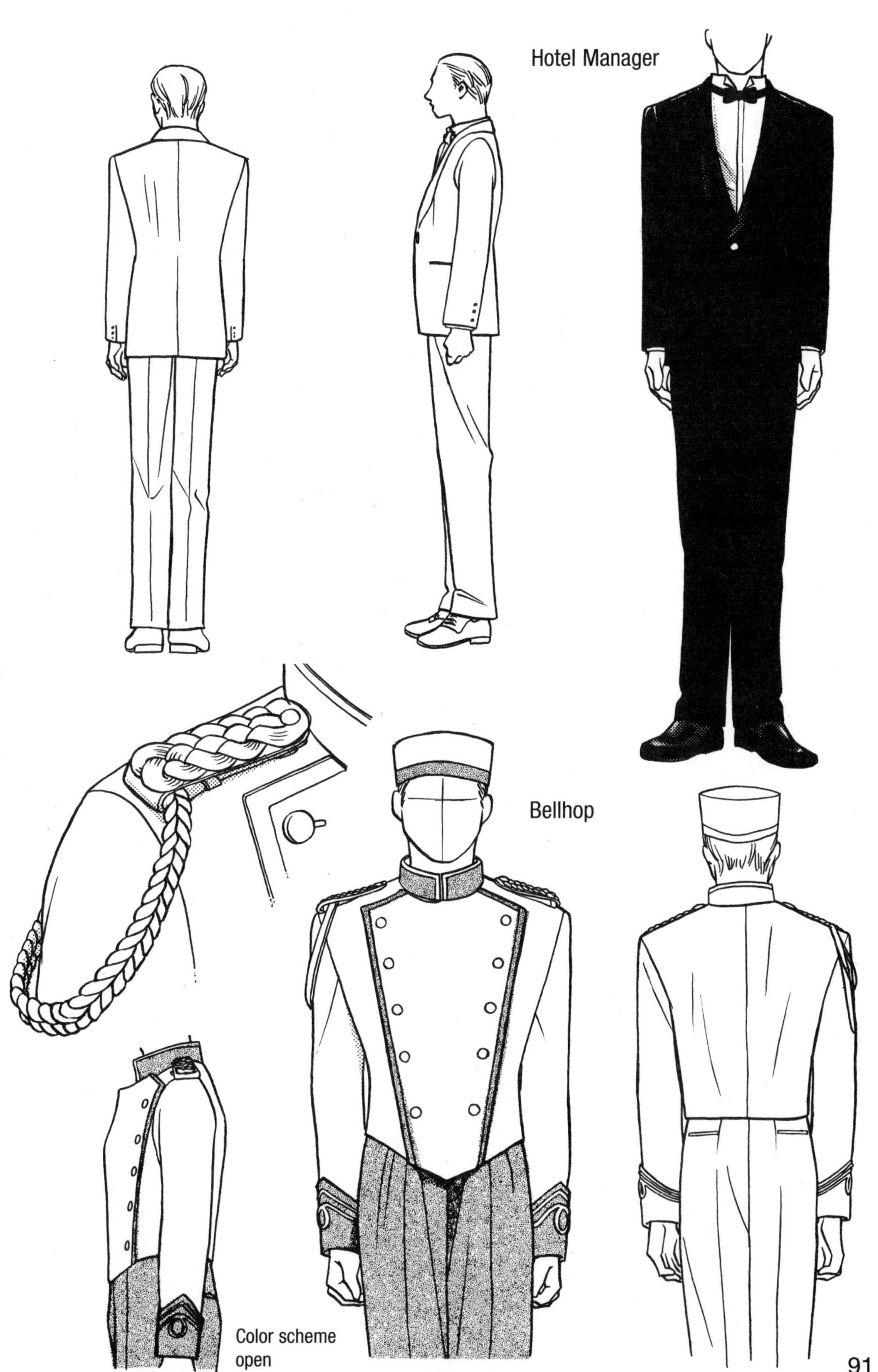
Hotel Manager
Bellhop
Color scheme
open

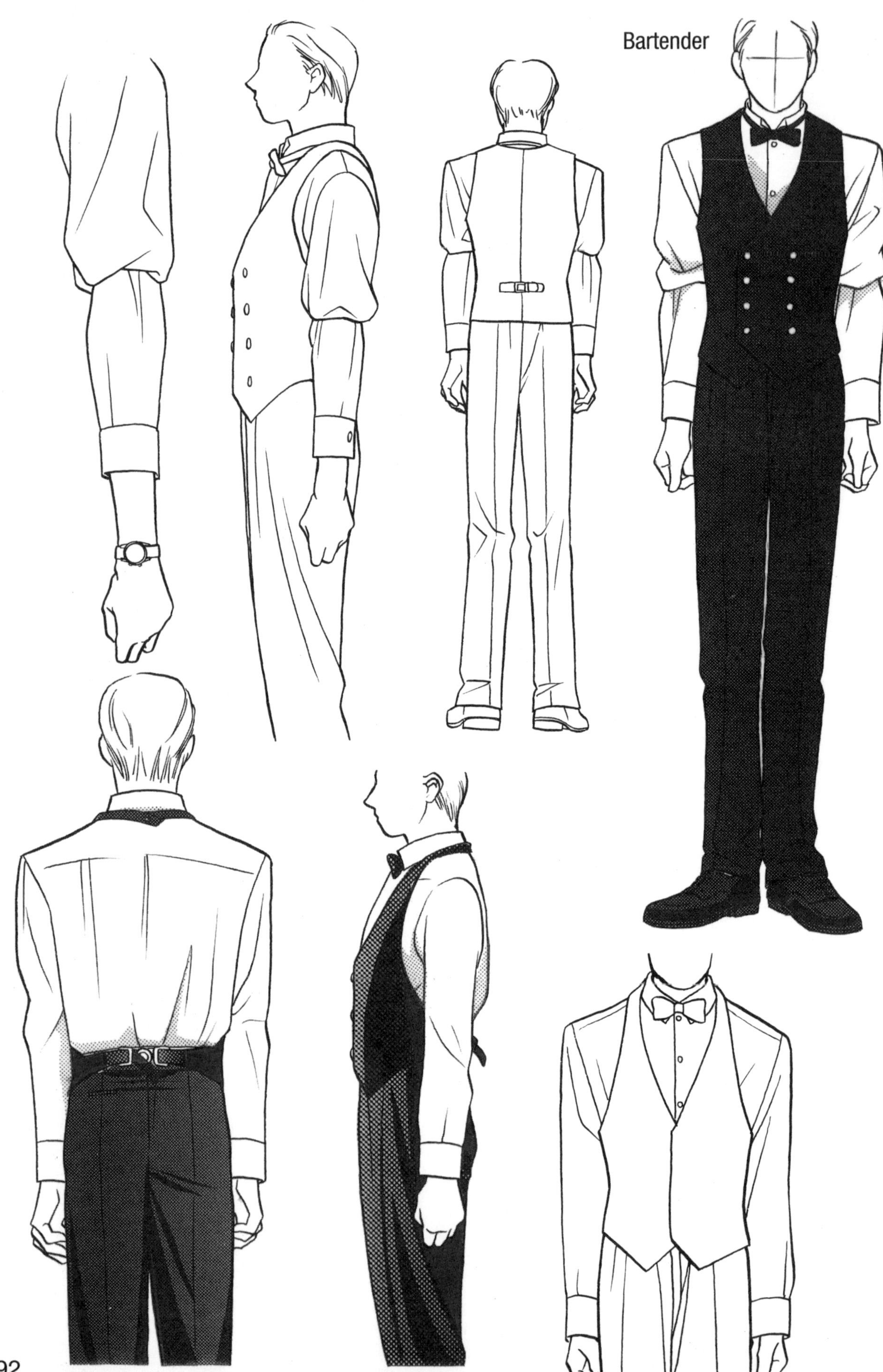

Bartender

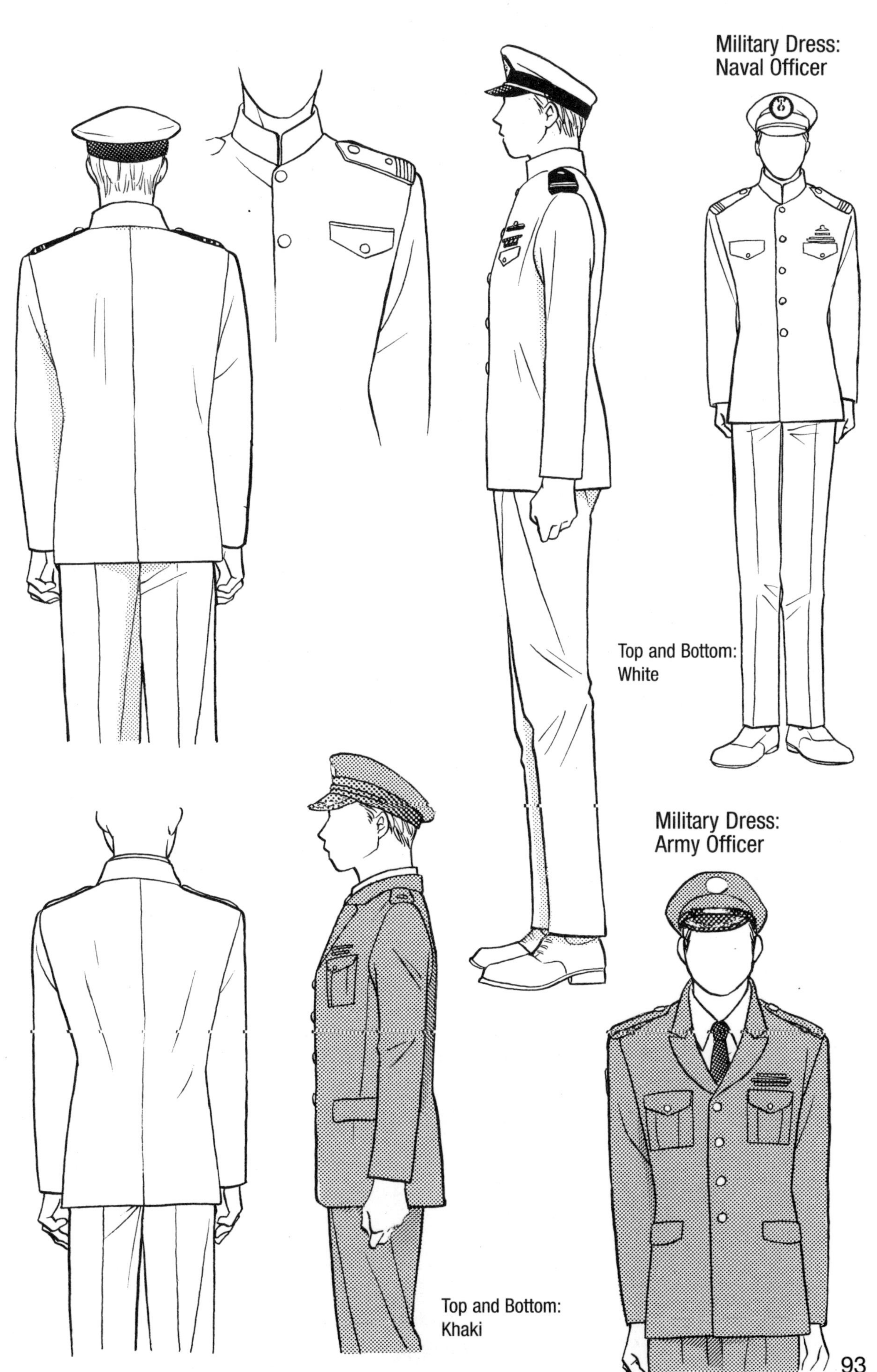
Military Dress:
Naval Officer
Top and Bottom:
White
Military Dress:
Army Officer
Top and Bottom:
Khaki

Japanese Dress (Kimono and Kinagashi)

1. Kinagashi (Without a Hakama)

Very similar to the yukata, kinagashi is the normal means of Japanese dress. The obi is either a thin, heko obi [obi used by young men] or a stiff kaku obi.

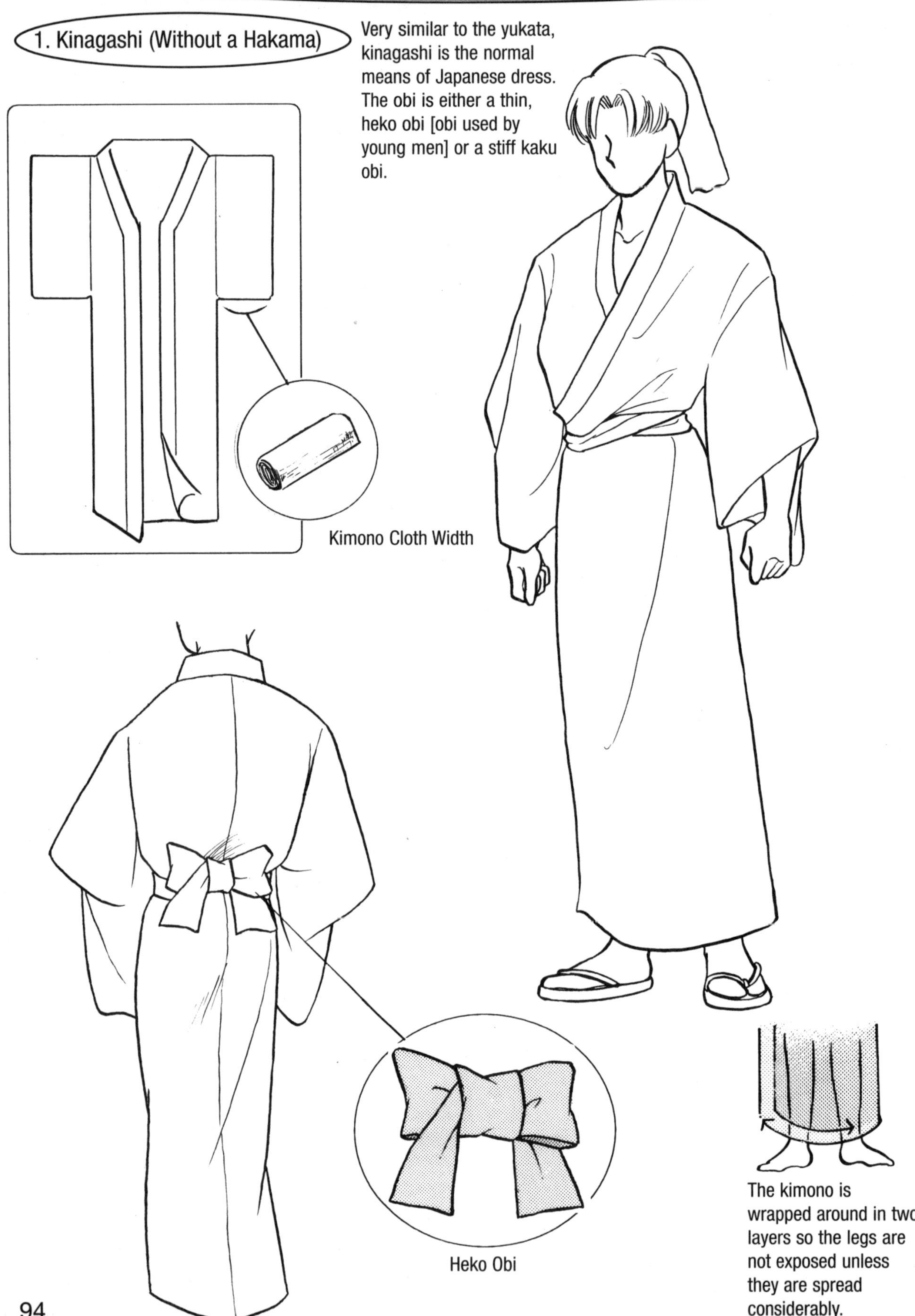

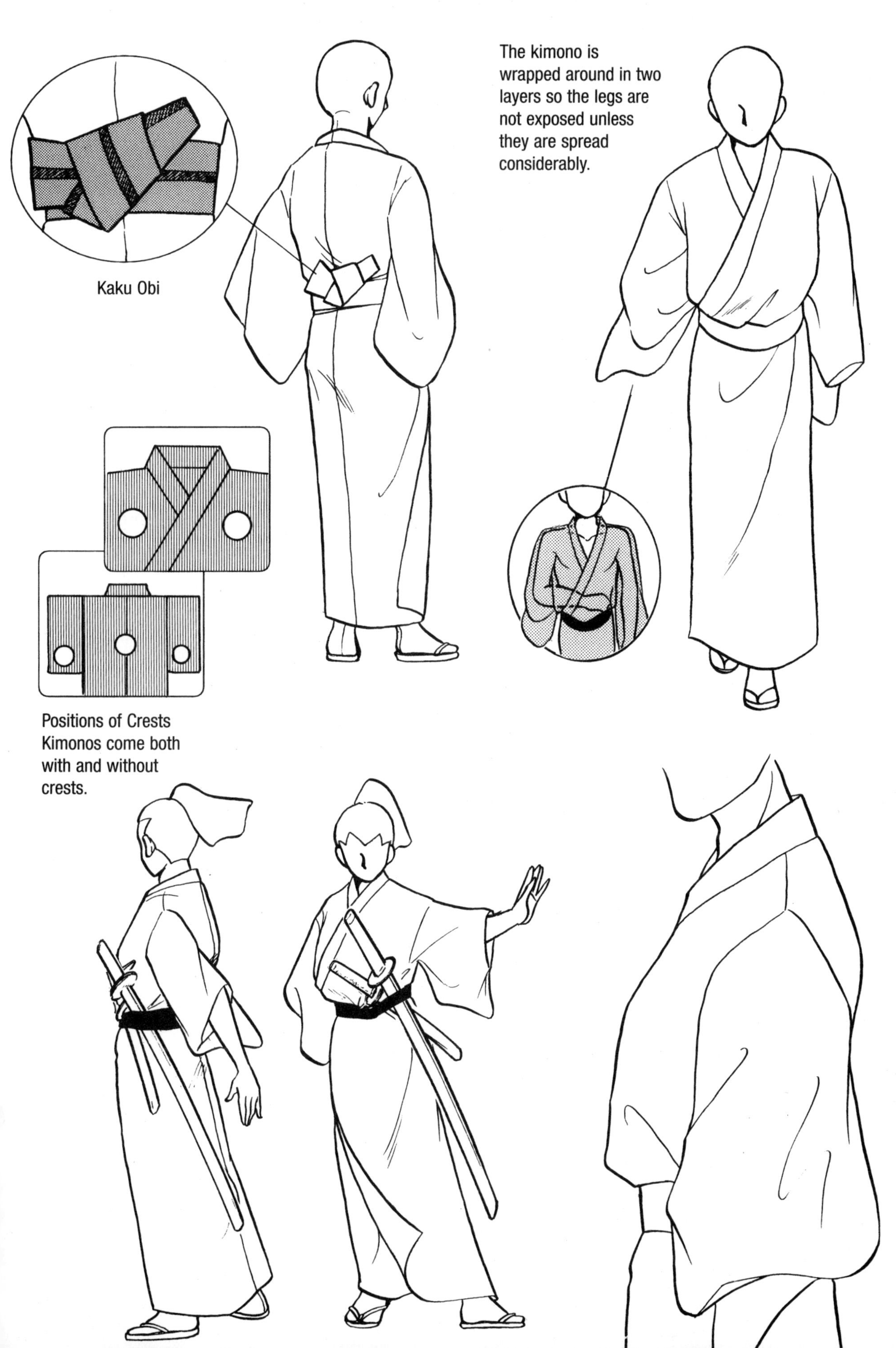
The kimono is
wrapped around in two
layers so the legs are
not exposed unless
they are spread
considerably.
Kaku Obi
Positions of Crests
Kimonos come both
with and without
crests.

Kimono (With a Hakama)

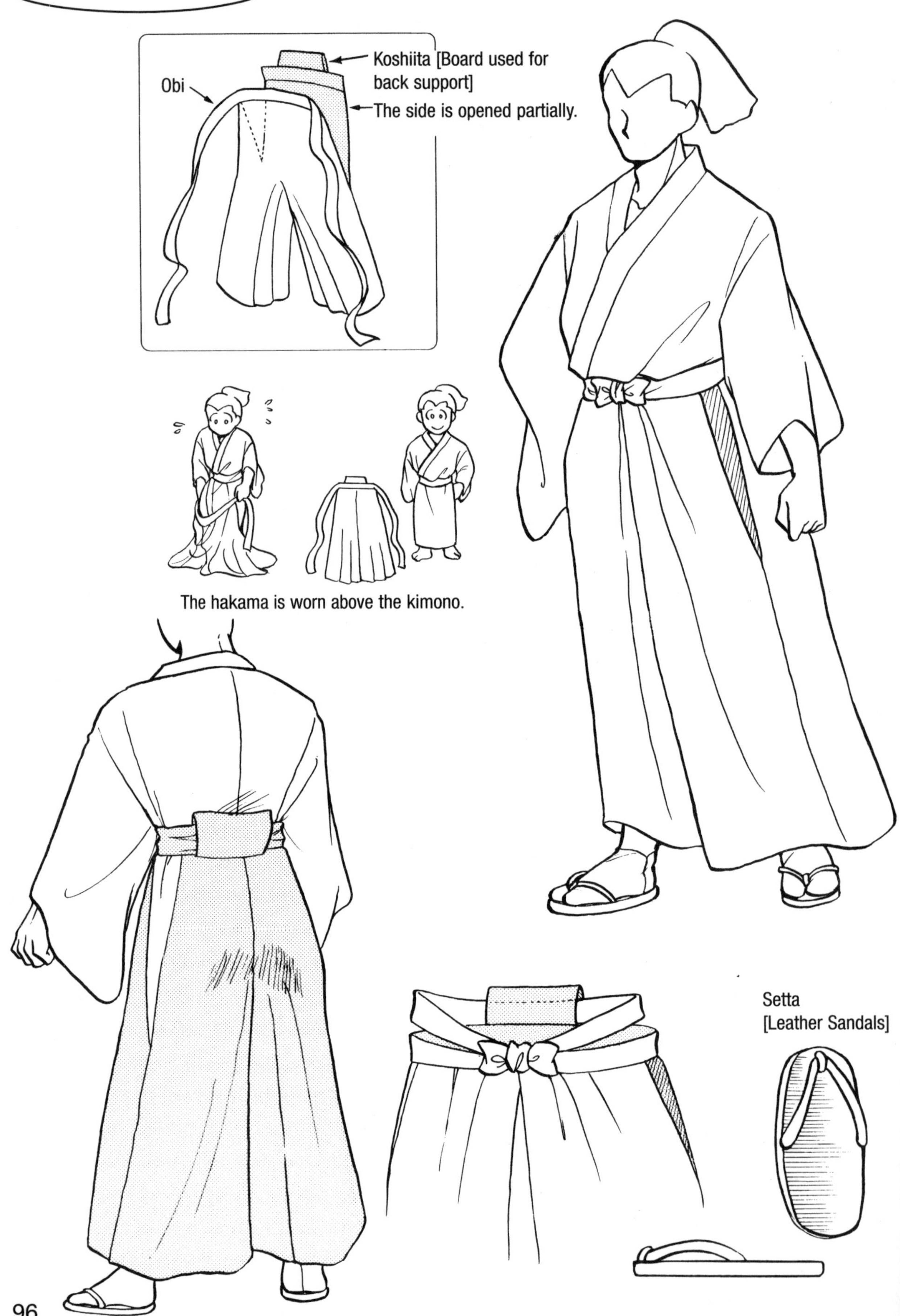

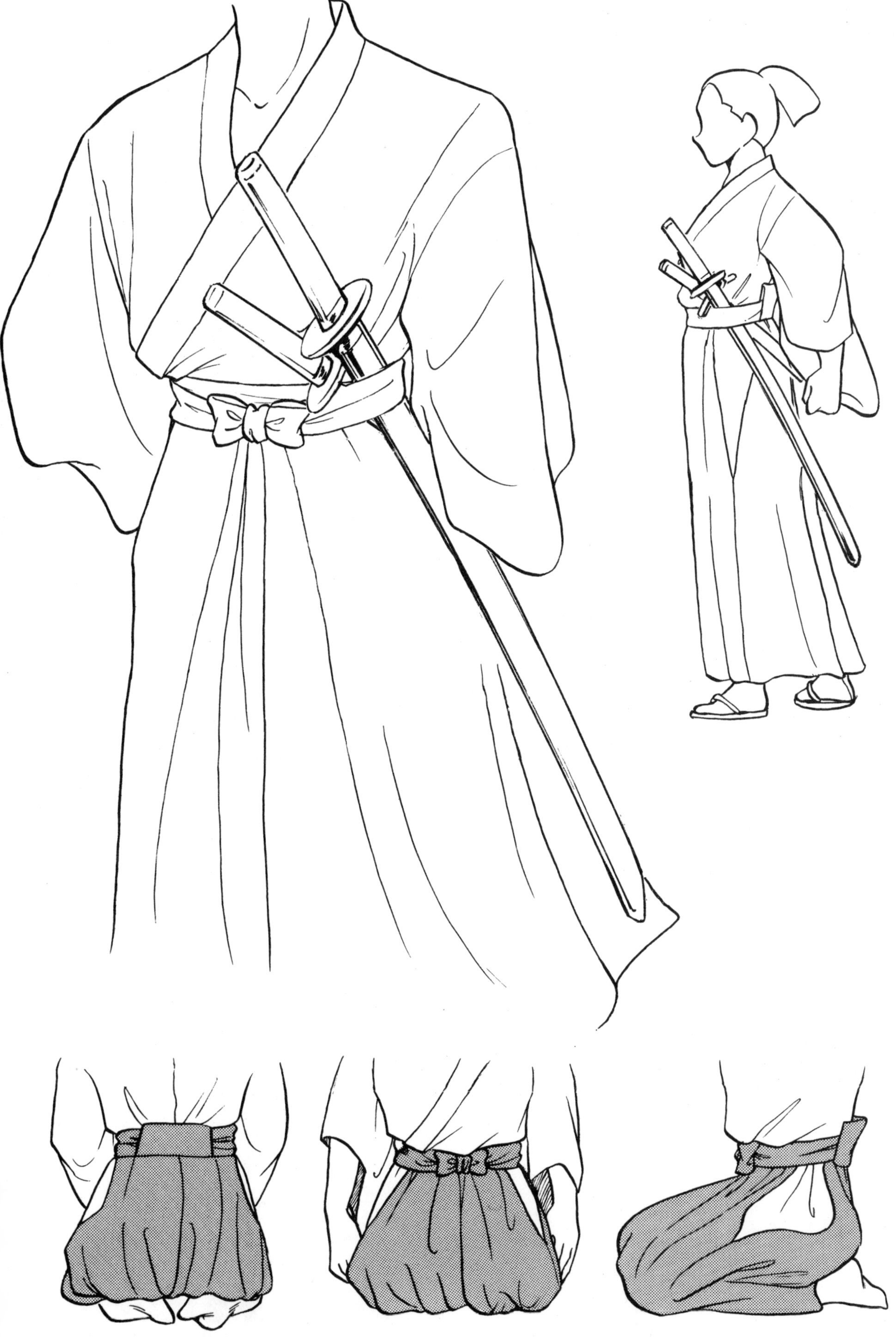

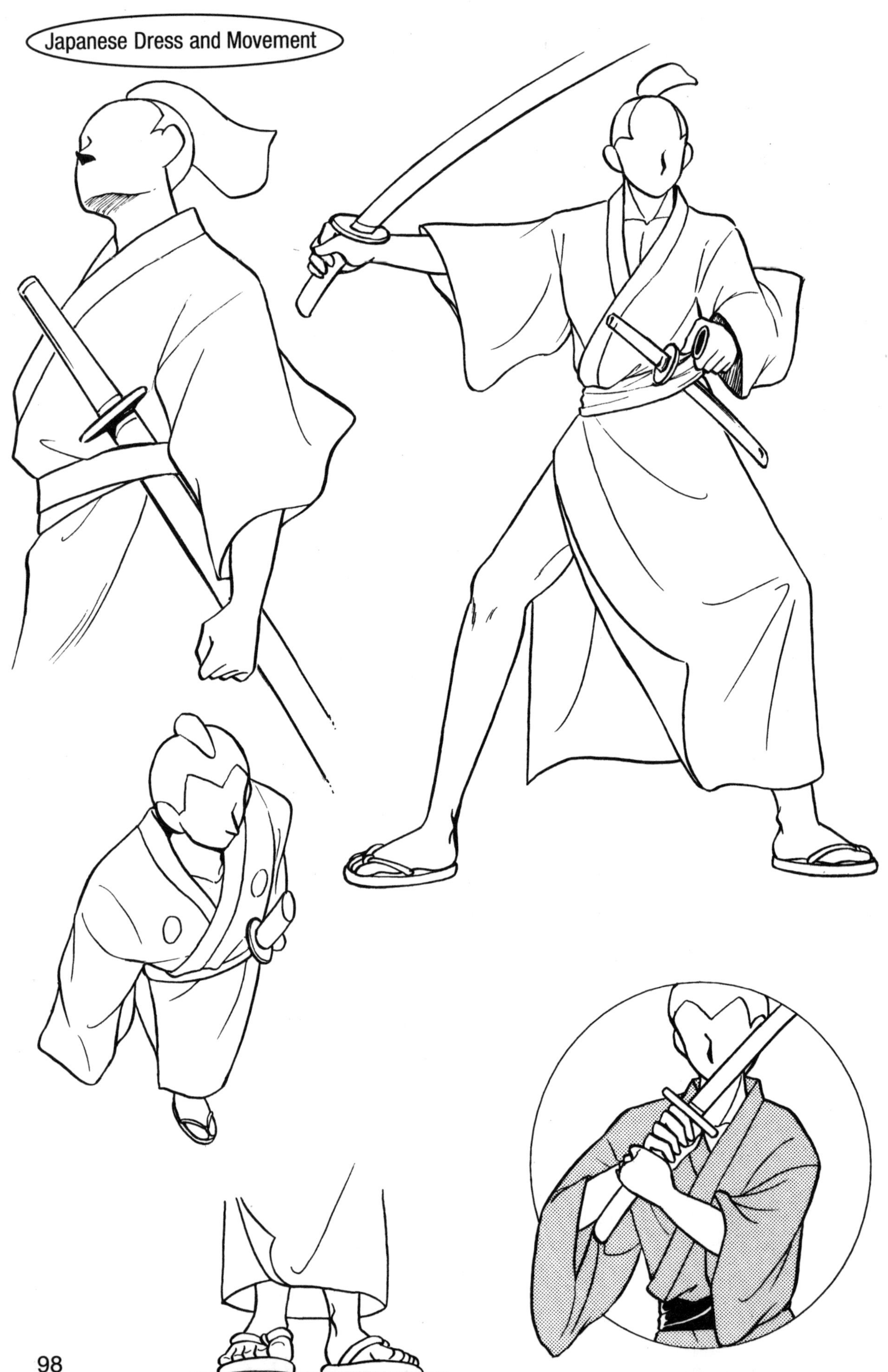

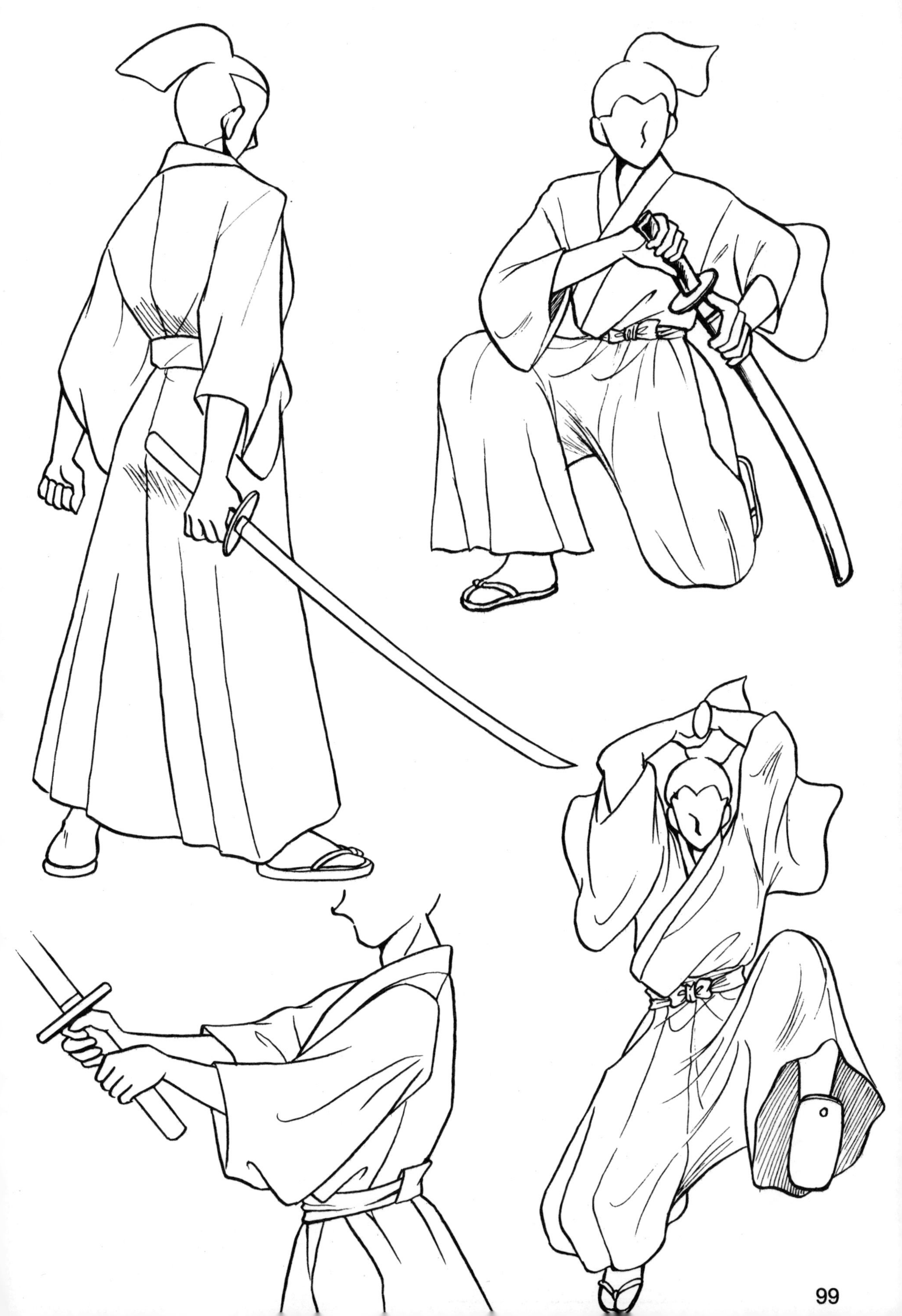

Rendering the Hand (Assorted Gestures)

1. Positions and Gestures

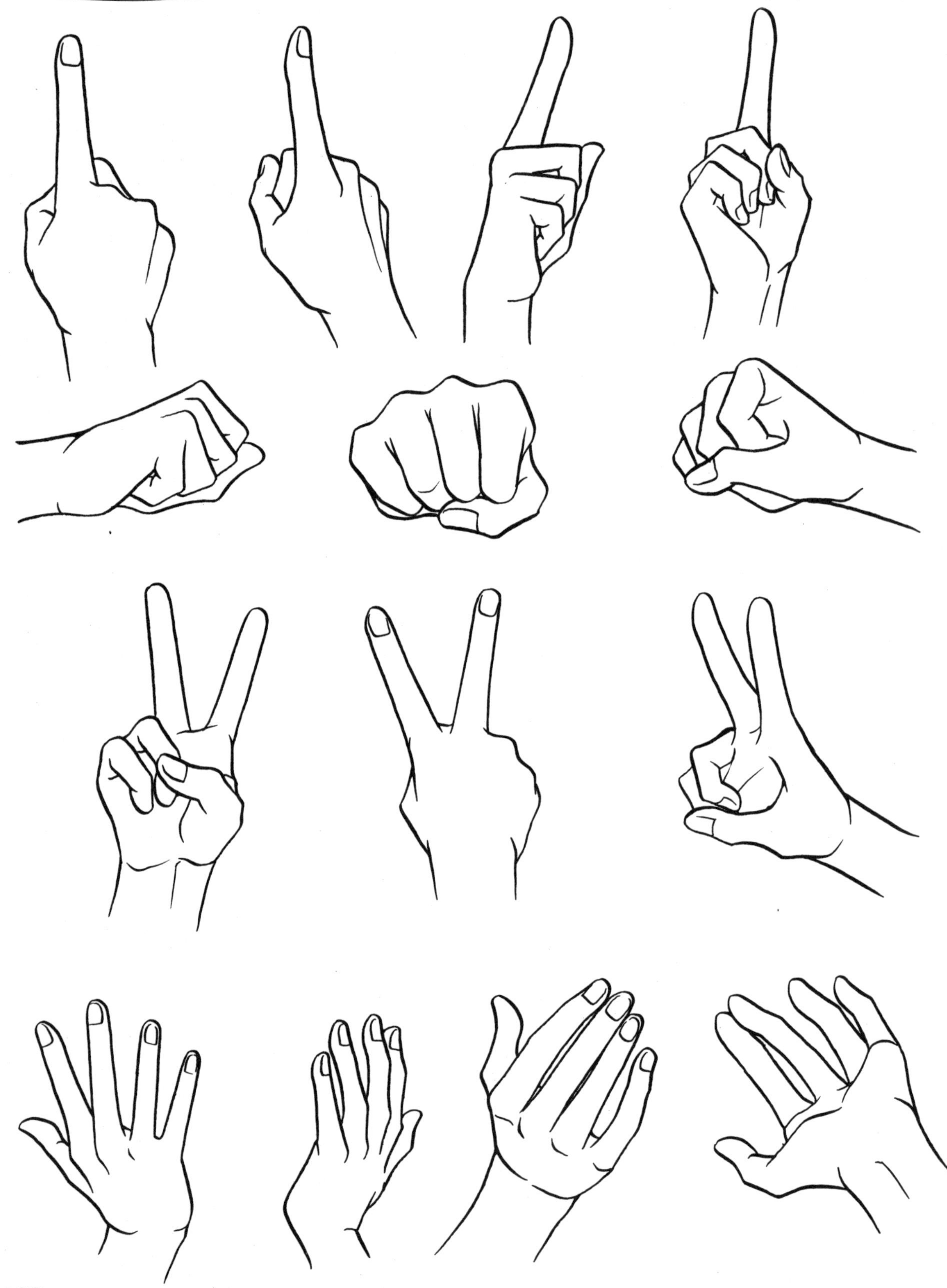

2. Touching the Face

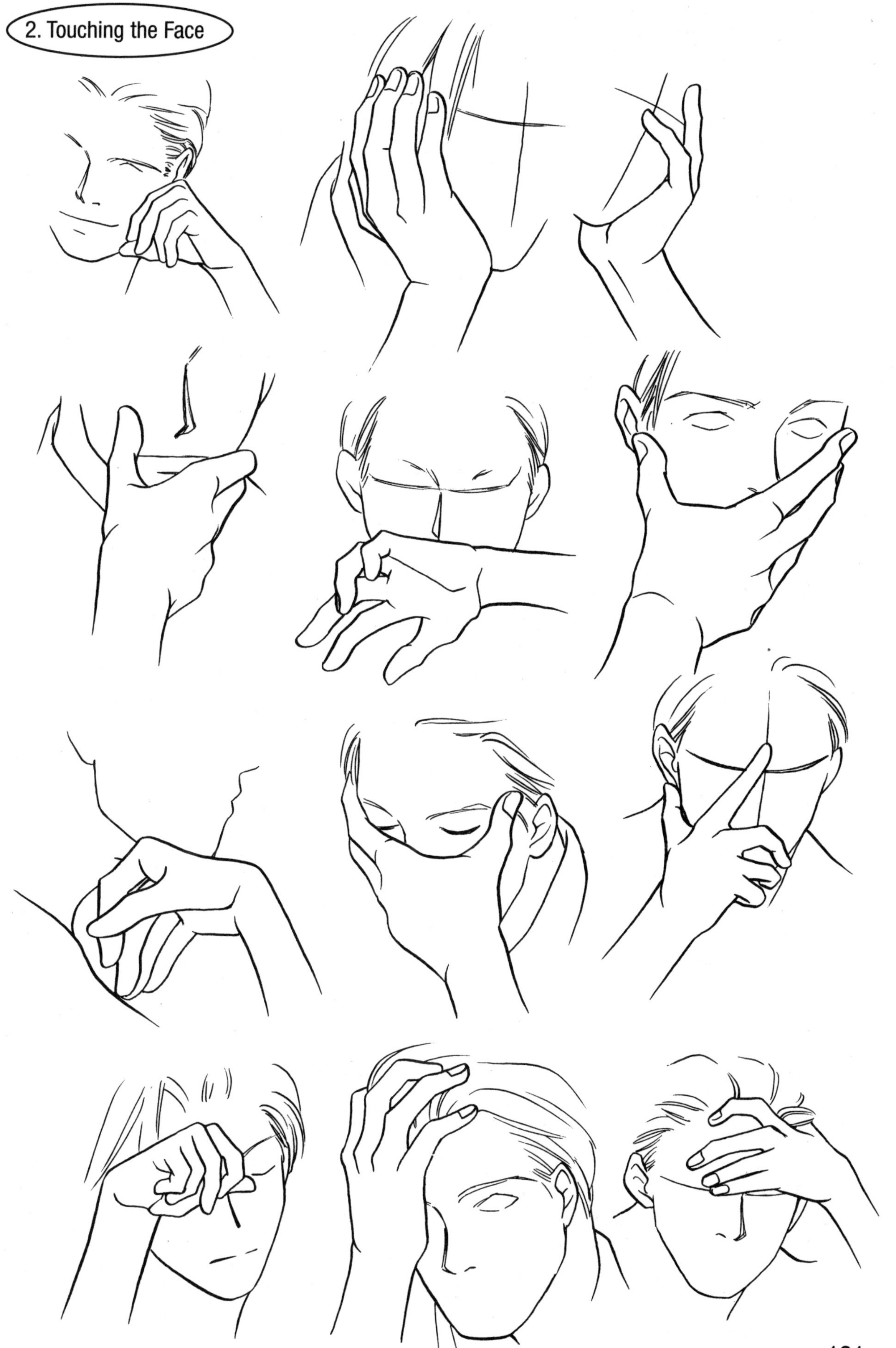

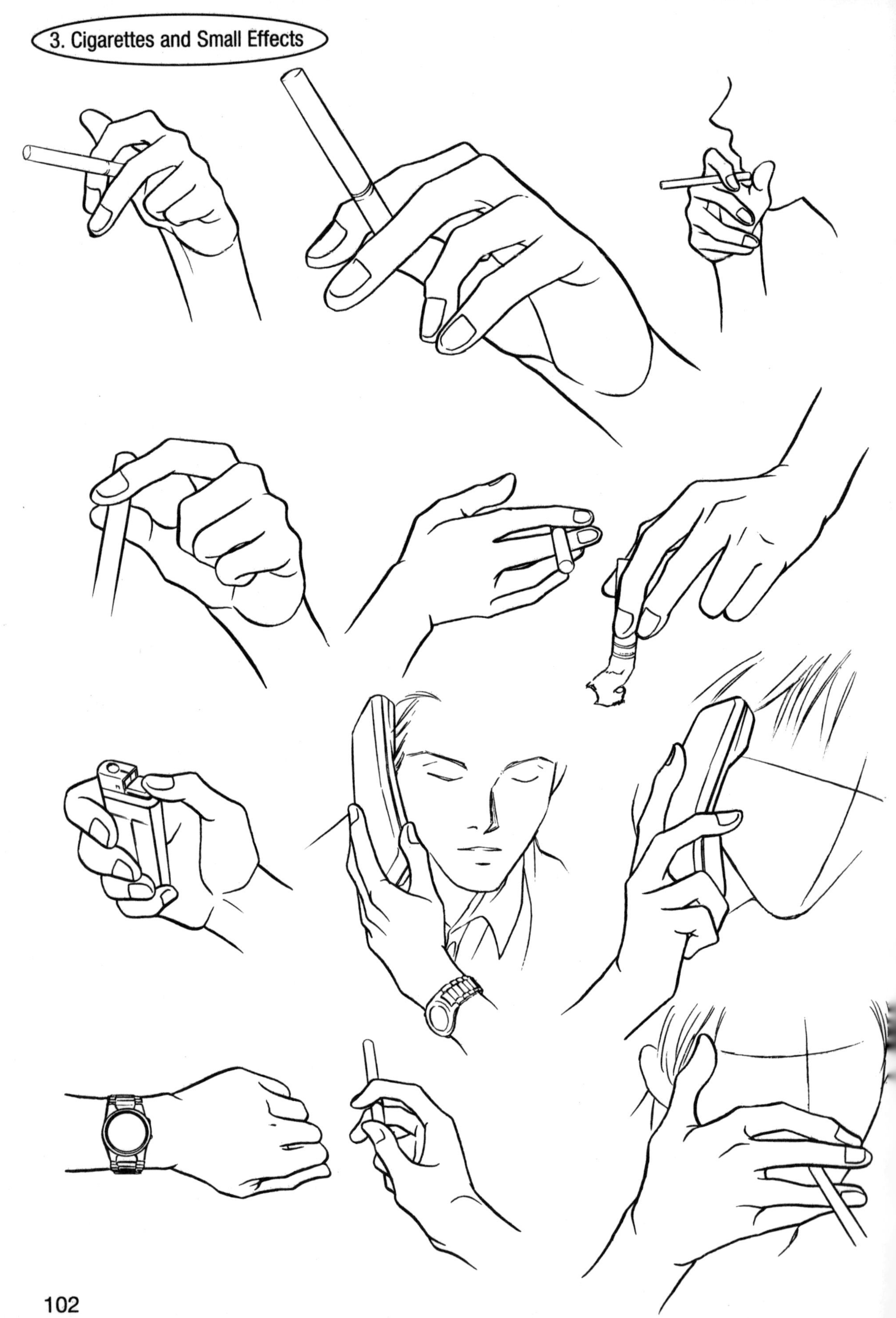
3. Cigarettes and Small Effects

4. Holding a Glass and Drinking

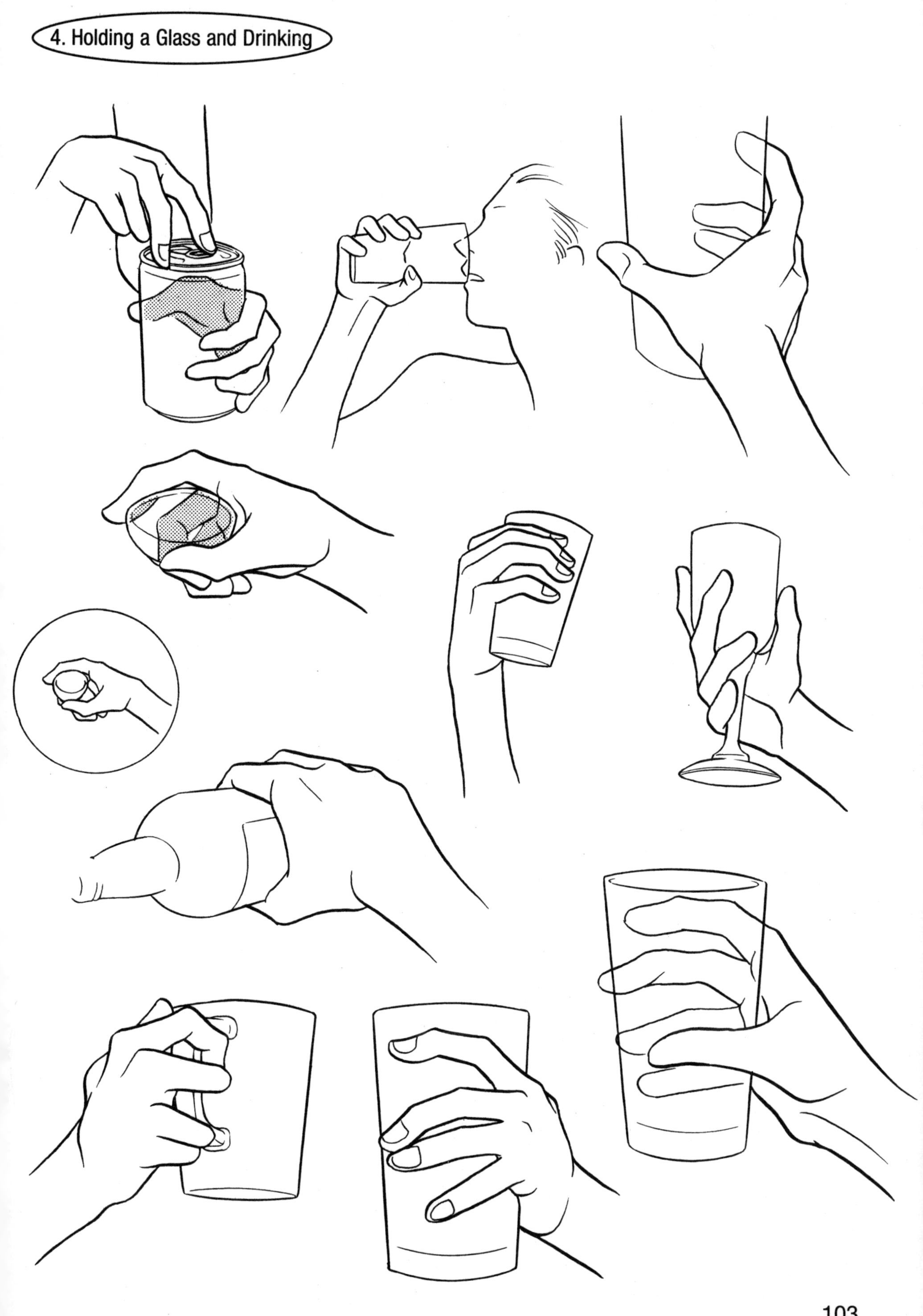

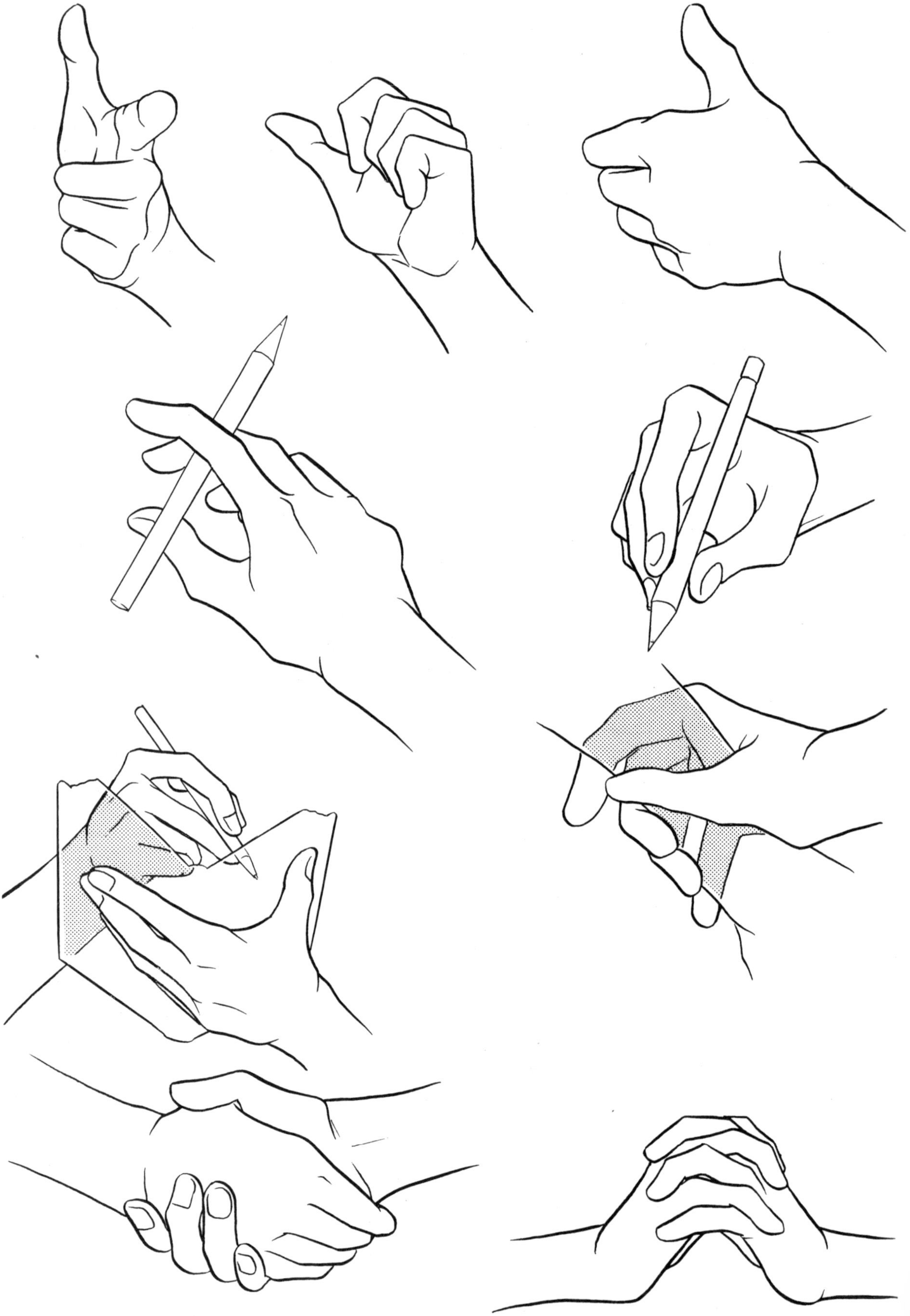

Eyeglasses and the Face

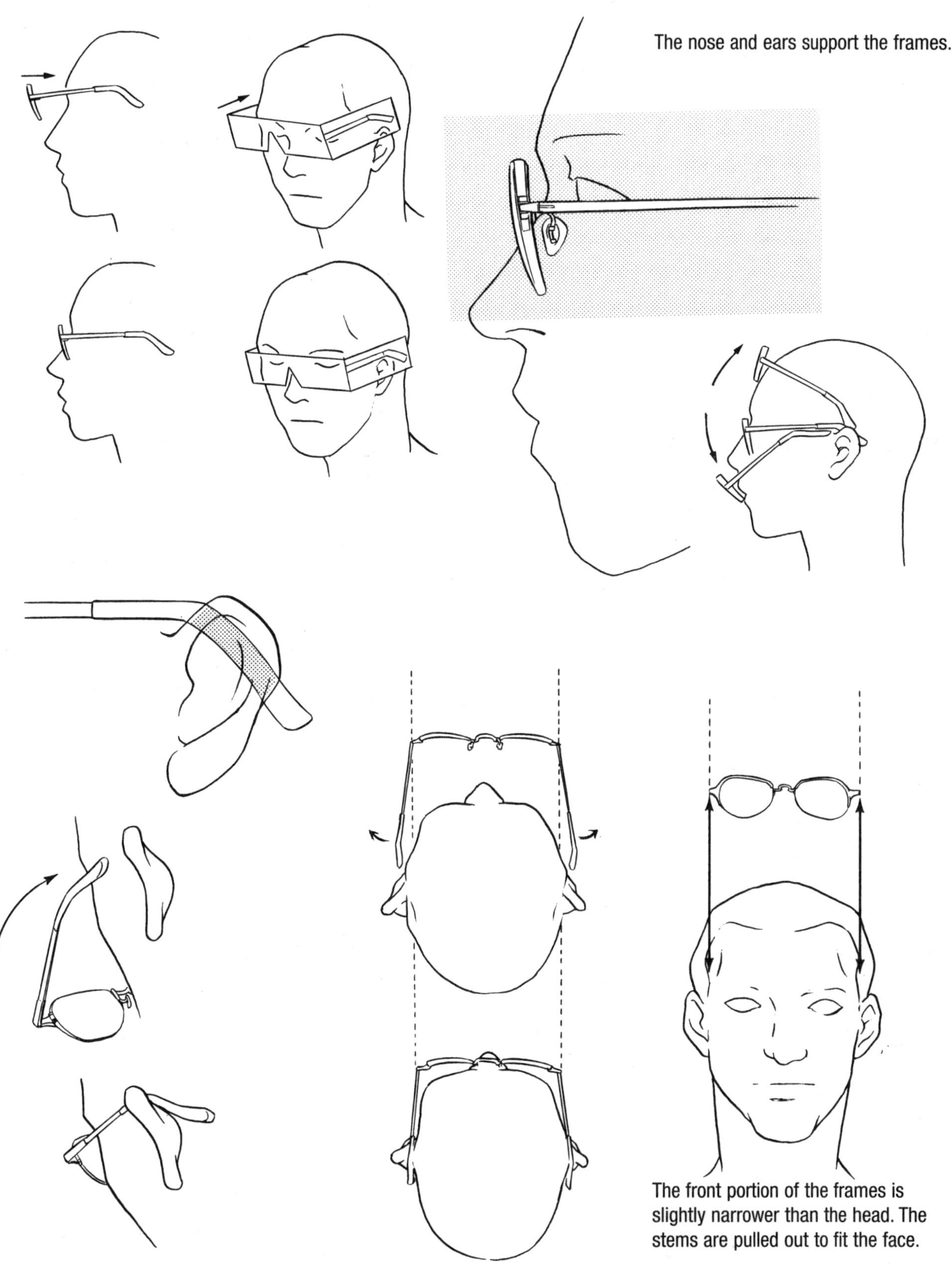

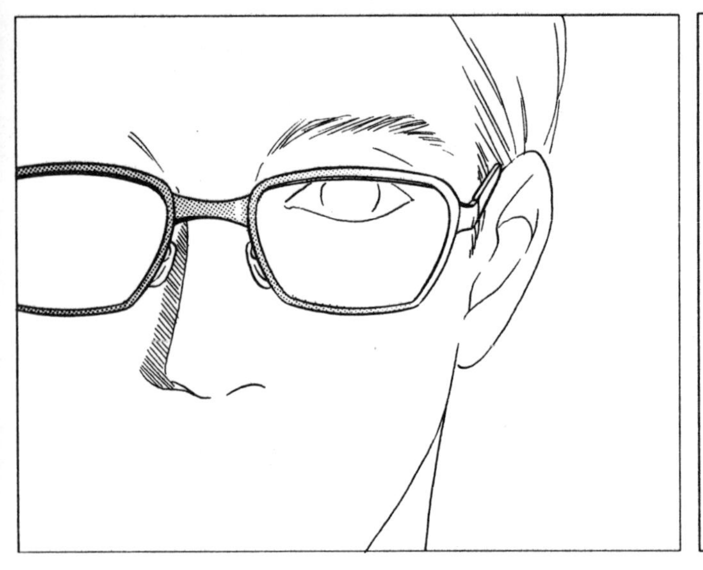

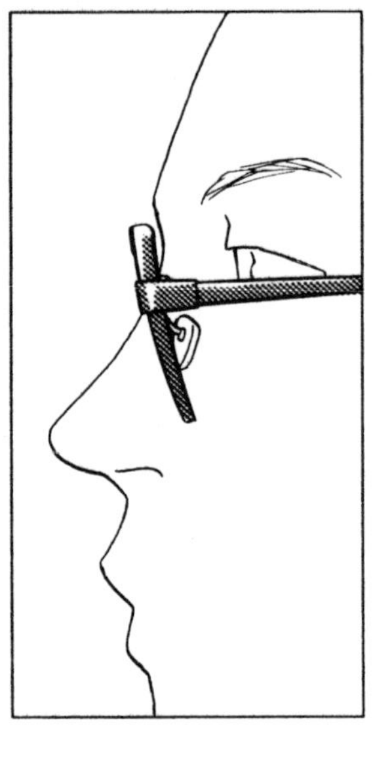

Silver Eyeglass Frames

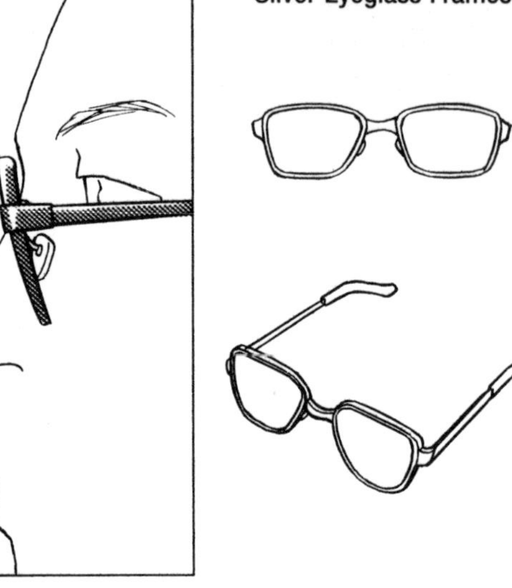

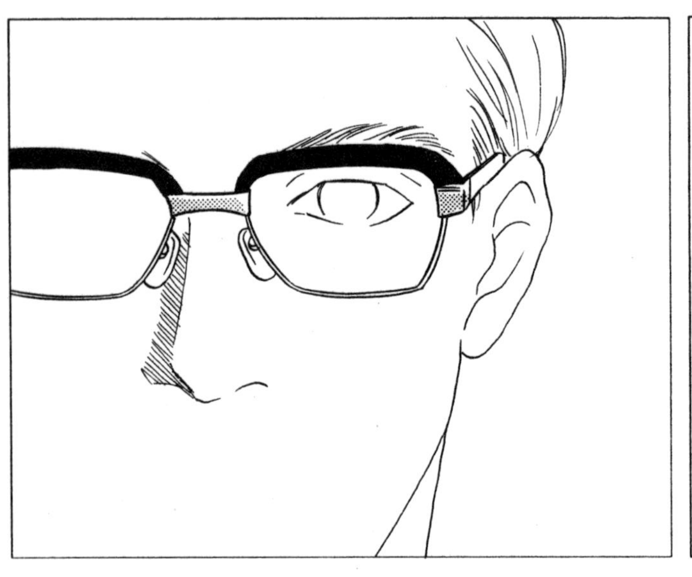

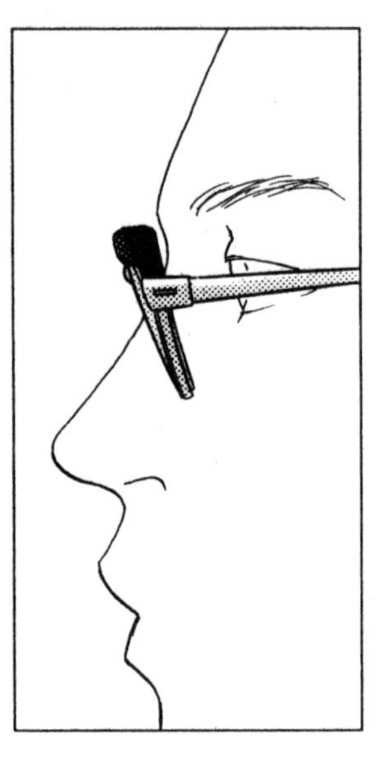

Black Frames

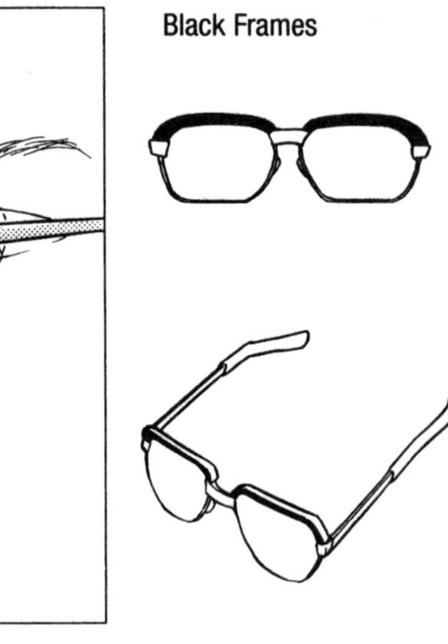

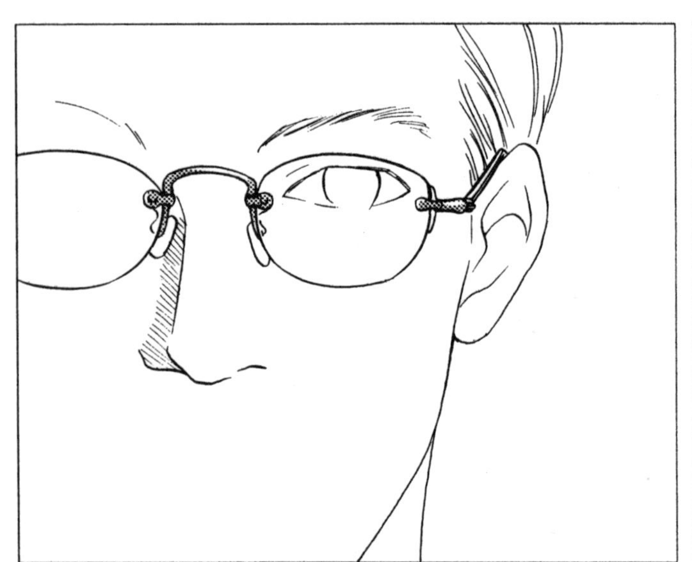

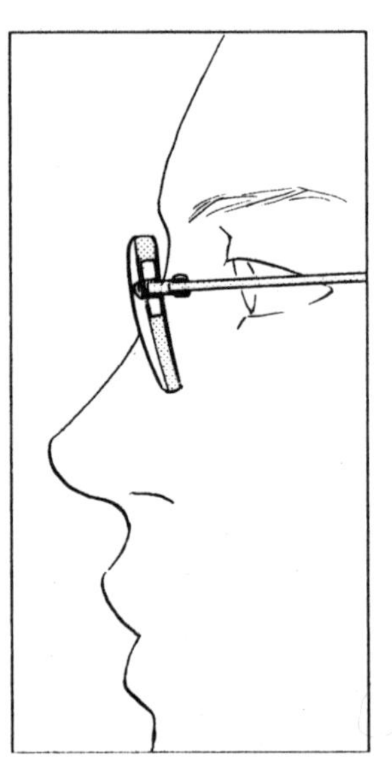

Rimless (Stems Only)

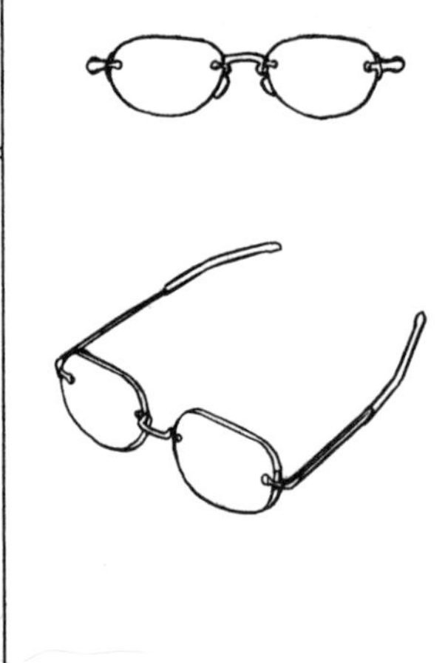

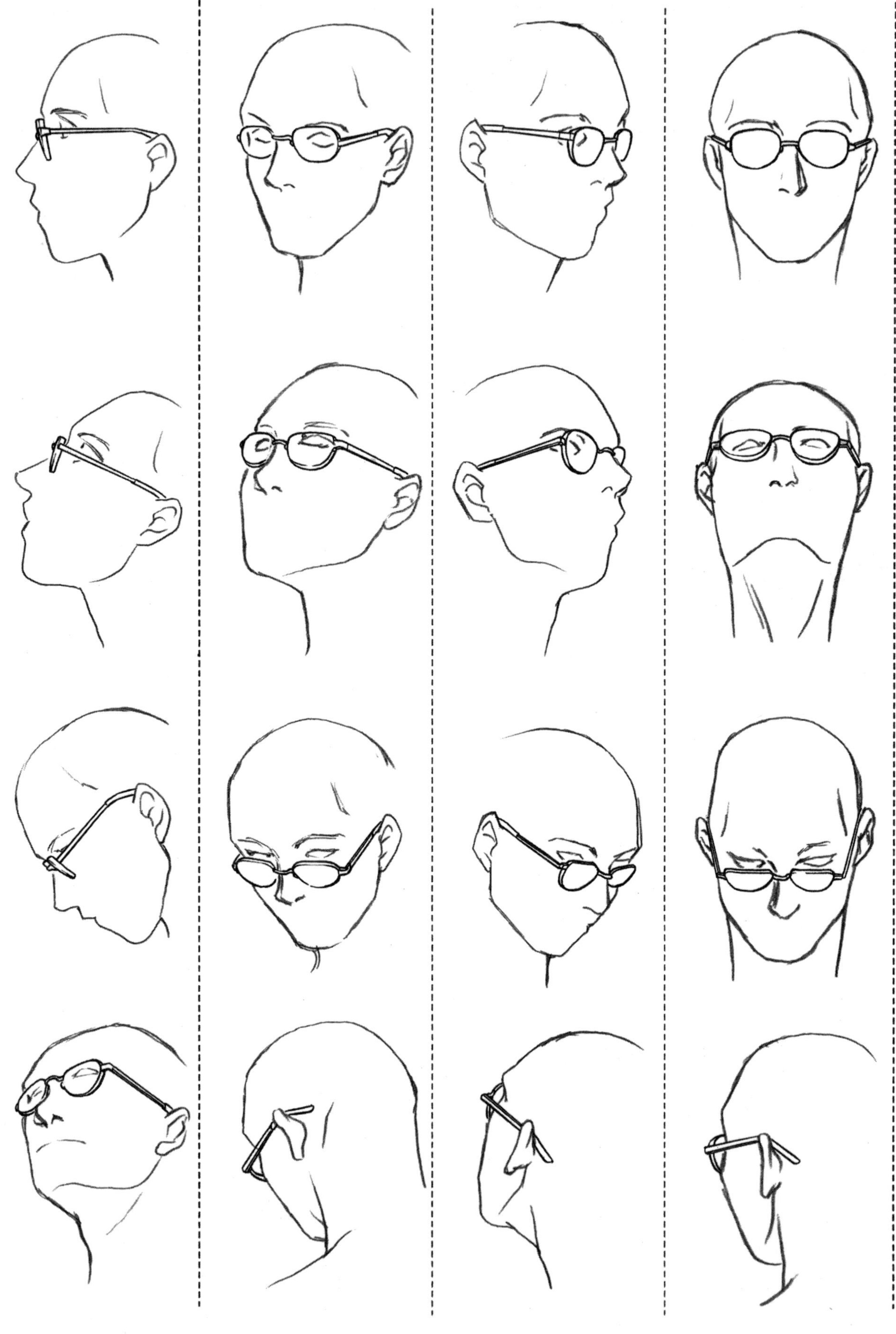

Handling Eyeglasses

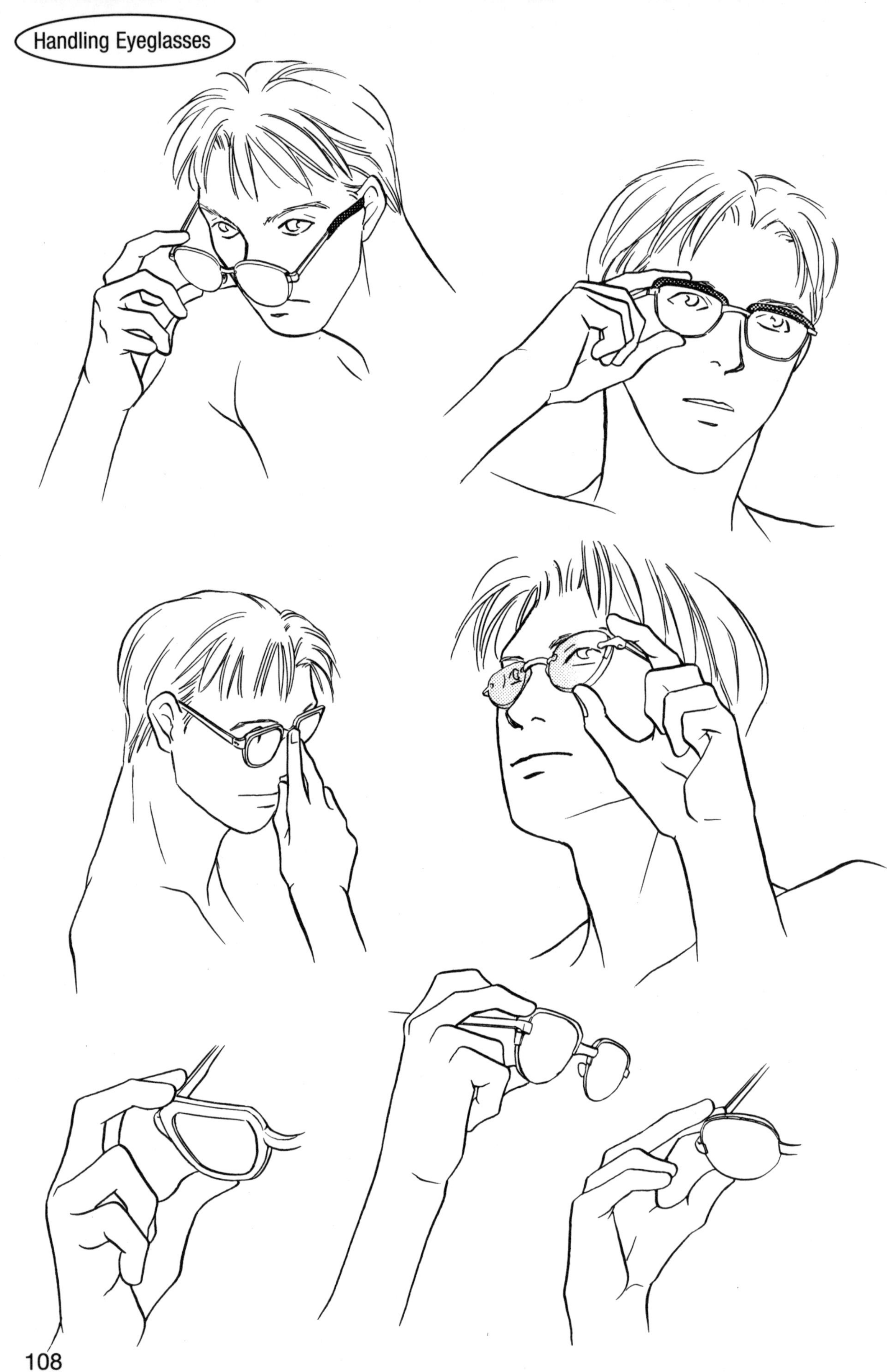

Shoes

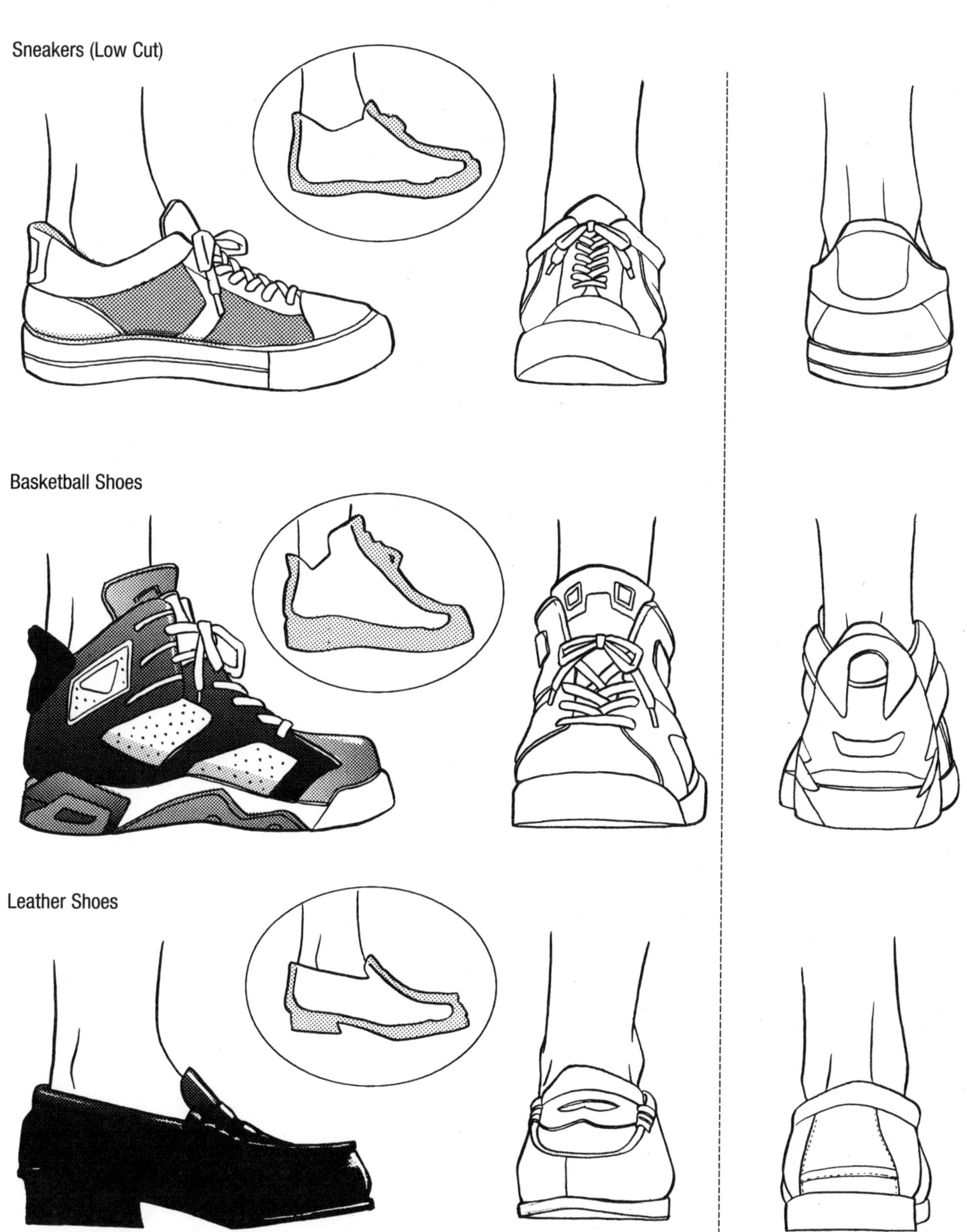

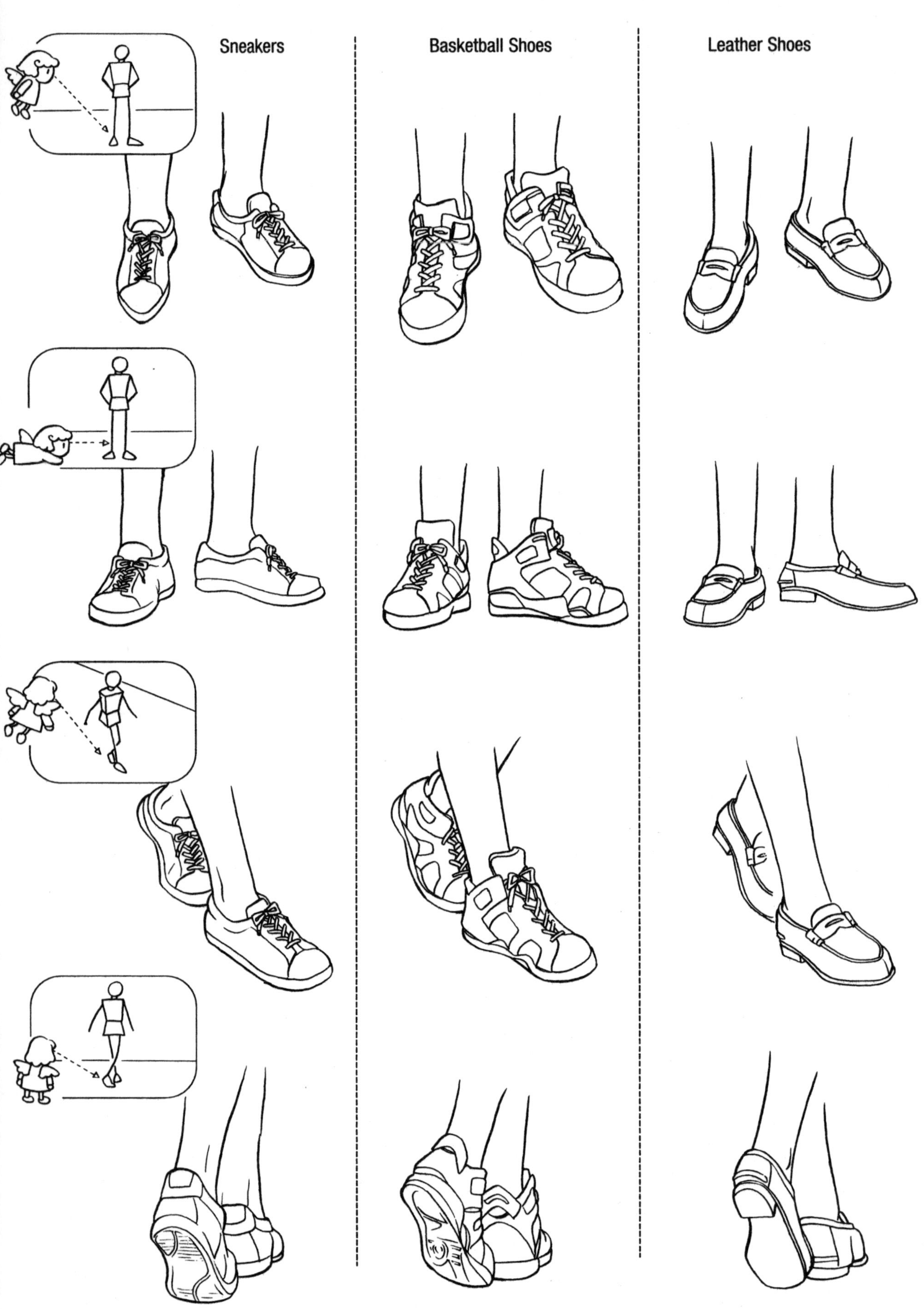
Sneakers
Basketball Shoes
Leather Shoes

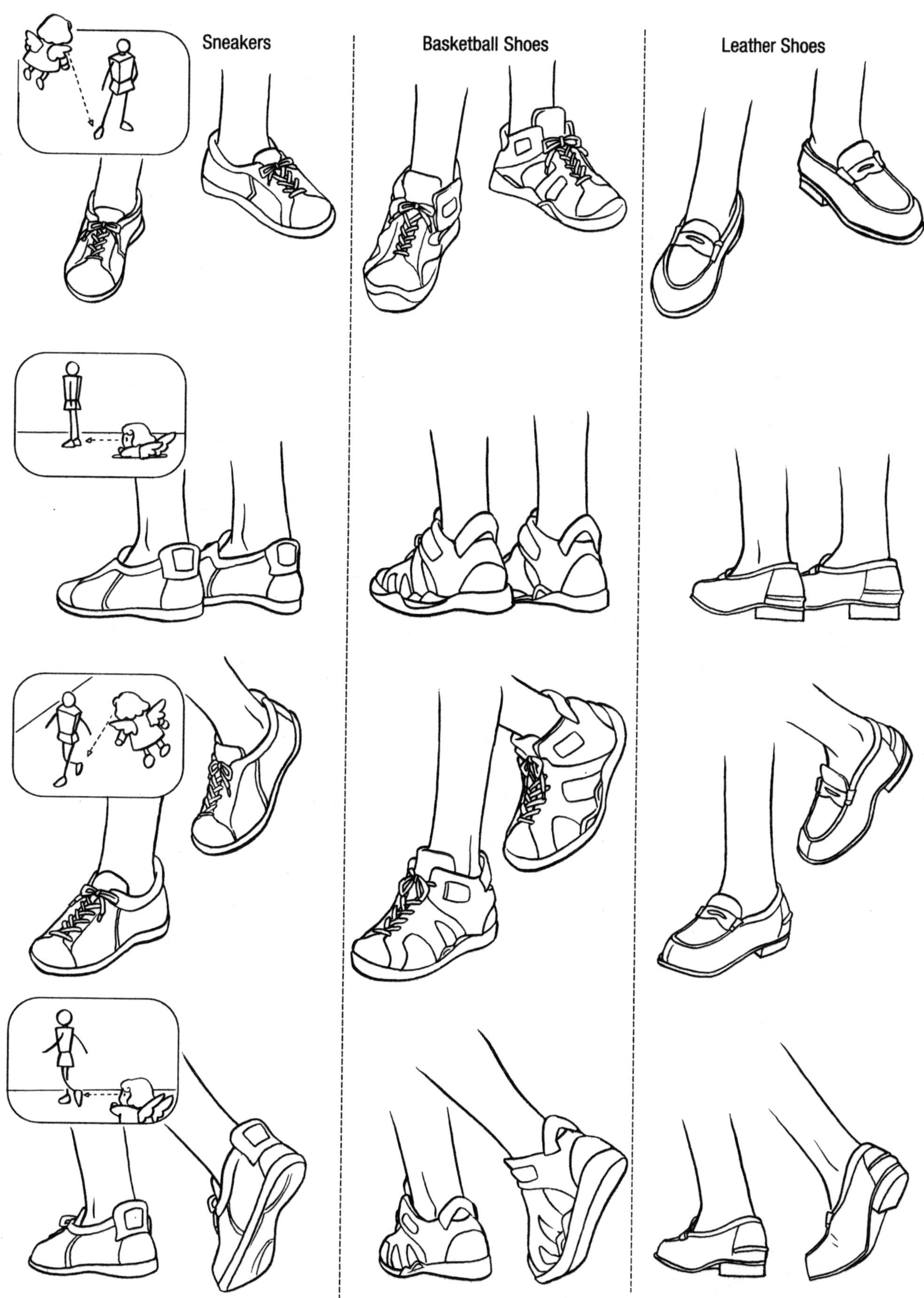
Sneakers
Basketball Shoes
Leather Shoes

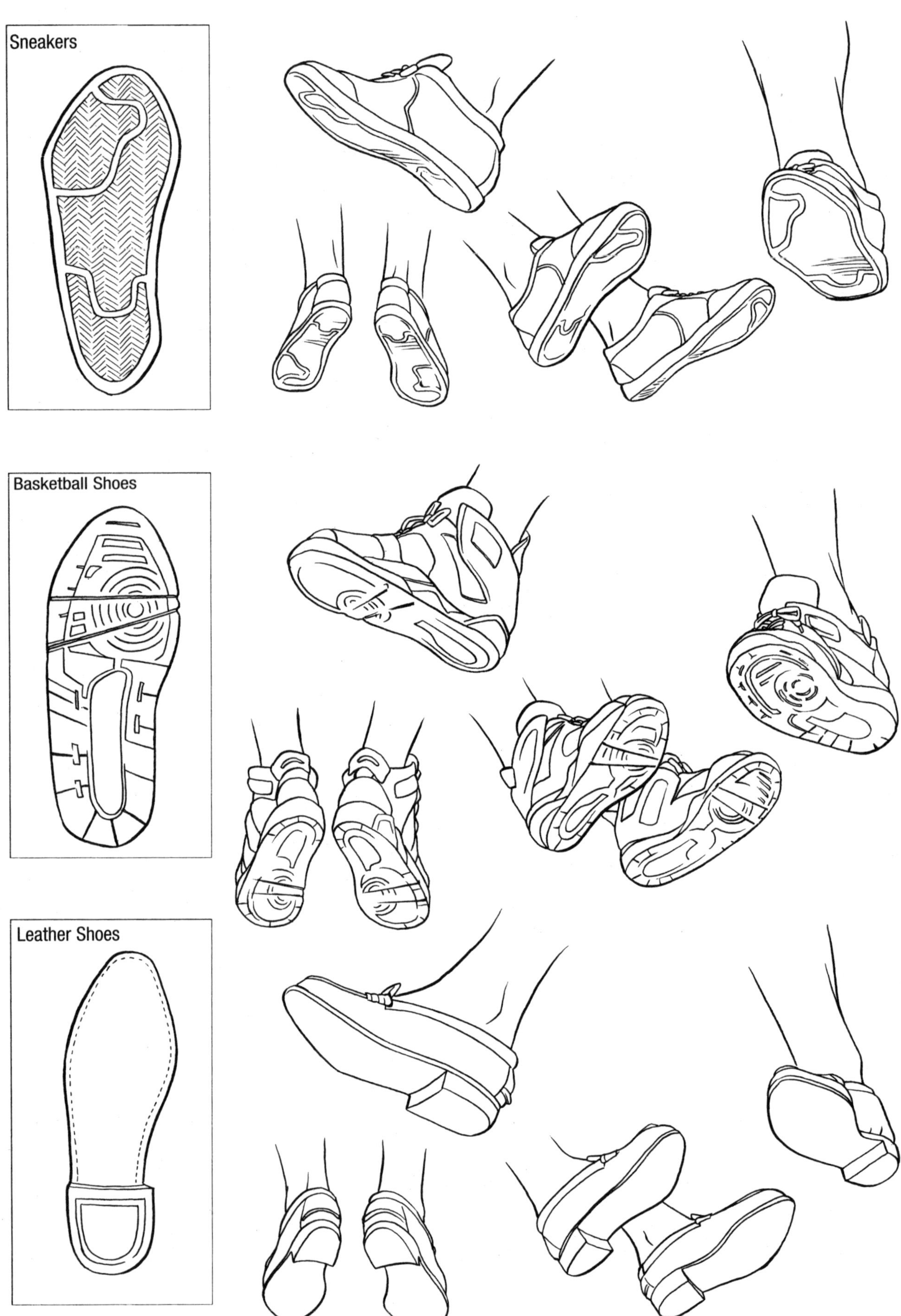
Sneakers
Basketball Shoes
Leather Shoes

Chapter 5
Representation Techniques Used by Manga Artists

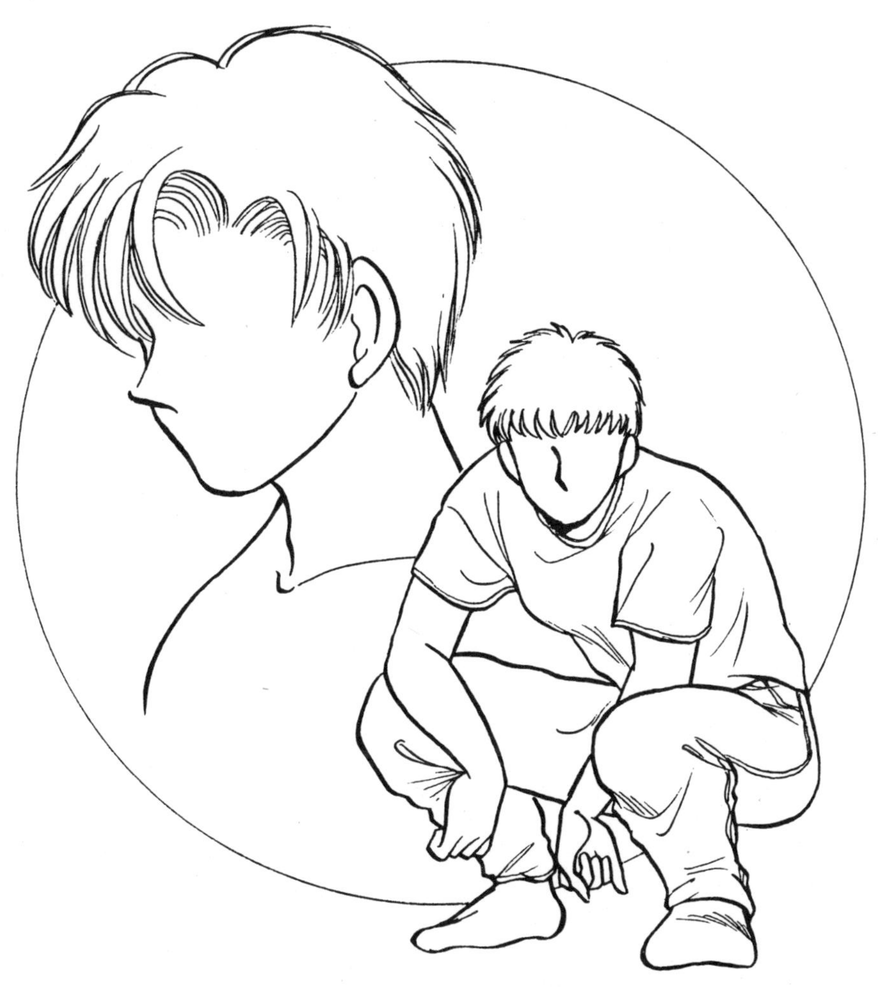

Contrast

by Jun Matsubara

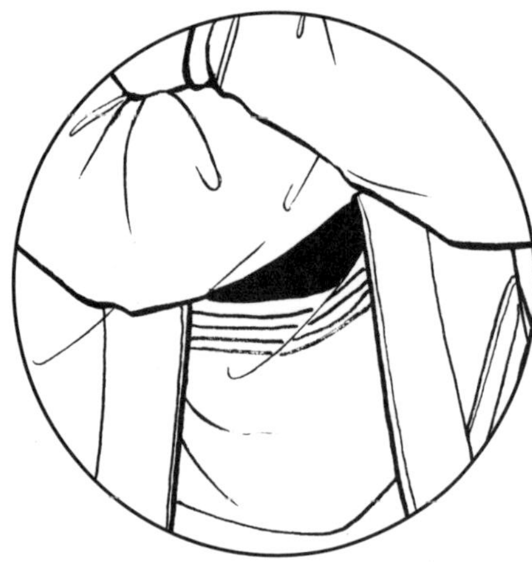

Matsubara has enhanced the feeling of volume in the male character from the waist to the hips and a sense of presence through the casual placement of a single crease in the T-shirt and adding a break in the stripes.

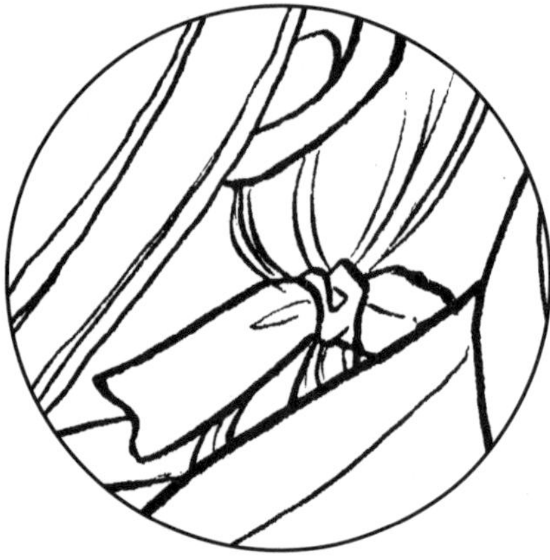

Ribbons and other effects offer hints into the characters' personalities. Here, the appearance of the ponytail even suggests the condition of the female character's hair.

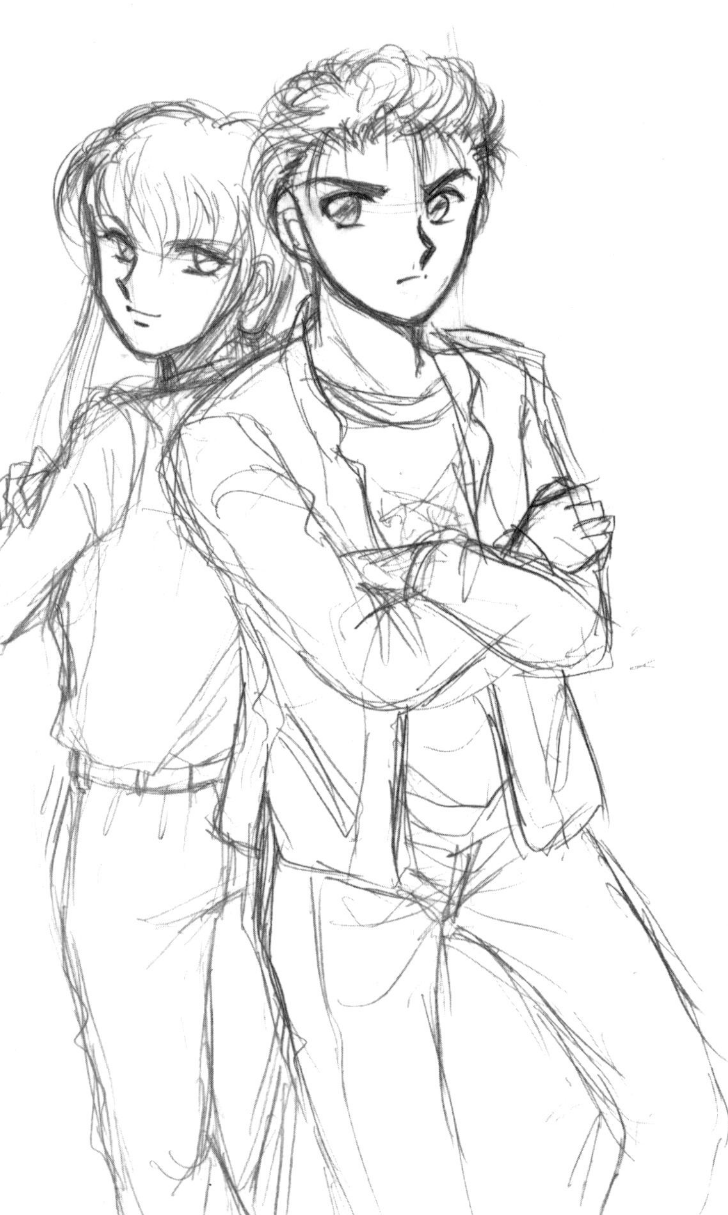

These two are an exercise in contrast, from the colors of their hair to the fashions they wear.

While one is garbed in street wear, the other is dressed in a more refined, softer fashion. Their faces contrast: male versus female. When combining the two, the artist took pains in the composition and drawing the one to contrast the other. The difference in hair color and height is basic to the concept. The artist included breaks with this as well, but still fundamental is that the reader is able to discern these contrasts at first glance.

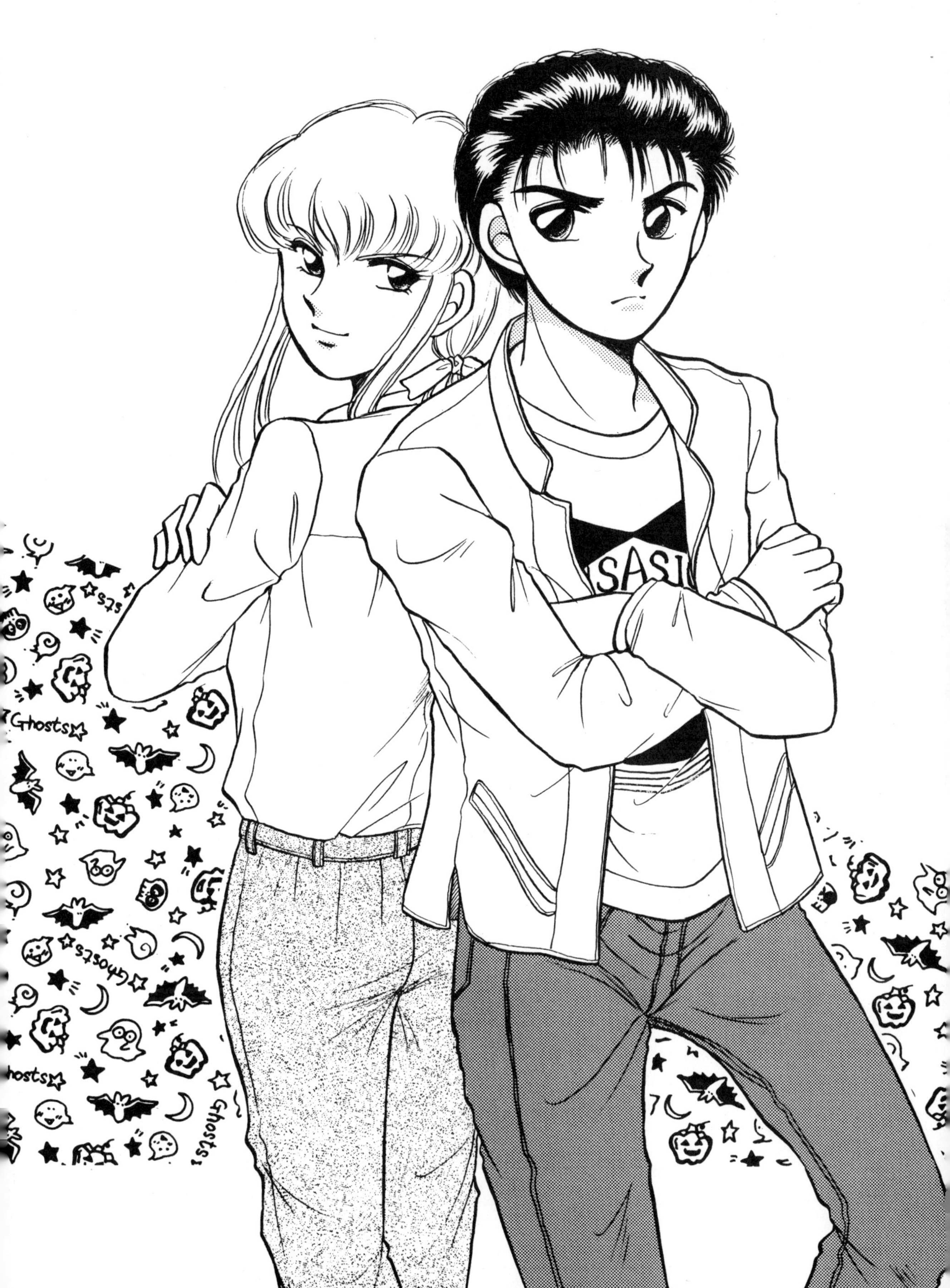
SASI
Ghosts
Ghosts
Ghosts

The Dreamer

by Kiyoe Yokoyama

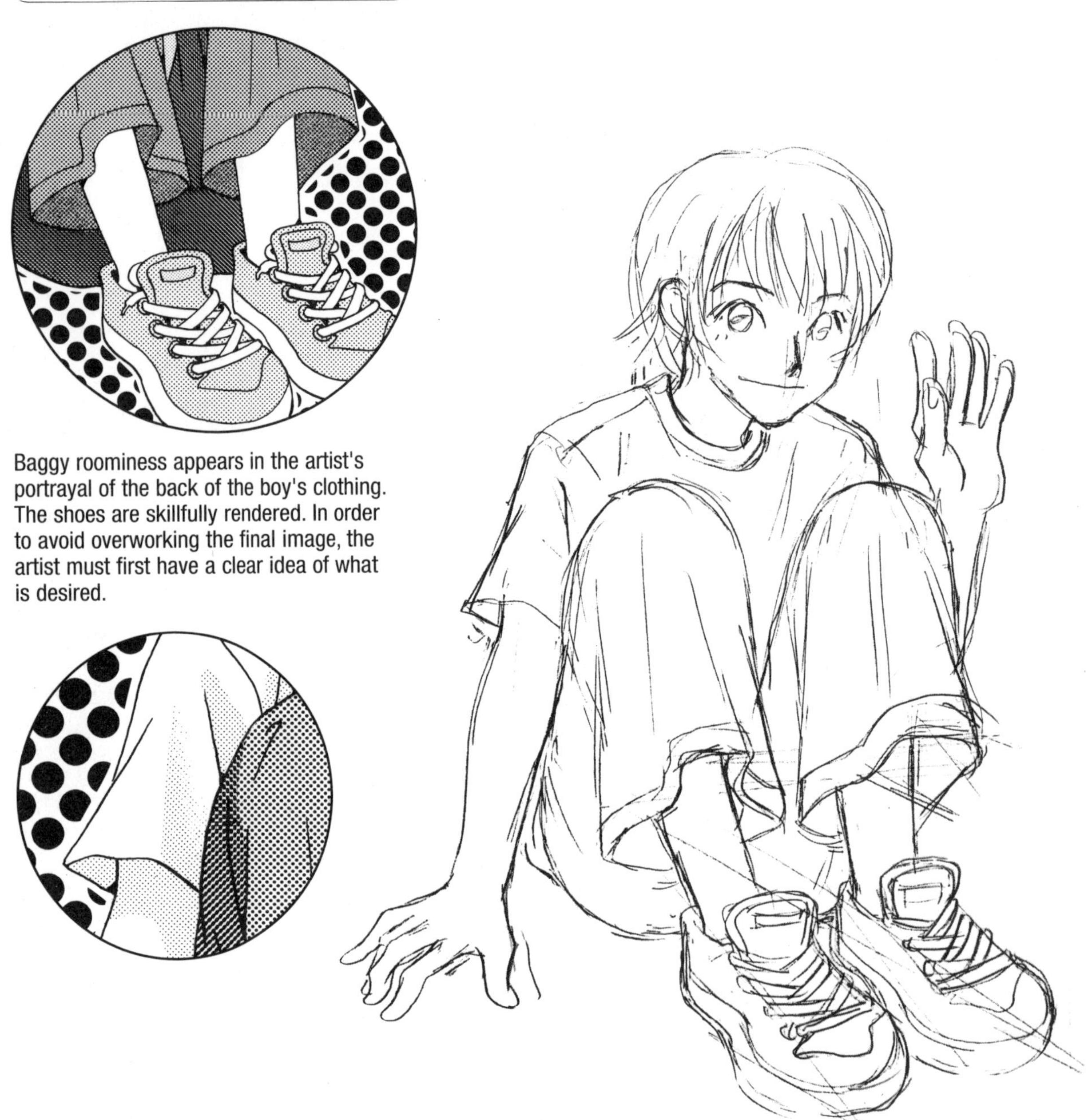

Baggy roominess appears in the artist's portrayal of the back of the boy's clothing. The shoes are skillfully rendered. In order to avoid overworking the final image, the artist must first have a clear idea of what is desired.

Let the image congeal before putting it to paper.

The baggy T-shirt sleeves and pant legs and oversized shoes send out both a pleasant feeling of freedom as well as one of carelessness. This space gives simultaneously a unique 3-dimensional sense and presence to both the character and the image as a whole. Further, use of a 2-dimensional sheet tone for the background generates a peculiar mood surrounding the presence of the character.

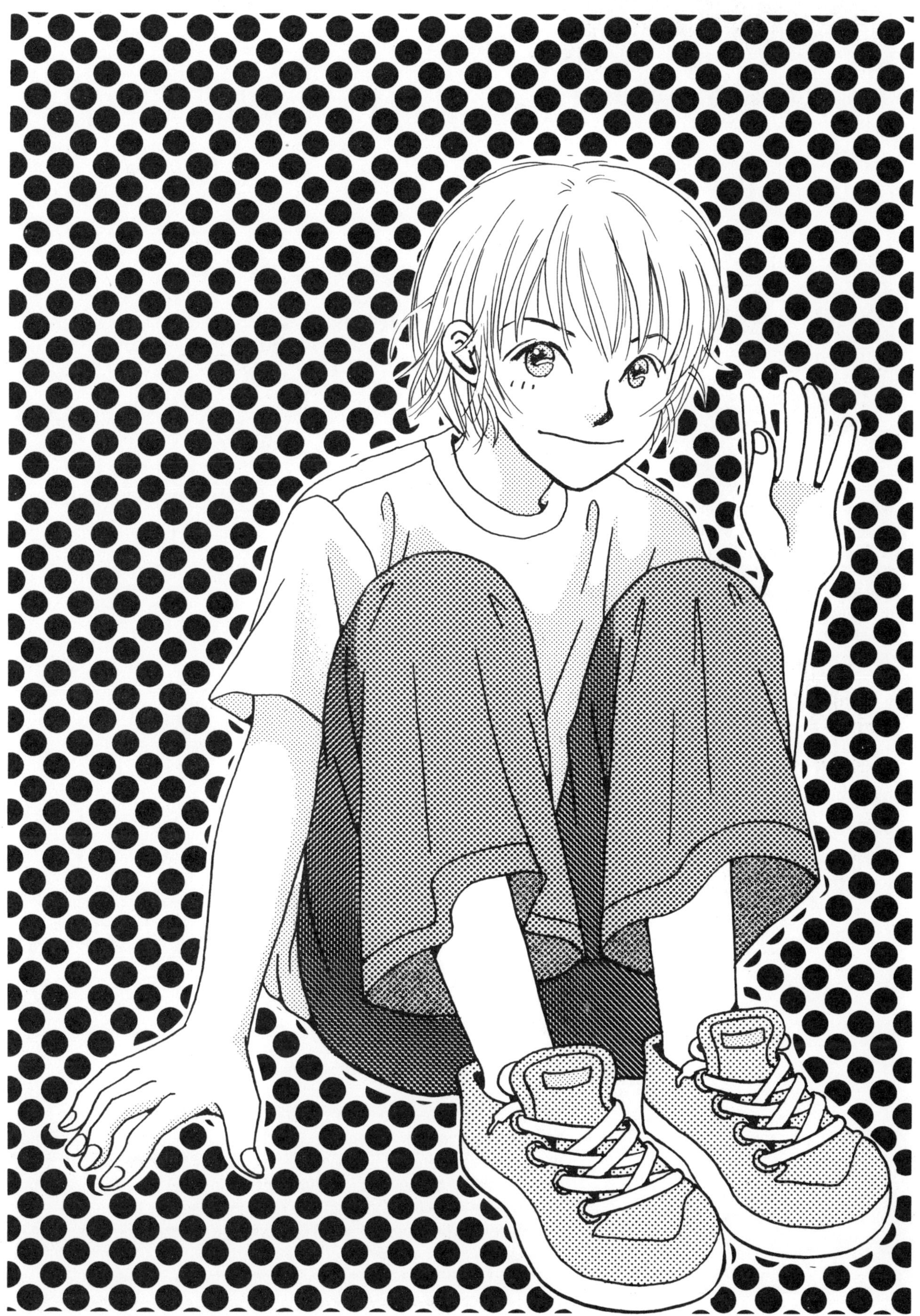

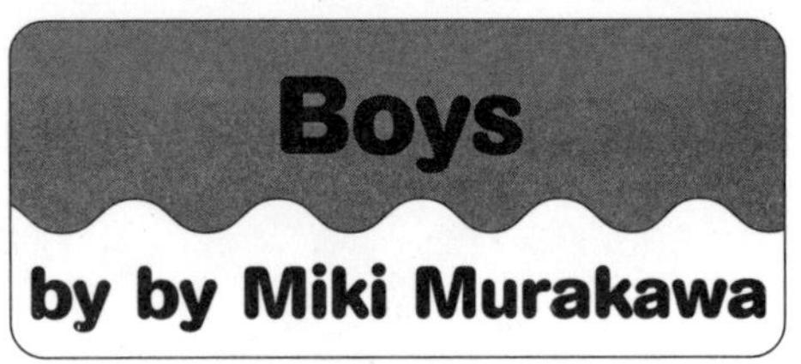

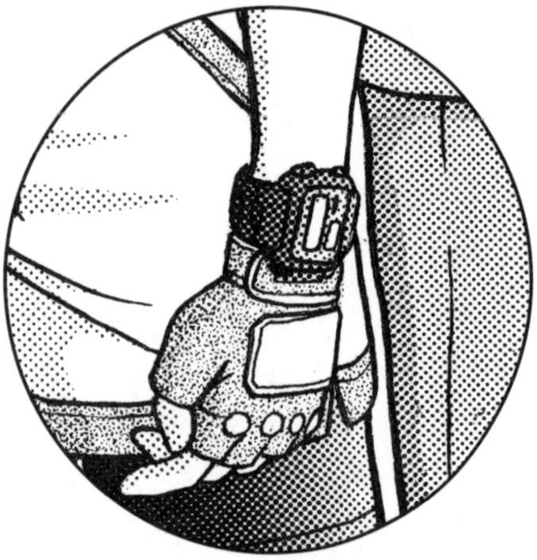

Although subtle, the significant elements of this work lie in the inclusion and rendering of small effects. Painstaking rendition of an inconspicuous wristwatch and shoelaces might take time, but it also gives the reader a sense of comfort and satisfaction with respect to the final image.

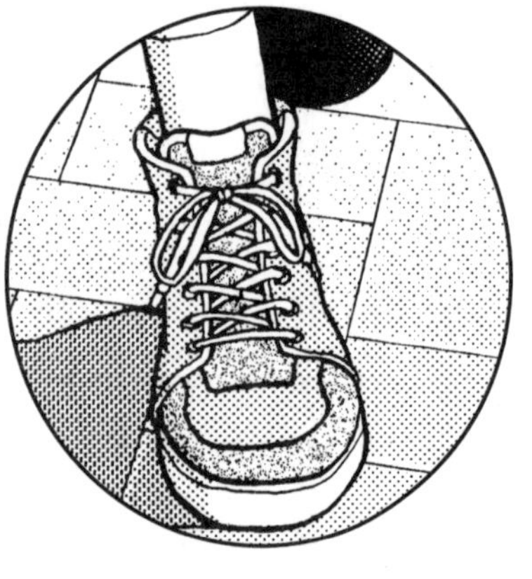

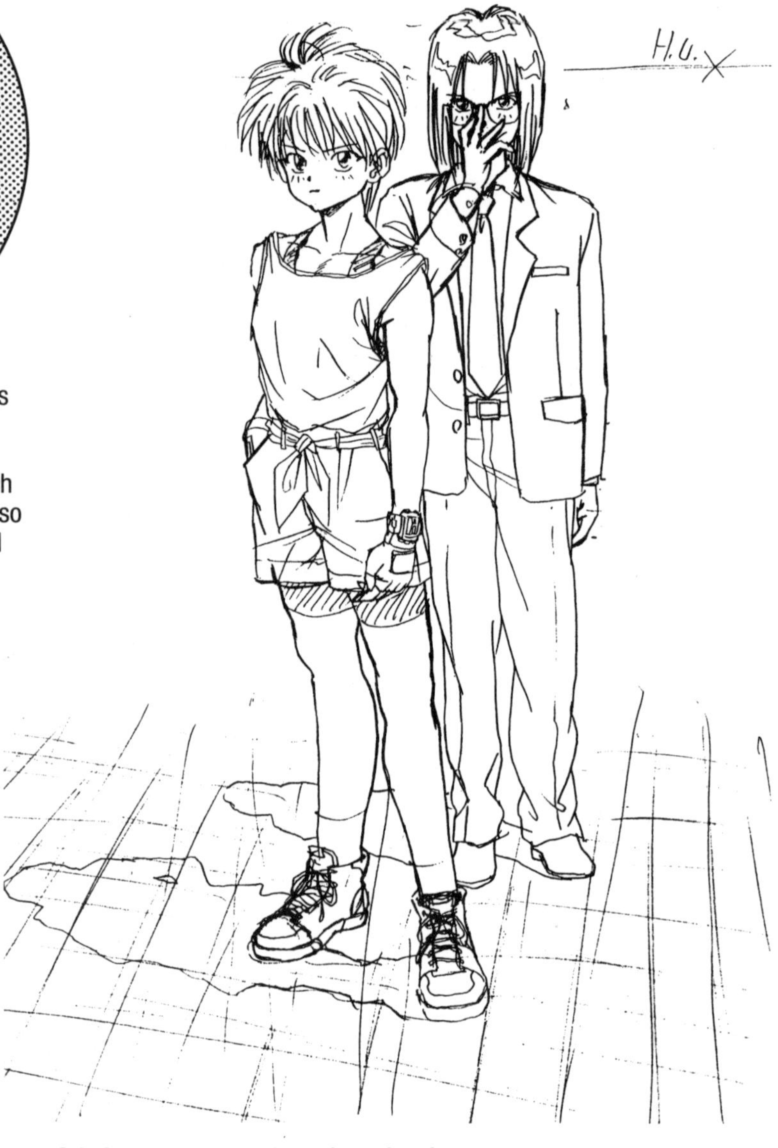

Stirring up the readers' imagination

This work gives the reader the immediate impression that these two are from different worlds. The angle suggests a subtle distance and calculated dance played where the two neither approach nor separate from each other. Similarly, the poses allow the reader to imagine the roles played by both characters, while conveying the differences established in their personalities. This causes a mood with a distinctive meaning to hang over the image.

The image is set up with distinctions made to the tiniest detail in order to drive home a strong impression of the characters and their individuality. Such meticulous rendering has tremendous impact on the reader.

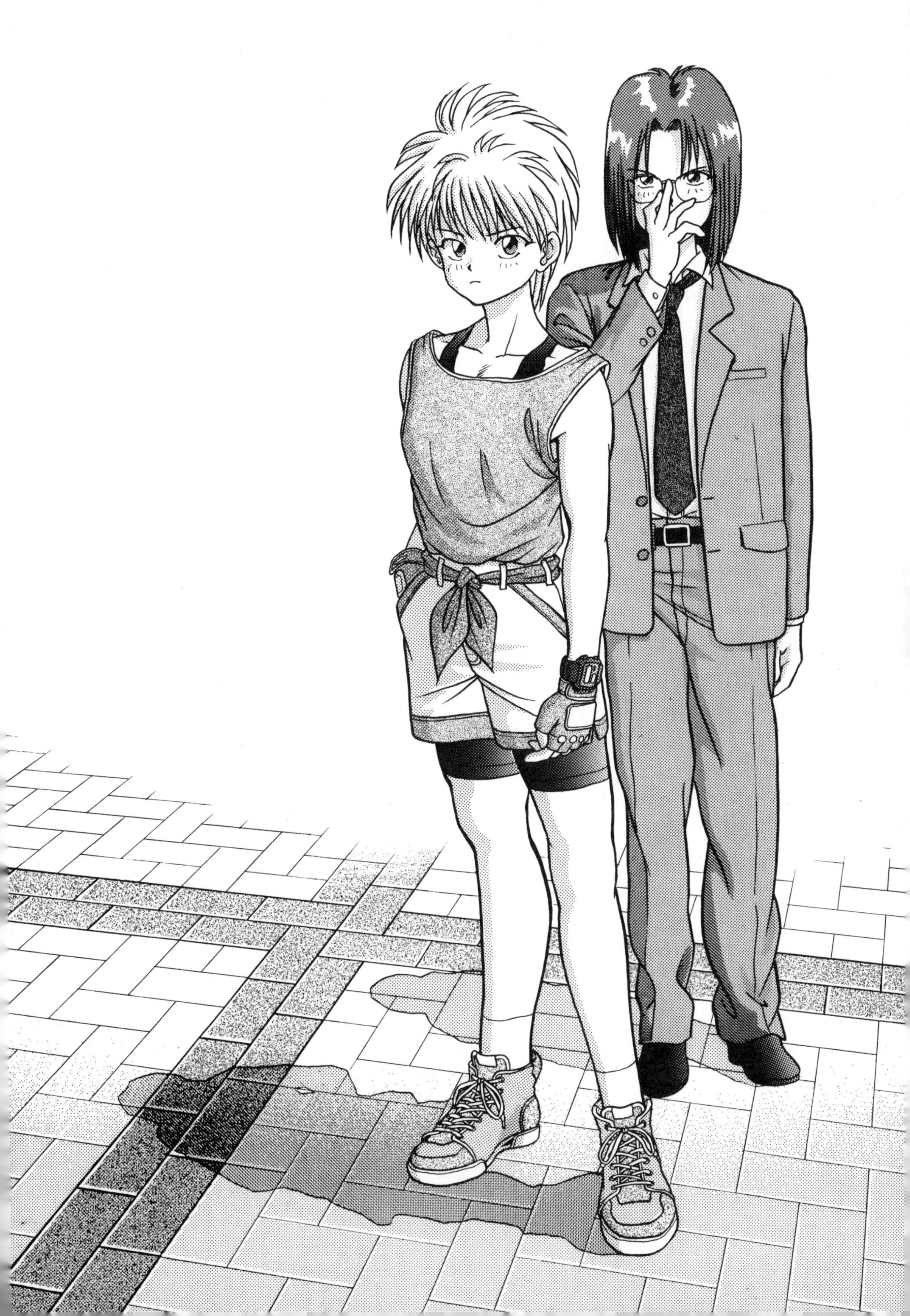

Holiday

by Yasuo Matsumoto

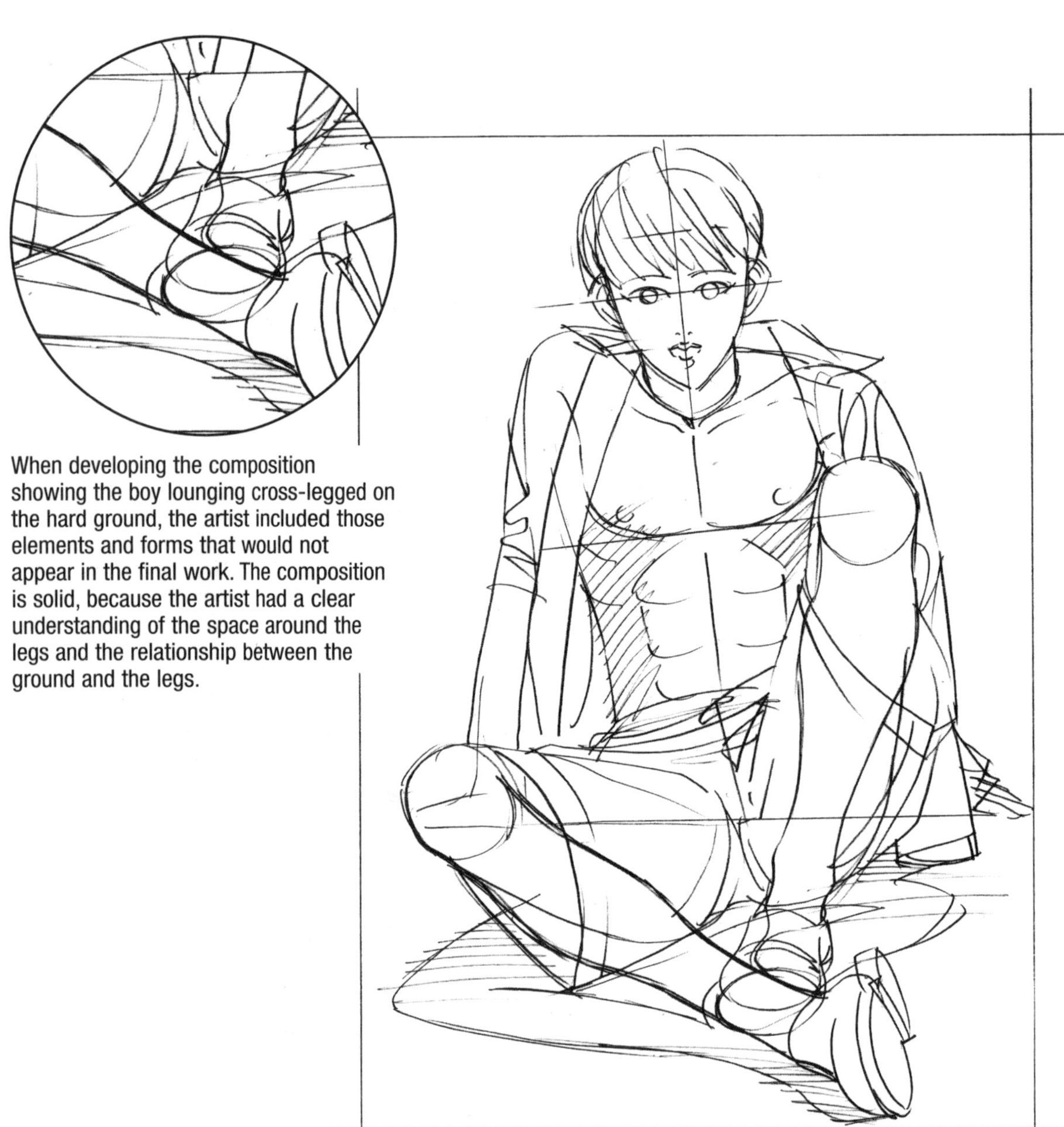

When developing the composition showing the boy lounging cross-legged on the hard ground, the artist included those elements and forms that would not appear in the final work. The composition is solid, because the artist had a clear understanding of the space around the legs and the relationship between the ground and the legs.

A slight incline in the upper body brings movement and calm to the image.

A relaxed mood is expressed in this composition of a character seated by having the figure's upper body lean slightly. At the same time, this gives a sense of movement to the image, creating a tranquil mood. When the artist rendered the body, adding shadows at angles and thus bringing attention to the physical structure, he created a sensual character, neither powerful nor frail. Finally, adding shadows in the same direction in which the character leans further enhances relaxed mood of the work.

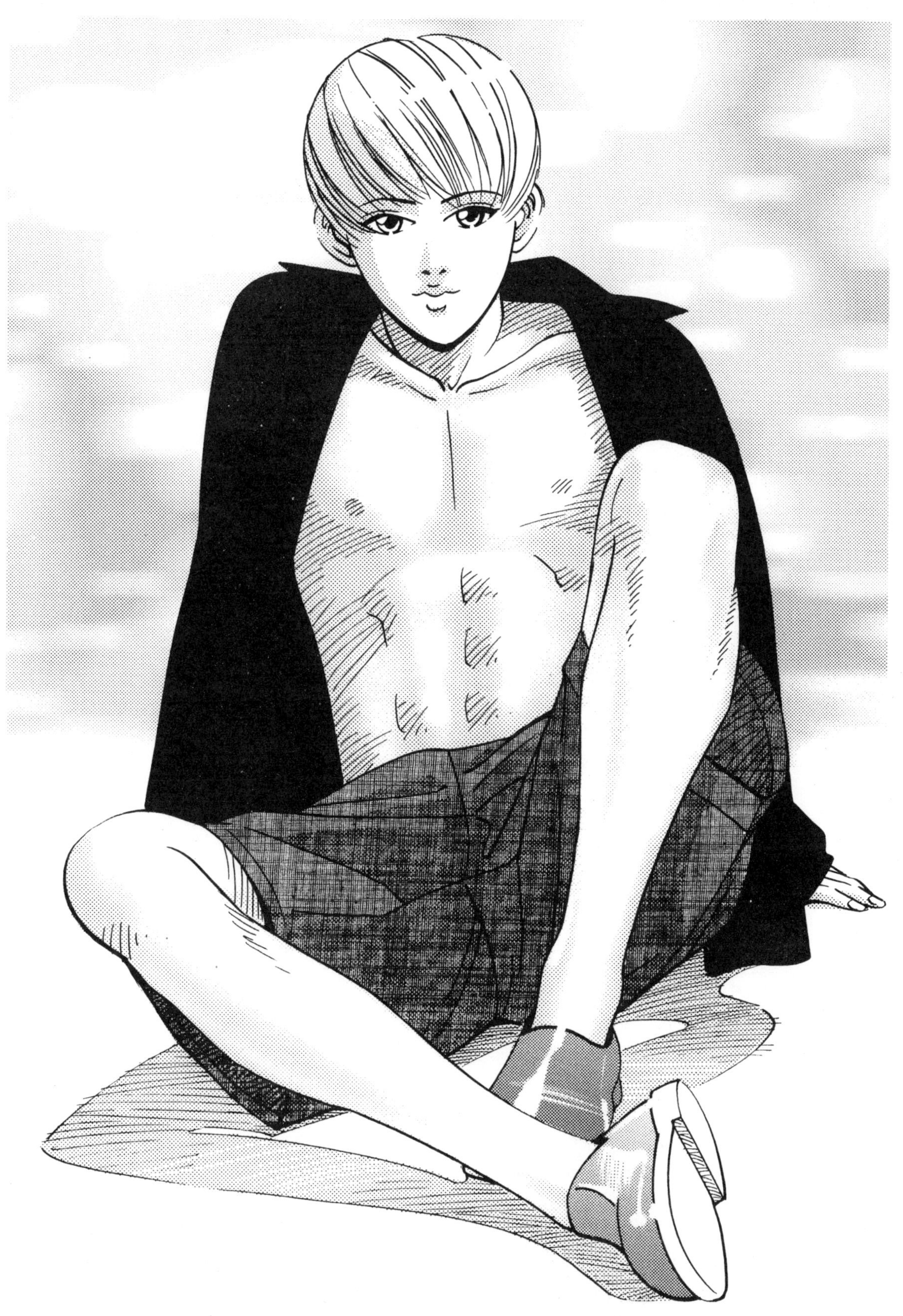

Entranced

by Kent Shimazaki

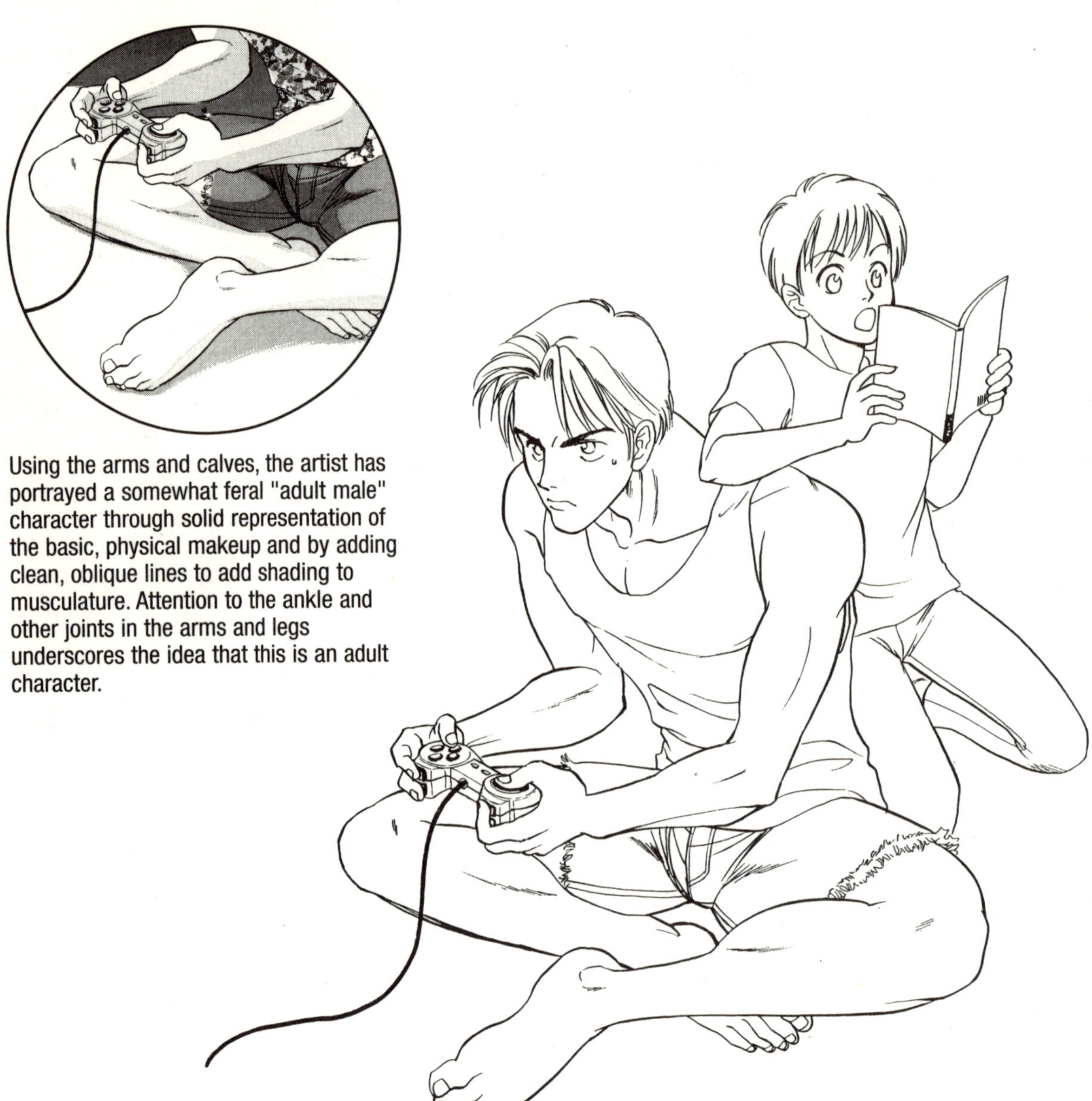

Using the arms and calves, the artist has portrayed a somewhat feral "adult male" character through solid representation of the basic, physical makeup and by adding clean, oblique lines to add shading to musculature. Attention to the ankle and other joints in the arms and legs underscores the idea that this is an adult character.

A striking image is created through a dramatic composition with subtle contrasts.

The artist has shown painstaking attention to all of the composition's components, from the characters, to light and shadow, to the direction the figures face. By having the young man and boy face different directions, the artist has created a dynamic scene being played out on a still image. Creases appearing on the form-conscious clothing of the physically fit "older brother" suggest a body with no extraneous flesh. They allow us to imagine a powerful chest and taut abdomen. The highlights in the hair and shadows on the figures due to the "light from the TV set" are calculated dramatizations. The artist has portrayed effectively the characters as well as the carefully rendered small articles.

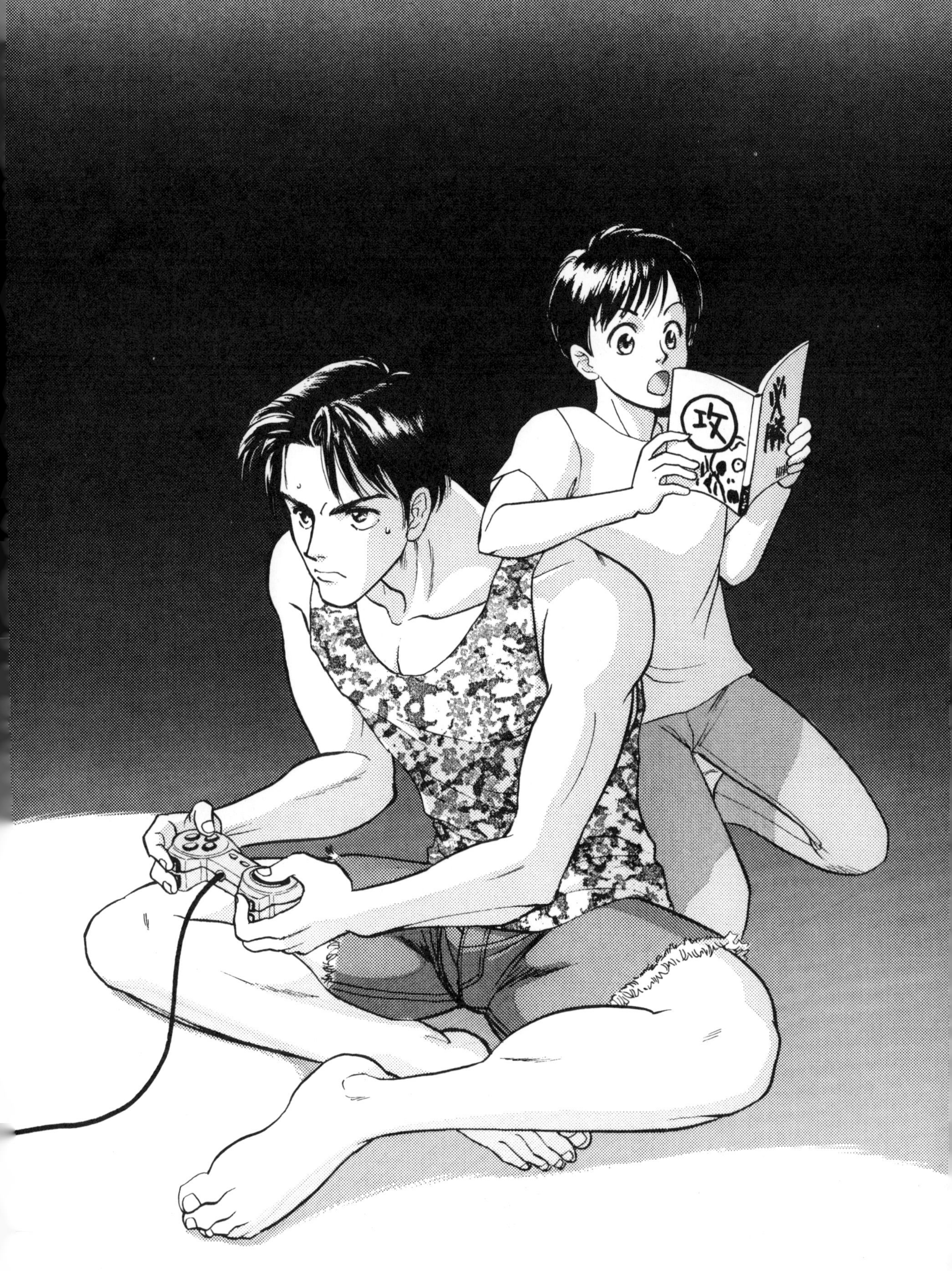
攻
必勝

The Wild One

by Yukai Asada

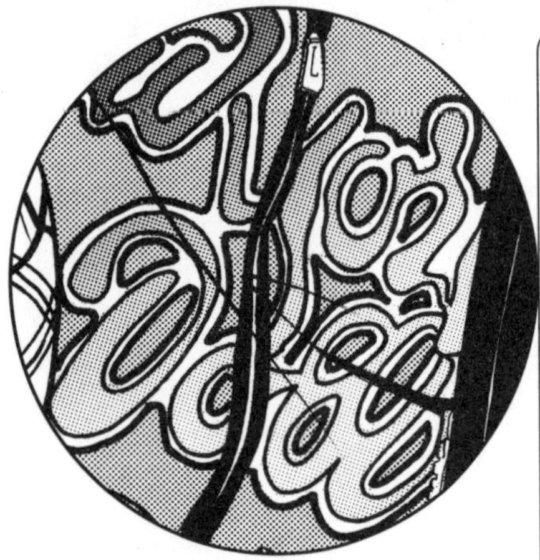

The elaborate logo lettering is simplified in the under drawing. Addition of outline and of the white border, balanced with the sheet tone, creates an individualistic atmosphere. Further, the thick line of the central zipper accentuates the impression of ripples in the jacket.

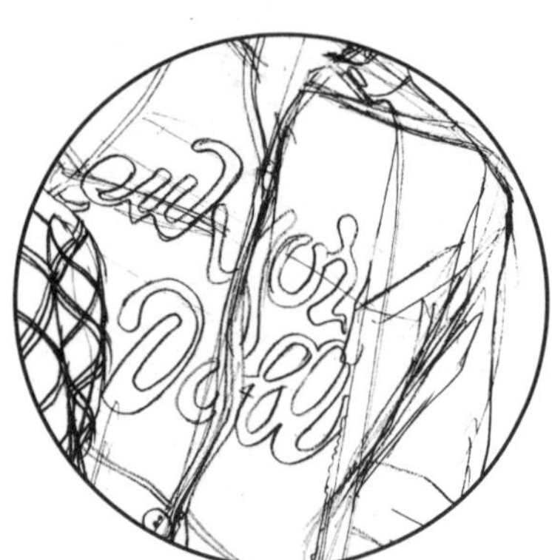

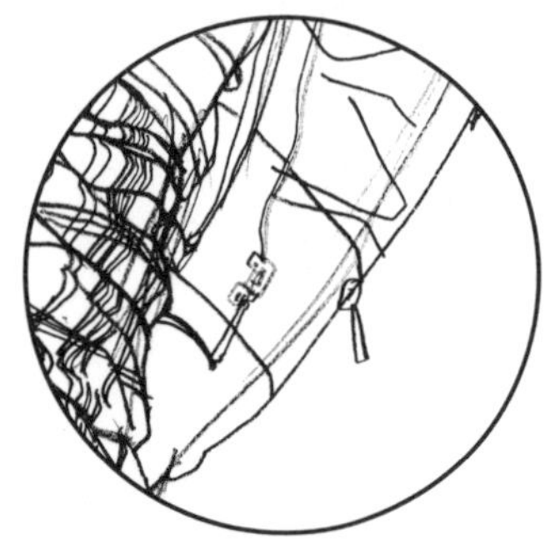

Note the collar buttons and zipper and other details the artist included even at the sketch stage.

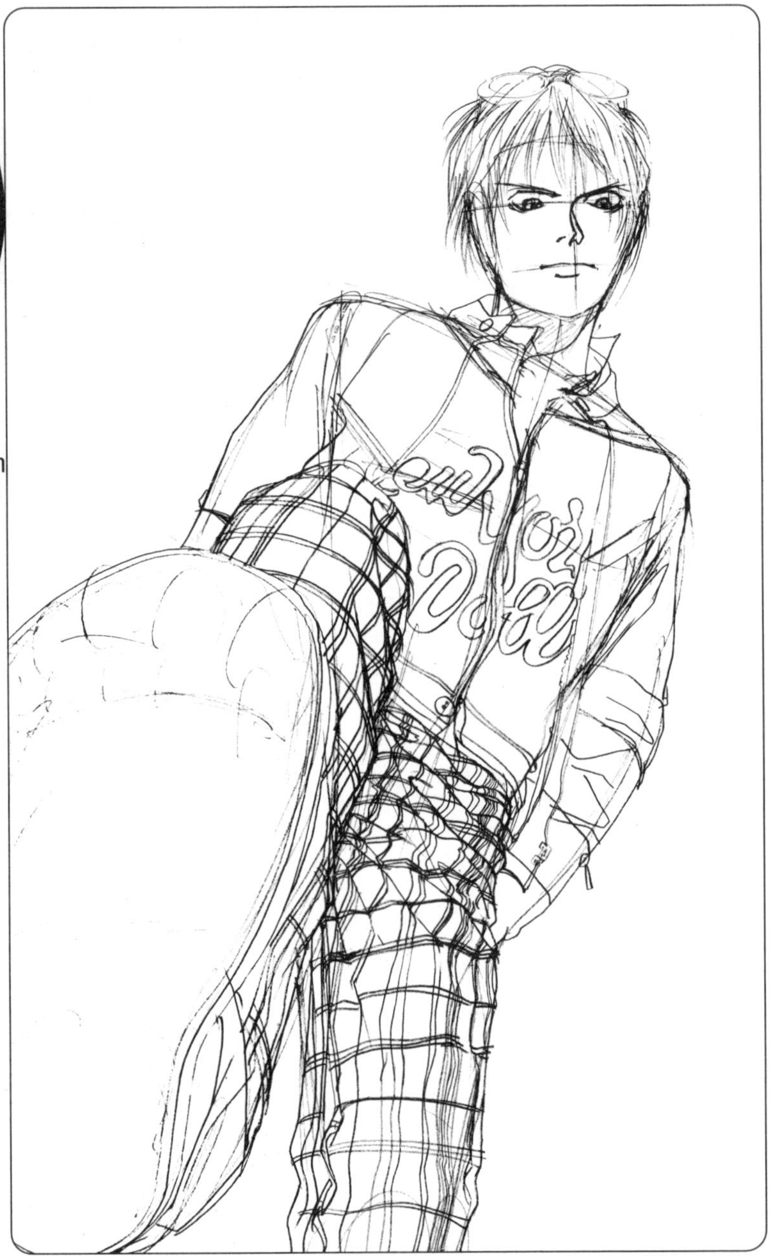

Confidence and a sense of balance produce an image with impact.

A dramatic angle and bold differentiation between filled in areas and lines of contrasting thickness generate a strong, balanced image. Dynamic lines were not just traced over those of the under drawing, but were confidently and decisively drawn to create the desired image. The simple shoe sole, the closest item to the picture plane, is an effective, sharp contrast to the detailed logo and pants. The artist carefully calculated those areas to receive detail and those areas to leave plain, resulting in a successful, well-balanced work.

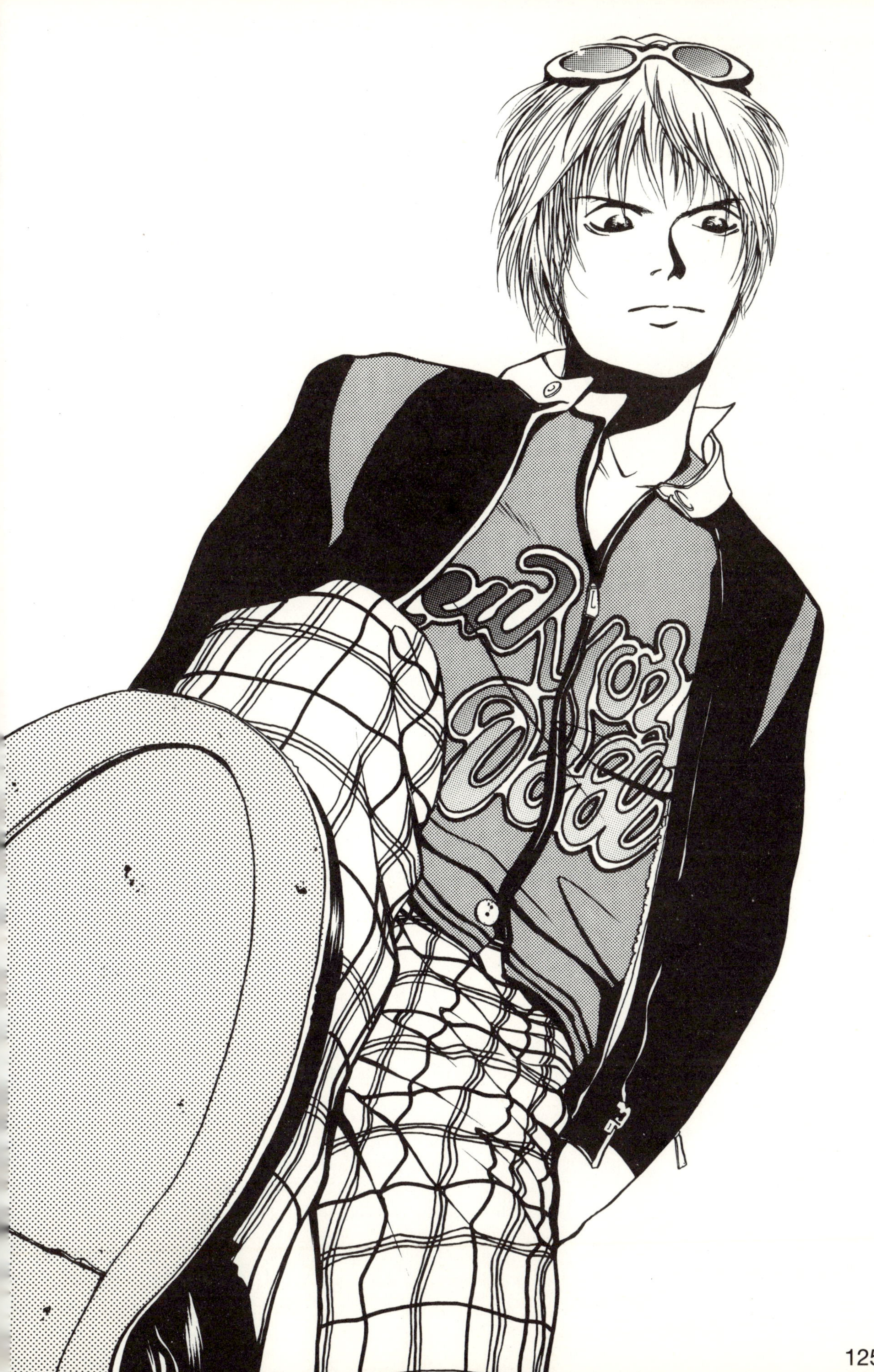

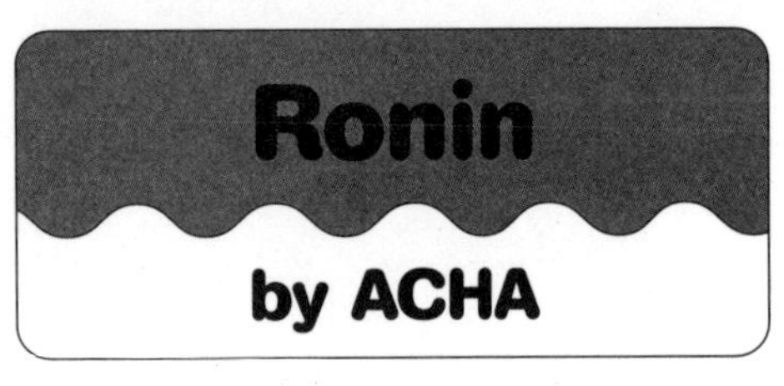

Ronin

by ACHA

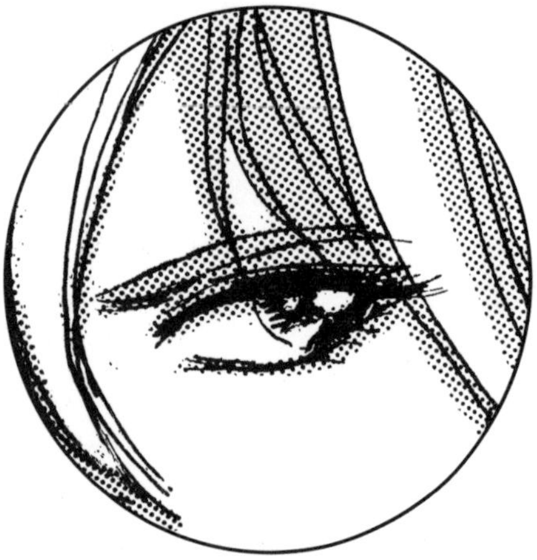

One technique is to affix sheet tone to the image along contours. This is a multipurpose technique used to arrest the reader's eye when conveying that indescribable something or adding that something extra, or creating a striking manga image. Where to apply this technique is up to the sensibility of the artist.

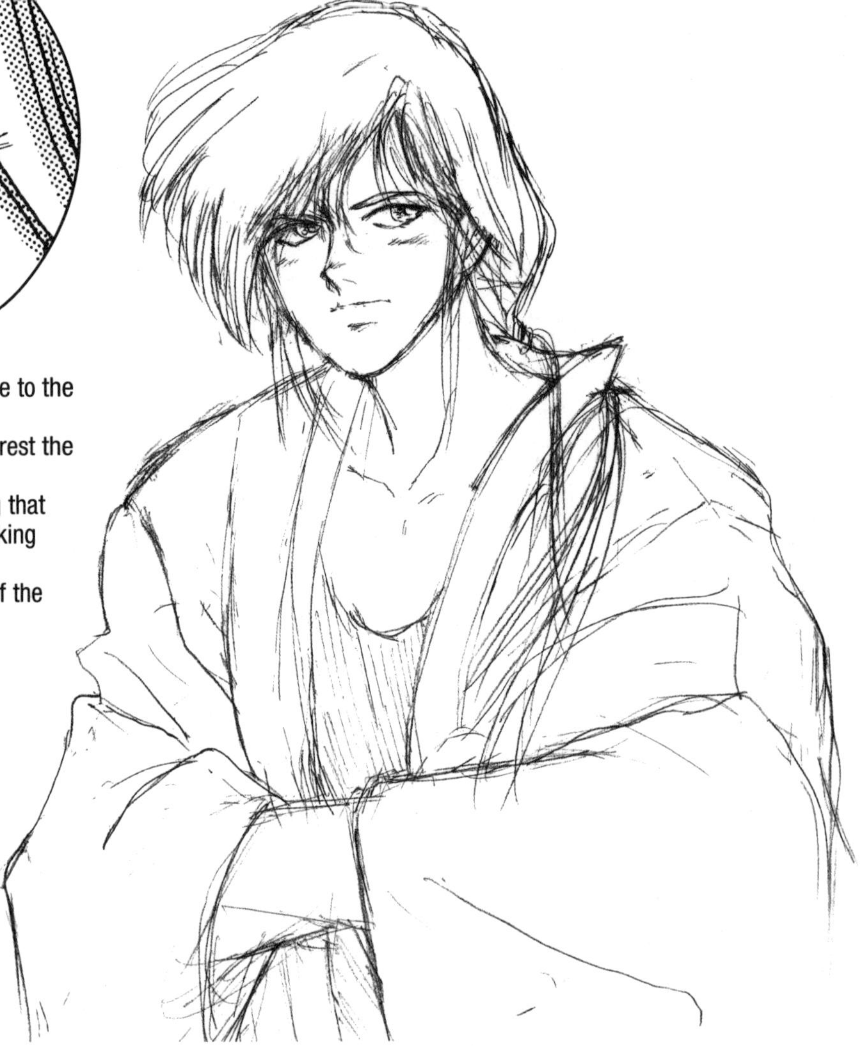

Maintaining the Artist's Sensibility-The Appeal to the Reader Lies in the Contrast between the Composition and Image

The artist has created a large-boned character without using particularly heavy lines. Balance, from the neck to the shoulders and along the body, gives a sense of physical mass and a distinctive weightiness and presence, creating a powerful image. The subtly sloped shoulders and crossed arms and restrained high angle generate this sense of presence. Further, attention to the bold solid block of ink and white areas testify the emphasis shown to light and shadow. The contrast in tones, as the visual effect of the image, forms the principal, decisive sensibility. It is this contrast that produces the odd presence of the image, which walks the tightrope between the real and surreal.

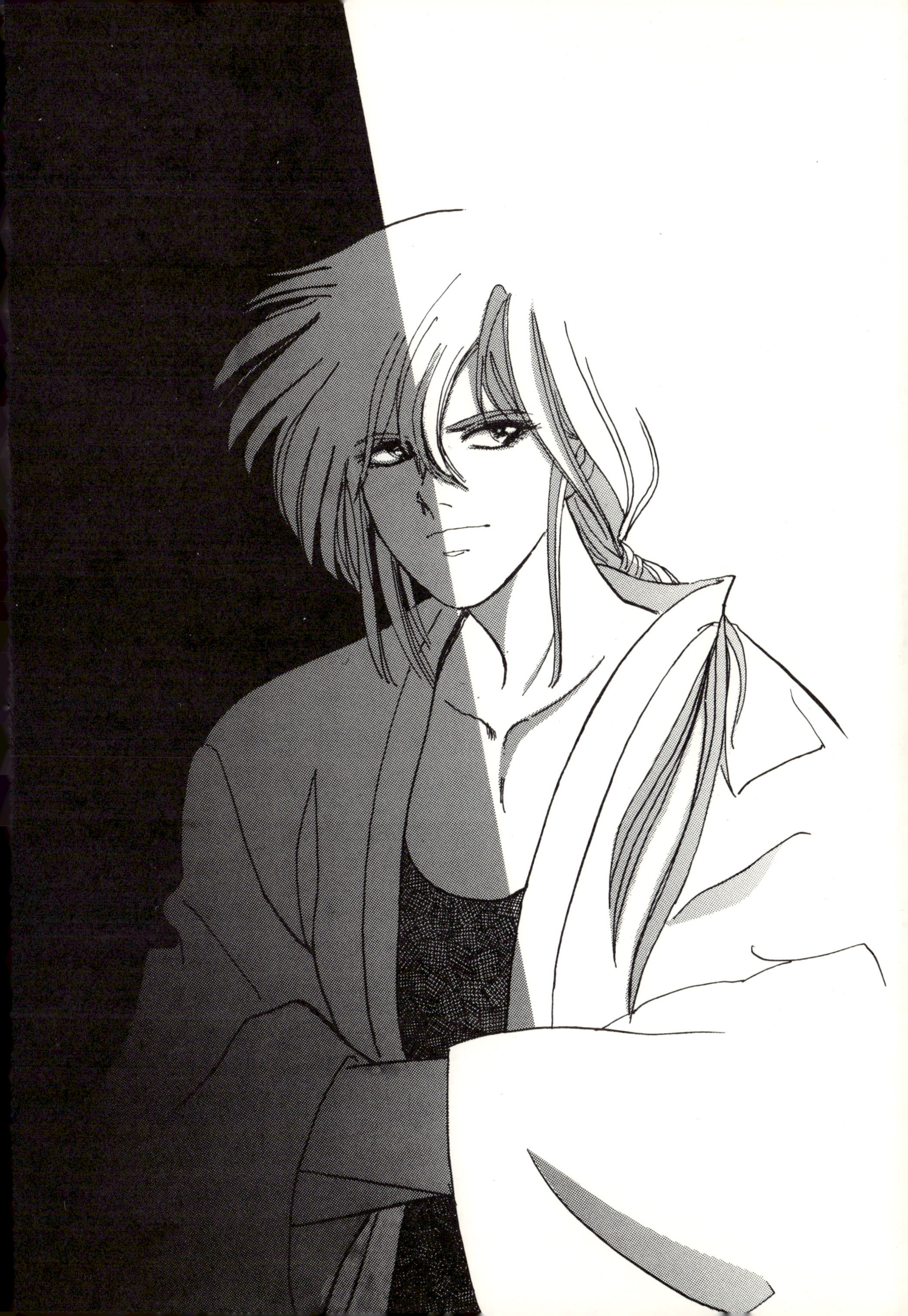